Castlem
Corkscrew

including
The Railways of Bournemouth
& Associated Lines

Volume Two: The Twentieth Century and Beyond

by
B.L. Jackson

THE OAKWOOD PRESS

© Oakwood Press & B.L. Jackson 2008

British Library Cataloguing in Publication Data
A Record for this book is available from the British Library
ISBN 978 0 85361 686 3

Typeset by Oakwood Graphics.
Repro by PKmediaworks, Cranborne, Dorset.
Printed by Cambrian Printers, Aberystwyth, Ceredigion.

A symbol of the years when the Waterloo-Bournemouth-Weymouth service had dedicated stock is shown as class '442' 'Wessex Electric' No. 2408 in the revised South West Trains livery passes Pokesdown on an up express on 30th July, 2002.   *J.D. Ward*

Title page: An undated view of an auto train approaching Hurn station with a Ringwood train.   *R. Smith Collection*

Front cover: A specially commissioned painting by Mike Jeffries depicts Drummond 'T9' class 4-4-0 No. 30120 between Wimborne and Broadstone with a Salisbury-Bournemouth West train. No. 30120 is today part of the National Collection and the sole survivor of a once numerous class.

Rear cover, top: 'West Country' class 4-6-2 No. 34007 *Wadebridge* passing through Holmsley station on 27th June, 1963.   *T.B. Owen*

Rear cover, bottom: In the beautiful Dorset countryside and representing the latest trains on the line, class '444' Desiro unit No. 444010 glides away from Wool with the 4 pm Weymouth-Waterloo service on 1st June, 2007 exactly 160 years after the opening of the Southampton & Dorchester Railway. In the siding behind the train can be seen a pile of sand and a sand wagon, the latest goods traffic to be handled at the station, whilst the bushes behind hide the now overgrown embankment of the former Bovington Camp Military Railway.   *Author*

Published by The Oakwood Press (Usk), P.O. Box 13, Usk, Mon., NP15 1YS.
E-mail: sales@oakwoodpress.co.uk
Website: www.oakwoodpress.co.uk

Contents

Bournemouth Central just after the turn of the century when the railways were reaching their zenith so often described as the 'Golden Age of Railways'. An unidentified later Adams 4-4-0 departs with a London express, the second coach a Pullman, a prerequisite for the better off on the principal Bournemouth expresses. *Author's Collection*

Acknowledgements

To assemble a work of this nature reference has been made to many documents, newspapers, published works and other sources. The surviving documents and minute books of the LSWR and the Southern Railway have been consulted, as have the principal newspapers of the area including *Bournemouth Observer*, *Bournemouth Visitors Directory*, *Christchurch Times*, *Daily Echo* Bournemouth, *Dorset Echo*, *Dorset County Chronicle*, *Hampshire Advertiser*, *Hampshire Independent*, *Poole & East Dorset Herald*, *Southern Daily Echo* Southampton, *Southern Times* and the *Western Gazette*. Various transport journals including the *Railway Times*, the *LSWR Gazette* and the *Southern Railway Magazine* have also been examined.

The assistance of the following organizations is gratefully acknowledged: Bournemouth Central Library, Bournemouth Railway Club, Christopher Tower Library Lyndhurst, Dorset County Record Centre, the Lens of Sutton Association, the National Archives at Kew, Poole Museum, Newton Abbot Library Railway Studies Section, Ringwood Library, the RE Museum and Library Chatham, Southampton City Archive, Southampton Central Library, the Tank Museum Bovington, the Signalling Record Society, the Somerset & Dorset Railway Trust, the South Western Circle, Weymouth Central Library, Wimborne Railway Club and the World War II Railway Study Group. Thanks are also due to the late George Pryer for his expert assistance on railway matters and his work on the manuscript at the early stages.

The author wishes to thank all who have so generously offered their knowledge and time with various questions that have arisen, in particular: J. Alsop, Maureen Attwooll, P.A. Brown, Wendy Brown, Dr J. Boudreau, C.L. Caddy, R.S. Carpenter, C. Chivers, P. Foster, A. Greatbatch, R. Grimley, D.M. Habgood, C. Harris, R.J. Harvey, M. King, B. Moody, C. Osment, N. Pomfrat, J. Read, the late R.C. Riley, R. Smith, C. Stone, P. Swift, B. Thirlwall, M. Thresh and A. Waller.

Many of the photographs in this work have been provided by various organizations and individuals and have been duly credited. Others have come from the author's collection, which has been accumulated over a number of years, many with their provenance uncertain. The SOUTHERN-IMAGES photographs are available from www.southern-images.co.uk

I should also like to thank the Oakwood team for their help and assistance, and finally my wife for her encouragement and forbearance whilst this work was being researched and written.

Introduction

Following on from Volume One of *Castleman's Corkscrew* which dealt with the 19th century, we now move into the 20th century by which time the railway map of Great Britain was virtually complete and the railways held almost a monopoly of inland transport. Within a few years the situation was to change, motor transport was to become the railways principal adversary in the coming years as the motor lorry, motor bus and private car rapidly developed, followed by improvements to roads and, much later, the construction of motorways. There was also the changing social scene as people had more free time and, following various Acts of Parliament, public and annual holidays for all gave everybody the chance to travel, with their choice of destination or mode of transport not so limited.

Thus it was against these options that the railways changed, firstly under the direction of the railway companies and later under Government control where political ideals came into play. With these complexities in the past hundred years it is necessary that certain events of a national nature be described to assist the reader through the minefield that has affected railways over the years.

During two world wars the Southampton & Dorchester line's involvement in both conflicts cannot be overstated, as part of the group of lines that connected the south coast ports with the remainder of the country. The London & South Western Railway (LSWR) in particular had vast experience with commuter, ocean liner specials and holiday traffic, also in the handling of large numbers of special trains for army manoeuvres or naval reviews. It was the well-rehearsed disciplines of these operations that proved so valuable in those troubled war years.

Following the publication of Volume One the question was asked, why the title 'Castleman's Corkscrew'? When the railway was conceived Bournemouth barely existed; by the turn of the century it had through meteoric growth become a County Borough, the result of which changed the entire demographic structure of the surrounding area making it the largest town west of Southampton. This resulted in a changed railway network where today both ends of the original Castleman's Corkscrew are still operational, and the centre section, in later years referred to as 'The Old Road', disappeared from the map, a victim of the Beeching era.

Therefore to write the history without referring in detail to these changes would be impossible, likewise the amount of information required to explain fully the development of the later lines serving Bournemouth would leave little for a further history to explain Castleman's Corkscrew; so the decision was taken to include all lines in the area as they all spring from Castleman's Corkscrew and are intrinsically linked.

In the past 40 years the elimination of the steam locomotive from the railway and much other equipment of the Victorian age has changed the traditional railway that many of the older readers grew up with beyond recognition; we now virtually have an electric railway. The countryside through which it runs has also changed from a relatively backward agricultural district into a popular holiday and residential area with a considerable number of light industries, thus shaping the requirements of the travelling public and the railways which serve them.

This book is dedicated to the railwaymen of the London & South Western Railway, the Southern Railway and British Railways who served the line over the years both in peace and war followed by the difficult years of rationalisation and uncertainty. Also to the late George A. Pryer who carried out so much research work on the line, in particular its signalling history.

Brian Jackson,
Weymouth,
2008

Upon entering the 20th century Castleman's Corkscrew was a line of contrasts: the busy main line sections, the less active Old Road and the tranquil Ringwood-Christchurch branch. This turn of the century photograph taken from the platform at Hurn looking towards Christchurch shows the signal box is in its original condition with the framework exposed on the outside of the planking. Beyond is the level crossing and to the left the down platform with the down starting signal. On the platform stands the old-type tapered milk churns, a reminder of the days before motor transport when milk was conveyed even short distances by rail.   *Paul Lamming Collection*

Chapter One

The Golden Age, 1900-1914

The new century was to herald what is generally described as 'The Golden Age of Railways'. By that time the system had, with the odd exception, reached its full potential; this was certainly true by 1914 when the line between Southampton and Weymouth was fully developed, with only the branch between Hamworthy Junction and Hamworthy having lost its passenger service.

The focus had also shifted to Bournemouth, the name of the new station being changed from Bournemouth East to Bournemouth Central on 1st May, 1899. The town's rapid development had given it a population of over 58,000 in 1900 and County Borough status. On the surface everything appeared calm, the LSWR having a monopoly on Bournemouth traffic. However, 1901 saw the incorporation of the Southampton & Winchester Great Western Junction Railway, intent on a further attack to penetrate the Bournemouth area. Fortunately for the LSWR the scheme was withdrawn during 1905 through lack of support from the Great Western Railway (GWR).

Inspired by the Light Railway Act of 1896 there were a number of schemes for light railways in the district around the turn of the century. Firstly, there was the Lulworth & Osmington Light Railway Company with Henry Weld Blundell of Whites Club, St James Street, London, 'acting as committee [sic] of the estate of Reginald Joseph Weld of Lulworth Castle', Frank Terrell of 7 Berkley Street, London, William Burchell Prichard of Eltham Road, Lee, Kent, and other persons, who made an application to the Light Railway Commissioners in November 1899 to build:

Railway No. 1 - 6 miles 6 furlongs 4 chains commencing in the parish of Arne by a junction with the Wareham and Dorchester branch of the LSWR about 1¼ miles west of Wareham station about 400 yards south west of the Wareham-Wool road bridge and then passing along or near to the villages of East Holme, East Lulworth, and terminating in West Lulworth near the Castle Inn.
Railway No. 2 - 3 miles 7 furlongs 4 chains would commence at that point proceeding westwards terminating at or near the boundary between the villages of Chaldon Herring and Owermoigne at a point about 1,080 yds in a northerly direction from the coastguard buildings at White Nothe Point.
Railway No. 3 - 3 miles 2 furlongs 9 chains commencing at the termination of the previous railway and proceed in a westerly direction to the north of South Down Farm and Osmington Mills and terminate in the parish of Osmington at a point in a field 50 yards from where the East Farm occupation road joins the main road from Poxwell to Osmington. [The application stated that the intended line was to be of standard gauge and that the motive power would be steam, electrical, or other mechanical power.

It would appear that the promoters were hoping that the LSWR would become involved as the application stated:] To authorise agreements with the London & South Western Railway Company with reference to the construction, working, management and maintenance of the railway and the traffic thereon, and also with regard to the use of Wareham station on such terms and conditions, pecuniary or otherwise, as may be agreed between the promoters and the LSWR; and the order will provide for the running over and using that company's line between Wareham station and the junction of the light railway.

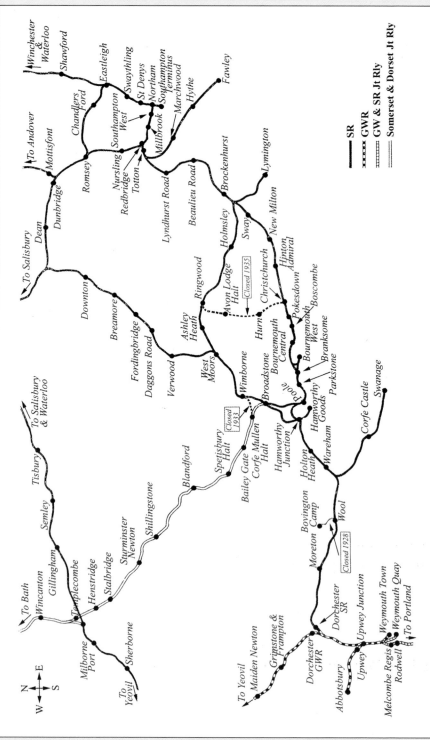

A general map of the railways of west Hampshire and south-east Dorset in 1930 showing the full extent of the network, although the Bovington branch had closed and the Ringwood-Christchurch branch would follow during 1935. (Several stations have been omitted for clarity.)

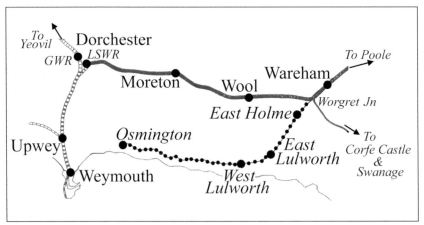

An outline map of the proposed Lulworth & Osmington Light Railway of 1899, showing its relationship to other railways in South Dorset and the route of the line from Worgret Junction with stations at East Holme, East and West Lulworth and Osmington where the line would terminate east of Weymouth.

However, to terminate the line on the east side of Osmington village appeared a little self defeating with Weymouth, a town that could provide both passengers and goods facilities, only four miles further west and passing through the village of Preston *en route*. On 24th February, 1900 the *Southern Times* was quick to raise the point stating:

> The promoters of the proposed light railway to Lulworth and Osmington from Wareham are still hopeful in being able to obtain the official sanction of the Weymouth Rural District Council through a portion of whose district it will pass. The local authority has taken up a diplomatic attitude in the matter, that the line will be a useful one none will deny, and Lulworth will be greatly advantaged by the development but unless the extension is carried on to Weymouth the Weymouth district authority do not see how their help can be expected. Weymouth people have no fear of such Lilliputian rivals as Lulworth and Osmington and they would do nothing to stop the scheme, but they naturally ask that the line should not stop at Osmington, Weymouth is the natural terminus for such a railway.
>
> A light railway running along this picturesque district would be a splendid thing not only for the two villages but for Weymouth and it is hoped that the promoters will see their way to carry the line a few miles further than they propose, and thus win not only the gratitude of the public, but the hearty cooperation of the Weymouth Rural District Council.

Had the scheme proceeded and had Weymouth been the western terminus of the proposed line it could of had a certain amount of trade in particular during the summer months. Unfortunately, little else was reported on the scheme which just faded away; ironically within a few years the introduction of the motor vehicle nullified the need for many of the lines that the Light Railway Act had set out to provide.

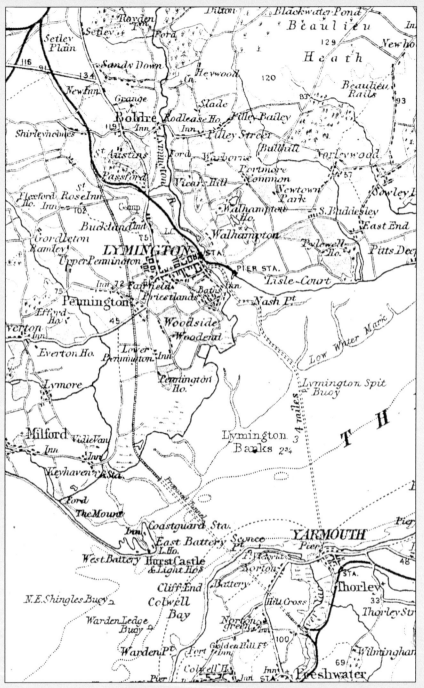

A map published during the early 1900s showing the route of the proposed railway and tunnel to the Isle of Wight, branching off from the Lymington branch near Passford going south and under the Solent west of Fort Victoria to join the Freshwater, Yarmouth & Newport Railway to the east of Freshwater.

In November 1902 a further scheme for the Fawley area was put forward by officers of the LSWR for a 10¾ mile branch to serve Hythe and Fawley. The fact that a number of bridges were planned, where, with light railways, level crossings were the usual means and the fact the line ended in the middle of nowhere at Stone Point gave the impression that the line's construction was a move to prevent others from entering the area. The Hon. Gerald Lascelles, the Deputy Surveyor of the New Forest, was sceptical in his report:

> ... this scheme seems to be sailing under false colours altogether. There is no sort of demand for a Light Railway in that part of the country, nor can there be any traffic to support it. Light Railways are not made with bridges over every road and of the same gauge as the railway they join and they do not usually terminate without rhyme or reason at a country lane with nothing anywhere near them but a single farmhouse. As presented the line does not reach the sea but there is little doubt that the present proposal is part of a much larger scheme for a branch line of the South Western Railway for the better facility of managing ocean traffic. In this there may be no harm but it would be better to extract the truth and ascertain what the scheme really is for. Whatever it may be it's not fairly described as the Totton, Hythe and Fawley Light Railway.

In February 1903 it was agreed to apply to the Light Railway Commissioners for a Light Railway Order to construct the line. However, this was as far as the scheme proceeded, the powers being allowed to lapse in November 1906. Fawley had to await other developments before obtaining its railway.

A scheme that would have had significant implications on the line between Southampton and Brockenhurst was proposed in 1903 for a line under the Solent to the Isle of Wight. An Act of Parliament incorporated the South Western Railway and Isle of Wight Junction Railway on 26th July, 1901, with a capital of £600,000 to construct a 7¾ mile line. It left the Lymington branch 1½ miles north of Lymington Town station then ran four miles to Keyhaven Marshes before descending a 1 in 40 gradient to enter a 2¼ mile single track tunnel under the Solent, rising up a further 1 in 40 gradient to join the Freshwater, Yarmouth & Newport Railway with a junction facing Yarmouth.

No doubt owing to the steep gradients at each end of the tunnel electric traction was to be employed. A power station would be constructed at Keyhaven to provide electricity for traction current, ventilation fans, and water pumps. The Act granted the company powers to electrify the branch to Brockenhurst and gave running rights into the LSWR station, and over the Freshwater, Yarmouth & Newport Railway and the Isle of Wight Central Railway on the island. The scheme also required the financial support and co-operation of the LSWR. However, as it appeared that the Great Central Railway had some involvement in the scheme the LSWR was reluctant to become involved. It had its own interests to safeguard, having in recent years invested a substantial sum in new steamers for both the Lymington-Yarmouth and Portsmouth-Ryde ferry services.

A further Act in 1903 allowed for the construction of a short branch at Keyhaven to a pier where liners would land passengers for rail transport to London. And in 1909 an additional Act gave extensions of time and allowed for an L-shaped pier suitable for the largest liners, and also gave the company the power to operate tugs.

Several stations on the Southampton & Dorchester route were situated a considerable distance from the places after which they were named and intended to serve. As early as 1888 there had been proposals to construct a 3 ft gauge electric tramway between Lyndhurst Road station and Lyndhurst. A public meeting in the October approved of the scheme for the line running alongside the road, although landowners and some members of the parish council opposed the scheme suggesting that the LSWR would use it as a precedent to extend the railway into the town.

The next proposal came after the turn of the century when on 23rd January, 1902 the Lyndhurst Electric Light & Traction Company obtained a Light Railway Order for the 2½ mile route into the town. Also included was a power station that would supply electric light to the town, the scheme costing £20,031. The Deputy Surveyor of the New Forest, Sir Gerald Lascelles, having feared a railway into town with the previous scheme, said, referring to the power station, 'a proposed factory-with a large chimney just outside of Lyndhurst should be objected to' and so the scheme faded away.

It was left to the railway to provide mechanical road transport into Lyndhurst, when the first railway bus operation took place in the New Forest area. During October 1904 two Milnes-Daimler 14-seat single-deckers Nos. A 4283 and A 4284 which had previously worked in Exeter, arrived at Lyndhurst Road station. The local press reported, 'that for several weeks they had been practising on the roads between Lyndhurst and the station. The service of fifteen journeys each way daily connecting with trains commenced on Monday 24th October, the single fare between the station and the Crown Hotel was 6d.' However, their stay was short-lived, there was an unprecedented number of breakdowns; it was not unknown for the horse bus operated by the Crown Hotel at Lyndhurst to overtake the new arrival! It was reported at the company's half-yearly meeting the following January that the motor omnibuses were not very satisfactory and had been a failure; in view of this the service was withdrawn on 11th February, 1905, the vehicles being sold to the Alexander, Newport and South Wales Dock & Railway Company. The corrugated garage erected for their use at Lyndhurst Road station remained as their memorial until dismantled as late as the mid-1960s.

In November 1904 the LSWR Traffic Committee had decided to purchase four 32 hp Clarkson steam buses, two fitted with 20-seat bodies for Exeter and two 18-seaters to operate between New Milton and Lymington via Milford and Pennington. The previous month the committee had decided upon petrol buses; no doubt the problems encountered at Lyndhurst had changed their minds and at the same time Messrs Thornycroft had run an experimental service between New Milton and Lymington using a 16 hp vehicle.

On 13th July, 1905 Lymington town council granted licences for the operation of the steam buses, a trial being conducted the same day, the outward journey taking 50 minutes whilst the return was made in 42 minutes. The *Hampshire Advertiser* said of the vehicles, 'They are beautifully fitted up in polished mahogany and ash, well ventilated and suitably upholstered'. The new service with vehicles Nos. LC 1434 and LC 1435 commenced on 15th July, running a weekday service three times daily each way at a fare of 1s. 3d. The vehicles were garaged at Lymington station in a corrugated iron shed.

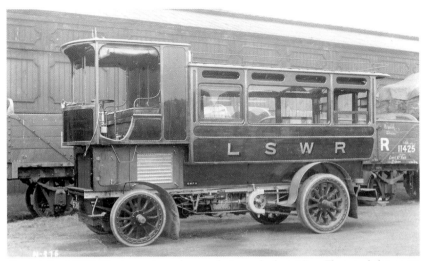

One of the LSWR Clarkson steam buses photographed at Nine Elms and for some unknown reason carrying the registration No. E 38. Steam was generated by a paraffin-fired water tube boiler to power the enclosed engine capable of giving a top speed of 15 mph. For a short period two of these vehicles operated between New Milton and Lymington.   *Author's Collection*

Despite the decision to use steam power as opposed to the still unreliable petrol engine, troubles still prevailed. Early in 1906 all four vehicles were returned to Clarkson's for the fitting of new water tube boilers, one of which burst on a Lymington bus on 11th September. The poor state of the roads in the area did little to help operations and the last service ran three days later on the 14th, the vehicles than being transferred to Exeter. Several years later Mr Stanley De'Ath operated a steam bus between New Milton and Lymington which continued until World War I.

At the January 1905 half-yearly meeting the General Manager, after discussing the failure of the Lyndhurst service, announced that it had been decided to test the traffic potential between Totton, Hythe and Fawley by running an experimental motor bus service before proceeding with the construction of the proposed Light Railway. In fact, no progress was made until the summer of 1906 when, following negotiations with Messrs Thornycroft, a 24 hp single-deck 16-seat bus was supplied at the cost of £900 to open the service. Allocated fleet No. 1M and carrying registration No. AA 2139, a service of two return journeys daily was undertaken.

It would appear that the management was satisfied enough with the service to expand it for the summer of 1907, resulting in the transfer from Haslemere of Thornycroft of 24 hp open-sided charabanc No. AA 2044. The revised service commenced on 10th June with four return journeys each way daily departing from Totton station at 8.25, 11.15 am, 3.15 and 4.52 pm. with return times from the Falcon Inn, Fawley at 9.55 am, 12.40, 5.00 and 6.50 pm.

Thornycroft 24 hp charabanc, registration No. AA 2044, having previously been in use on the Farnham-Haslemere service, was transferred to the Totton-Fawley bus service during 1907, only to be moved to the Exeter-Chagford route in November 1908.   *R. Grimley Collection*

Photographed at Hythe is LSWR Thornycroft 24 hp bus registration No. AA 2139, a 16-seat vehicle that operated a service from Totton to Fawley between August 1906 and November 1908.   *Author's Collection*

Like all early bus services there were difficulties: on the third day of operation it was reported that the bus had been involved in a collision with a motor van near Totton station. There was also the problem of the gravel roads of the period bringing complaints from the highway authority concerning the damage caused by the narrow tyres of the vehicles, and likewise the railway complaining about the condition of the roads. Tragedy struck on 12th May, 1908 when a new conductor on his first day of employment fell off the rear platform of No. AA 2139 at Dibden and was killed. The service failed to develop as anticipated and, with little public notice, was withdrawn on 14th November, 1908, thus bringing to an end railway-operated bus services in the area. The Light Railway was not constructed and it was not until the coming of Hants & Dorset Motor Services that public transport returned to the Waterside area.

Whereas the railway-operated bus service had been unsuccessful in rural areas, at Weymouth the GWR had commenced a service between Radipole and Wyke Regis on 26th June, 1905, which continued until 31st August, 1909. Its sudden withdrawal was blamed on complaints from residents concerning the nuisance the motors caused. Their introduction had been brought about by threats of proposed electric tramway services in the area. In larger centres of population local tram services became very successful, and were to cause concern for the railway companies. The LSWR, with stations at Poole, Parkstone, Branksome, Bournemouth West, Bournemouth Central, Boscombe, Pokesdown and Christchurch, was the principal provider of transport within the area. However, the introduction of electric trams at both Poole and Bournemouth was to change the situation.

The Poole & District Electric Tramway commenced a service between Poole station and County Gates via upper Parkstone and Branksome station on 6th April, 1901, and Bournemouth Corporation trams commenced running between the Square and County Gates via Bournemouth West station on 18th December, 1902. In June 1905 Bournemouth Corporation took over the Poole system and on 3rd July through running commenced. In addition an extension via Boscombe and passing Pokesdown station to Christchurch opened on 17th October, 1905. Furthermore, an additional route had opened from Bournemouth Square to Boscombe via Bournemouth Central and Boscombe stations.

The through tram journey between Poole railway station and Christchurch was over a distance of 11 miles; this at the time (London excepted) was the longest tram route in the South of England. The entire journey took an average of 72 minutes, whereas a train from Poole to Christchurch took 36 minutes stopping at five intermediate stations. A train from Bournemouth West to Christchurch with three intermediate stops took 22 minutes. This has to be balanced against the fact that few tram passengers made the complete journey, but as Bournemouth West was at the western extremity of the town and Central was anything but central, for those with business in the towns the tram with its frequent and convenient stops proved very popular. During 1906 alone the system carried over 11 million passengers and without a doubt had abstracted many potential railway passengers.

The LSWR had not been idle to the threat: in February 1905 the General Manager recommended that two steam motor carriages be provided to

The short-lived Meyrick Park Halt, Bournemouth photographed on 28th August, 1907 with Adams 'X2' class 4-4-0 No. 586 passing with the 12.50 pm Weymouth-Waterloo express.

R. Smith Collection

West Moors showing the armoured (reinforced concrete) footbridge constructed during 1902 making it one of the earliest structures of its type. Photographed on 16th May, 1964 just after the withdrawal of passenger services 97 years of railway history waits to be slowly destroyed. Today only the gate house (No. 19) on the left survives, the site of the station being occupied by sheltered housing appropriately named Castleman Court. *C.L. Caddy*

supplement the existing train service in the locality of Bournemouth with the object of meeting the tram competition. In May approval was given at an estimated cost of £167 to the provision of a halt consisting of two short wooden platforms and huts situated in a cutting with two flights of steps leading to the bottom end of Meyrick Crescent, situated 55 chains west of Bournemouth Central. This would serve the growing suburb of Winton and the nearby Meyrick Park, which had amongst its attractions a golf links. Thus on 1st March, 1906 steam railmotors commenced running on local services between Bournemouth West and Christchurch with certain journeys extended to New Milton and Ringwood.

Although the trams had already staked their claim, at the halt's opening the *Bournemouth Guardian* remarked: 'A few years ago this convenience would have been greatly appreciated by the residents of Winton, who probably will mostly use the trams, but the golfers will be able to get an easier access to the links'. Indeed, the residents of the area had, as early as 1894, petitioned the company for the provision of a halt; however, human nature being what it is, even if it had been provided, the later introduction of the trams would have tempted passengers away with their more flexible service.

Whilst expansion was taking place around Bournemouth, in October 1904 it was decided that the Hamworthy branch (which had lost its passenger service in 1896) would be reduced to single track. This took place on 10th September, 1905, the former branch platform at Hamworthy Junction having been converted into a down loop during February 1901.

The matter of station names arose during 1906 in two cases where the particular stations served a large rural area. In June Ringwood Rural District Council suggested that Holmsley should be altered to Burley. In October the parish councils of Hampreston and West Parley, together with other interested parties, suggested that the words 'For Ferndown' be added to the name board at West Moors. Both suggestions were declined, but in later years 'For Ferndown' was added to the latter station name.

West Moors station had also been drawn to the attention of the Board of Trade following complaints over the alleged danger of the level crossing at the west end of the station, which at the time consisted of hand-operated gates. In late 1901 plans for a footbridge were submitted with estimates for: timber construction £280, concrete £310, and light iron with brick piers £338. Approval was given for the bridge to be constructed in armoured (reinforced) concrete. This was an interesting decision as this was a very early date for a structure in this material, the work being completed by late 1902.

In January 1904 the subject of the level crossing was again raised and it was decided to move the signal box from its site opposite the junction with the Salisbury & Dorset line to a position alongside the crossing. This would enable the gates to be operated from the box. The estimated cost for this work was £541 and would also render unnecessary the services of two gatemen; work was quickly taken in hand, the new box opening on 4th December.

During this period there had also been various developments on the commercial side. A letter was received from Branksome Urban District Council with a petition from tradesmen in December 1901 asking for a goods depot to be established at Branksome. This was declined following a report from the goods manager, no doubt the company considering that the two nearby goods yards at Bournemouth West and Parkstone could handle the anticipated traffic. In July 1905 approval was given for a siding to be laid at Wimborne to serve the gas works, and the following year it was decided to lay an extra siding in Wimborne goods yard owing to difficulties encountered with the previous arrangements.

Developments on the outskirts of Southampton at Millbrook were progressing. In October 1906 it was reported that land had been acquired to lay out a goods yard and that it was to be filled to the level of the railway and a siding laid which would form part of the improvements to be eventually carried out. At Poole the request of the British Petroleum Company (at the end of 1907) to establish a motor spirit depot at Poole station was not approved, whilst at Wool additional land was acquired for sidings and cartage space.

It has to be noted that the Southampton & Dorchester and associated railways had been free from serious accidents, although two accidents took place in the Bournemouth area in the early 1900s. If luck had not intervened these could have had serious consequences, and both involved Drummond 'T9' class engines. On 8th March, 1900 No. 704 suffered a broken driving axle whilst travelling between Hinton Admiral and Christchurch. The second mishap took place on 19th September, 1903; having worked light engine from Bournemouth Central coupled to Adams 4-4-0 No. 662, No. 709 was uncoupled at Gas Works Junction and proceeded towards Bournemouth West to be attached to the 7.50 am Waterloo express. When approaching platform 3, tender leading, the driver realised he was unable to stop the engine, he put it into forward gear and opened the regulator in an attempt to bring it under control. The fireman and guard who were also travelling on the footplate jumped onto the track, the driver leaving it to the last moment, leapt onto the platform as the engine smashed into the coaching stock at about 15 mph.

Luckily, platform staff alerted to the situation shouted to passengers to stand clear and this resulted in only minor injuries to three persons. At that point the crewless engine in full forward gear with an open regulator set off out of the station; fortunately the spectacle of a 'Greyhound' in full flight was averted when a goods guard sprinted across the tracks and jumped aboard and stopped the runaway!

Damage was severe, the rear of the tender stove in, bogie brake third No. 114 and bogie composite No. 581 had their ends smashed in and Pullman car *Princess Margaret* had the vestibule beam at the front end smashed. The next two carriages received only minor damage whilst the rear coach was derailed and damaged and the buffer stops were displaced. Work on removing the damaged stock was quickly put in hand whilst other services were maintained.

Of the crew, the fireman received a fracture to the base of the skull and the guard had three toes amputated. Retribution was swift: having failed to connect the brake hoses of the engine and for approaching the train at reckless speed both driver and fireman were dismissed, whilst the guard received seven days suspension. The goods guard who stopped the engine received three days extra pay and £10.

Engineering matters attended to during that period included bridge No. 49 at Holmsley, which carried the main Southampton-Bournemouth Road (A35) over

A pre-1914 view looking towards Bournemouth West from the Branksome direction. In the background is the Somerset & Dorset Branksome shed, to the left Branksome goods yard. Over the years there were several plans to relocate the Bournemouth Central engine shed to this site. *South Western Circle Collection*

the railway east of the station. The original cast-iron girders and timber decking were replaced by a steel structure, and in 1908 permission was given to strengthen Rockley viaduct. In the same month a proposal for a new running shed at Bournemouth West near the triangle to replace the shed at Bournemouth Central was discussed. Although powers were sought the following year, opposition from both local residents and Bournemouth Council, fearing noise and smoke would affect the value of adjacent properties, caused a change of mind and no action was taken, although the plan resurfaced on several occasions in future years. At Wimborne the two elderly buildings used as engine sheds by the Somerset & Dorset company were replaced by one structure during 1909.

Improvements became pressing at Southampton in November 1904 when the Town Clerk drew attention to the unsheltered state of the western portions of the platforms at Southampton West station, which were exposed to winds across the upper reaches of Southampton Water. As early as January 1905 a report with plans was received from the superintendent of the line for additional shelter on the down platform. One proposal was for a screen on the outside of the platform estimated to cost £490, the second costing £2,556 was for a screen and additional roofing; no doubt reflecting Southampton's importance to the company the second scheme was approved.

The following year attention was turned to the old Southampton West station which had been disused since 1895. It was recommended that the buildings be removed except a small portion of the platform and roof on either side which could be used for small goods traffic. In the event very little of the up side building was removed, it remaining with the shortened platforms until the rebuilding of 1934.

Further work was carried out at Southampton West after approval was given in March 1909 for the extension of the down platform, alterations to crossover roads and sidings, also a slight diversion of the public footpath and seawall.

COUNTY OF SOUTHAMPTON
PLAN

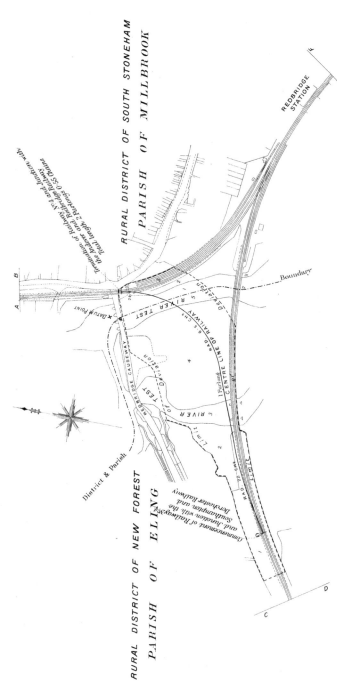

Plan for the proposed 2 furlong 55 chain curve linking the Southampton & Dorchester line with the Andover and Redbridge line to the west of Redbridge, a scheme which, if proceeded with, would have given greater flexibility of working in particular during two World Wars.

Southampton Record Office

'Q' class 0-6-0 No. 30548 heads a down train away from Redbridge viaduct; the original arched road bridge that carried the A35 into Southampton can be seen in the right background. A triangular junction with the Salisbury line would have been formed at this site if plans of 1906 had been proceeded with. *South Western Circle Eyers Collection*

Plans had also been put forward to form a triangle between Redbridge and Totton when on 20th July, 1906 an Act was obtained to construct a 21 chain curve, which would have included a bridge over the River Test from Redbridge crossing to a point seven chains west of Redbridge viaduct on the Southampton-Bournemouth line.

The *South Western Gazette* for October 1907 reported that:

Some time ago parliamentary powers were obtained to construct a short bridge over the river at Redbridge, so that trains may proceed direct from Romsey to Lyndhurst and the New Forest. It is understood that the work will be proceeded with this winter, and that the line when finished will be utilised to take some of the traffic that now proceeds from Weymouth and Bournemouth to Waterloo through Southampton, and which instead will travel via Romsey, Fullerton, and Hurstbourne Junction.

However, in the event the spur failed to materalise. In 1909 there were unsuccessful attempts to alter the proposed curve to 45 chains radius, and although extensions of time were obtained in both 1911 and 1913, the LSWR Board decided in June 1917 to allow the powers to lapse, an implausible move in view of the war situation.

Further south improvements on the Portland branch had increased the capacity of the line and taken the branch trains away from Weymouth station where space was at a premium. On the traffic side it was decided that from 13th March, 1911 to make the return halves of tickets between London and Weymouth and Dorchester available by either the LSWR or GWR routes.

The *Southern Times* for 8th June, 1912 reported that, 'from 1st July the entire staffing at Weymouth station both in regard to passenger and goods services will be managed by the GWR with one station master and one head of each department instead of the two as at present'. In the goods department previously the LSWR had used the west side and the GWR the east side. Under the new arrangements the west side became 'goods outwards' and the east side 'goods inwards', there was also a rearrangement of the agreements involving the carriers who delivered the goods around the town. The *Southern Times* also mentioned the hopes of a new station to be constructed nearer to the Portland branch; unfortunately, World War I and the difficult years that followed were to prevent progress in that direction.

Railway-operated buses were also reintroduced in Weymouth on 19th July, 1912 when it became a joint service between the GWR and LSWR. In reality the GWR provided the vehicles and staff and apart from both companies' names on the sides of the vehicles which were in the GWR livery, the LSWR did little more than take its share of the profits and add its good name to the proceedings.

Unrest in the mining industry resulted in the national coal strike at the beginning of March 1912, in an age where homes, industry and the railways relied on coal heavily. Not only did the railways deliver the majority of coal from the pits to various stations but they were also major consumers. This resulted in the LSWR quickly curtailing its goods services and advising that it would be unable to receive for conveyance rough traffic including bricks, clay, gravel, stable manure, sand, stone, slates etc. In the first week it was reported that both Wimborne gasworks and waterworks had a sufficient supply for some time. However, it was noted that activity at the station was much less than was the custom for an important agricultural centre. The *Southern Times* for 16th March reported that little more than a Sunday service was operating and that as from the 18th March excursion, weekend and all other cheap tickets except workmen's would be suspended.

By 30th March, Dorchester Brewery and other businesses in the town stated they were managing owing to stocks of coal they held, although the delivery of goods was delayed by the disruption of services; the LSWR were running eight up and 10 down trains through Dorchester. With the strike coming to an end in early April the LSWR put on additional trains over the Easter period but did not reinstate cheap rate fares; these had to wait until later in the month when an excursion from Weymouth and other Dorset stations was run to the FA Cup Final at Crystal Palace to see Barnsley draw 0-0 with West Bromwich Albion.*

The inhabitants of the rapidly expanding and progressive Borough of Bournemouth attempted to improve their rail facilities during 1910 when the company received a memorial from the tradesmen of Pokesdown and West Southbourne calling attention to the inadequate accommodation at Pokesdown and the need for providing for goods traffic. They also suggested that the station be renamed Bournemouth East, a suggestion that was refused. However, plans and estimates were to be drawn up for a new station at Pokesdown; unfortunately it was to be a further 20 years before Pokesdown's wish was granted. At Holmsley, where accommodation of goods traffic was considered insufficient, an additional siding and cart road were provided.

The residents of Burton, no doubt aware of the success of the steam railmotors in the Bournemouth area, petitioned the company for a halt to be constructed between Christchurch and Hinton Admiral, a suggestion that was declined. However, although the provision of halts by the LSWR pre-1914 was far less prolific than its neighbour the GWR, there were plans drawn up in 1913

---

* Barnsley won the replay 1-0 at Sheffield United's Bramall Lane ground a few days later.

to provide a halt between the road overbridge and Lymington Junction signal box for the use of visitors to the Brockenhurst Manor Golf Club. Perhaps it was felt that the necessary returns would not be forthcoming or world events caused the scheme to fade away as it was never built.

Along the line a number of crossing gates were still manually-operated and not interlocked with the signalling. In May 1914 a crossing keeper at East Burton was killed in tragic circumstances. It appears that he mistook the warning bell from Wool for that from Worgret Junction, and upon hearing the down express approaching at 60 mph rushed out of his cabin to open the gates. Unfortunately, the train was upon the crossing as he reached the gates resulting in both the keeper and the gates being struck by the express.

At this juncture an appraisal of the services provided during the period when the railways were at the pinnacle of their influence is not out of place. The first 14 years of the 20th century saw improvements in the train services of most railways, whereas on the LSWR the Old Road had lost much of its importance. The growth of Southampton with its business and shipping interests and Bournemouth with its upper class residents and flourishing holiday trade both required an improved service. New more powerful locomotives and modern rolling stock were introduced: in 1903 ten corridor sets were ordered for the Exeter and Bournemouth lines and this was followed in 1905 by the introduction of restaurant cars on certain Bournemouth expresses and the beginning of the replacement of Pullman cars. Further corridor stock was added during 1906-7 although it was only the restaurant car trains that were provided with this luxury.

At the time the fastest train of the day was the non-stop 4.10 pm Waterloo-Bournemouth Central covering the distance in 2 hours 6 minutes, where after a four minute stop a portion proceeded calling only at Poole and Dorchester, arriving in Weymouth at 7.15 pm and covering the entire journey in 3 hours 5 minutes. The best two GWR trains took 3 hours 40 minutes and 3 hours 55 minutes respectively from Paddington. The corresponding up train was the 8.00 am from Weymouth, combining at Bournemouth Central with portions from Swanage and Bournemouth West and reaching Waterloo in 3 hours 10 minutes. These two expresses and the 1.57 pm Bournemouth Central-Waterloo and the 2.00 pm Waterloo-Bournemouth passed through Southampton without stopping, although the latter train, which included a Pullman car in its formation, stopped at Christchurch and took 2 hours 27 minutes to Bournemouth.

Wareham, despite being the junction for the Swanage branch and at that period the most important station between Poole and Dorchester, was also passed by the Weymouth portions of the 10.15 am, 12.30, 4.10 and 6.55 pm expresses from Waterloo and the 8.00 am and 4.15 pm up workings from Weymouth.

The Old Road was served by a through train departing Waterloo at 2.10 pm calling at Basingstoke, Winchester, Southampton West and Brockenhurst before stopping at Ringwood, Wimborne and Broadstone Junction. After rejoining the main line, further calls at Wareham and Dorchester gave a 6.09 pm arrival at Weymouth.

From July 1911 two up and two down expresses were running the 108 miles between Waterloo and Bournemouth in 120 minutes. Although this had only

Drummond 'L12' class 4-4-0 No. 429 stands in the up platform at Dorchester with the 9.55 am from Weymouth which contained LNWR through coaches for Liverpool and Great Northern coaches for Kings Cross, both sets being detached at Clapham Junction. The LNWR coaches are behind the engine in the photograph taken during May 1906.   *G.A. Pryer Collection*

An unidentified Adams 'Jubilee' class 0-4-2 runs into Ringwood station with an up train. The number of people on the platform and their dress would suggest an outing of some description, the details of which have unfortunately been lost in the mist of time.   *Author's Collection*

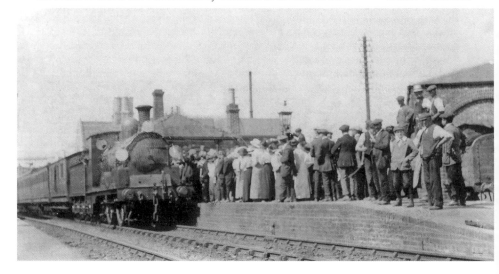

clipped six minutes off 1900 timings it was that magic 'two hours', a coup for the publicity department!

The new century also saw the development of through services with other companies. Previously passengers wishing to travel for instance from the Midlands or North of England to the South and West had to change trains two or three times during their journey, often involving the difficulties of passengers and luggage having to cross London. The first move to alleviate this practice was the provision of through coaches that were attached and detached at points where the companies met: the Somerset & Dorset after the opening of the Bath extension providing a through coach between Birmingham and Bournemouth, to be followed by coaches serving Bradford, Leeds, Sheffield, York and Newcastle. On 1st October, 1910 a year-round Manchester-Bournemouth restaurant car express commenced, later to become the 'Pines Express'.

Through working between Portsmouth and Cardiff with the GWR commenced in July 1896 with a Portsmouth-Bristol service added in 1903. In July 1902 a through service between Bournemouth and Newcastle commenced, originally the stock was detached and attached at Waterloo before and after transfer to the Great Central Railway. In July 1903 a GWR coach for Birkenhead was added and the down train ran independently from Basingstoke, the northbound service becoming a separate service from 1st July, 1905. The working by this time was formed of four GWR coaches for Birkenhead and Great Central vehicles including a buffet car for Manchester, Bradford and Newcastle. The Birkenhead service ran as a separate train from 1st July, 1910, departing Bournemouth West at 10.15 am, running non-stop to Eastleigh and hauled by an LSWR engine through to Oxford, the LSWR providing stock including a restaurant car for the Birkenhead portion with the GWR providing stock for the Manchester portion.

From 1st July, 1905 a train departed Weymouth at 9.55 am served both the London & North Western Railway (LNWR) and the Great Northern Railway Railway (GNR). From Clapham Junction the LNWR coaches proceeded to Willesden Junction for a service to Liverpool (later Manchester) whilst the GNR coaches continued via the widened lines to Kings Cross. Here the passengers only had to make cross-platform connections for afternoon trains to the North. The return working left Kings Cross at 2.35 pm arriving at Weymouth at 6.52 pm, this unusual working being withdrawn in October 1910.

Another through train during this period was the Brighton-Plymouth travelling via Southampton West and Salisbury. This began in July 1907 and from July of the following year coaches for Bournemouth West were added, these being detached at Southampton West. The *Southern Times* for June 1908 carried an advert for new and accelerated services between Weymouth, Dorchester, and Swanage to and from Brighton and other South Coast stations. Again these services continued with the Bournemouth portion becoming a separate working.

Excursions were popular in the years before World War I; with the motor charabanc yet to arrive the railways had a monopoly in the pleasure-seeking public. There were various types of excursion, firstly the ones organized by the railway which could be a complete train travelling to and returning from an advertised destination or event. There were also the one way excursions, with facilities to travel home on a later date by normal services, or just simply pre-advertised cheap fares offered on ordinary services to certain destinations. A perusal of the local newspapers, handbills and station notices of the period showed a varied selection of venues including seaside resorts, beauty spots, exhibitions and other public events.

One example was the 1902 August Bank Holiday which saw a number of people taking advantage of the cheap excursion fares on offer. From Dorchester LSWR 450 passengers travelled to Weymouth (the GWR station reported they carried 500), 150 went to Bournemouth, 37 to Swanage and seven to Corfe Castle, 11 to Wool and 13 to Southampton West.

An annual event in the years before World War I was a grand fete that included a fairground held at Brockenhurst Park in aid of the LSWR Widows & Orphans Fund with greatly reduced rail fares including admission available from all stations west of Eastleigh and Portsmouth. The annual Dorset Police Sports held at Dorchester would also attract large patronage from as far afield as Southampton, with additional coaches added to trains and special excursion fares available.

Also run were what the railway classed as guaranteed excursions where the organizer of the excursion paid a set price for the train, hence the railway was guaranteed the money regardless of the patronage. These usually included companies' works excursions, outings for religious, political and other groups or by private individuals. In the days before paid annual holidays the annual works outing was an event to be looked forward to often subsidised by the employer.

One such local event was the yearly excursion organized for the employees of Eldridge Pope, the Dorchester brewers, it also embraced the workmen of other employers in the town including Lott & Walne, the gasworks, the laundry, the town council, Dorchester butter factory and several other small employers. The 1907 outing was a 14-coach train consisting of eight picnic saloons, two corridor lavatory thirds, one lavatory third, one ordinary third and two lavatory composite brakes to convey the 550-plus excursionists. Departing just after 6.00 am, stops were made at Ringwood and Eastleigh before arriving at Waterloo shortly before 10.00 am. The return from the metropolis left just after midnight arriving back in Dorchester at 4.00 am, although a lesser number returned, the railway making the tickets available by any train during the following week.

Although the Victorian era had passed the traditions and beliefs of the public were slow to change, so deep-rooted were Victorian values. The Sabbath was universally regarded as a day of rest and contemplation. Although the railways from the beginning had run Sunday trains they were circumspect in their operations: at the outbreak of World War I 14.5 per cent of the LSWR system was closed on a Sunday, mostly branch and minor lines, no doubt lack of trade and financial considerations also being taken into account. However, change was taking place and a few seaside branches began to operate a limited Sunday service just in the summer months.

The religious revival of Victorian times had the effect by the early 1900s of an 80 per cent attendance of children at Sunday schools with the reward of an annual Sunday school outing. This always depended on the funds or goodwill available for the distance travelled, and could vary from a short trip in a borrowed farm cart to a train journey to a nearby seaside resort of beauty spot, and understandably never on a Sunday!

One of the shortest recorded Sunday School journeys undertaken took place on Saturday 20th June, 1914. Twenty members of the Moordown Band of Hope travelled the 1 mile 60 chains from Bournemouth Central to Pokesdown a journey taking seven minutes in an additional carriage attached to the 1.19 pm from Bournemouth West, the party returning from Pokesdown at 7.52 pm. Three days earlier 280 members of the Boscombe Band of Hope undertook the 1 mile 72 chain journey from Meyrick Park Halt to Boscombe on the 7.40 pm Bournemouth West-Christchurch service. The usual push-pull train had to be replaced for the occasion by a locomotive and four coaches and a member of staff from Bournemouth Central was sent to the halt to supervise the loading of what was probably the greatest number of people ever to board a train at that point!

Running on a parallel track to the aspirations of the religious revivalists was the National Sunday League. Formed in 1855 its original intentions were to secure the Sunday opening of parks and museums for the enjoyment of the working classes. Within 25 years it was organizing Sunday railway excursions, during the summer of 1913 around 500 specials were run throughout the country, the LSWR usually running three excursions each summer Sunday from Waterloo. Records from June 1914 reveal a number of excursions to both Swanage and Bournemouth. On the 14th an 8.55 am departure complete with dining saloon called at Southampton West and Brockenhurst before proceeding via the Old Road then calling at Wareham and Corfe Castle and arriving in Swanage at 12.27 pm, with a return departure at 7.08 pm. Two excursions run on the 21st June were more complex departing from Waterloo at 8.55 and 9.00 am respectively, both consisting of 10 coaches including a dining saloon. The 8.55 am called at Vauxhall, Wimbledon, Surbiton, Basingstoke, Eastleigh, Southampton West, Brockenhurst, Ringwood and Wimborne where the front three coaches were detached before the train proceeded to Poole, Parkstone, Branksome and arriving at Bournemouth West at 12.43 pm. The 9.00 am departure made the same stops except Clapham instead of Vauxhall and arrived in Bournemouth at 12.59 pm, the return workings departing at 7.20 and 7.30 pm respectively. The final excursion for the month departed from Waterloo on the 28th at 8.55 am with a 12-coach load including a dining saloon, four coaches being detached at Wimborne.

Amongst the number of private individuals who organized excursions was Henry John Edgson of Weymouth. Originally employed as a butler in Berkshire he had become a passenger guard on the LSWR at Dorchester by 1871, and 10 years later he owned a gift shop in Weymouth, resigning from the LSWR in 1882. The first advert for his excursions appeared in August 1889, they were usually to destinations on the LSWR system, some trips having facilities to return by other services, whilst other excursions, including half-day excursions, used timetabled trains. These popular excursions continuing until shortly before his death aged 82 in January 1910 when the local press referred to him as the local 'Cook'.

A further inducement to travel was the introduction of the 'Bournemouth Holiday Season Ticket' a forerunner of the popular runabout ticket. The advertising described them as, 'An Open Sesame to, The Evergreen Valley, Hardy Country, and the historic New Forest'. A choice of four tickets was available, the prices in 1913 ranging from 10s. to 16s. for one week's travel. The area varied according to price, covering Swanage in the west, Lyndhurst Road to the east, and to the north Hurn and Wimborne; unfortunately it was not available eastwards over the Old Road.

Two forms of public entertainment that heavily relied on the railways were the circus and the theatre. Whereas funfairs in general tended to travel on a short circuit using both horses and road locomotives to haul their equipment, the circus travelled the length and breadth of the country, usually involving special trains. The parade of animals and equipment from the station to the circus site generated much local interest and publicity. The *Southern Times* reporting on the arrival of Buffalo Bill's Wild West Show from Taunton at Weymouth on 4th August, 1903 stated: '... to accomplish this gigantic task requires an army of men and three special railway trains, made up of twenty-one cars-each constructed on American lines and each measuring nearly sixty feet in length'. It had to be a finely tuned operation, following two performances at Weymouth in front of 20,000 spectators it was off to Bournemouth the following day and then to Salisbury. The following year the same circus performed in Taunton, Dorchester, Poole and Southampton on successive days.

Theatrical specials usually moved to the next venue on a Sunday, the thespians travelling in a carriage with the scenery, props and other items loaded into covered carriage trucks or similar vehicles (the LSWR only possessed one scenery van). There obviously were movements to and from theatres at Southampton, Bournemouth and Weymouth over the years. However, an interesting noted movement was of Hayes Portable Theatre on 9th March, 1914 from Dorchester to Wimborne requiring the use of about 13 railway vehicles, suggesting the arrangement was something on the lines of a circus marquee or other type of sectional building. Theatrical specials declined quickly after World War I with the introduction of the motor pantechnicon; today only a few of the specially printed tickets for such traffic survive as a reminder of a past chapter in railway history.

Dorset and West Hampshire was predominately agricultural, the line west of Southampton had none of the heavy industrial goods traffic of others, but it did serve the ports of Poole and Weymouth and carry the stone traffic from Portland. Otherwise, the main traffic apart from the delivery of general goods was coal, which during the early part of the 20th century coal was extensively used by industry and domestic households (house coal in 1911 cost £1 5s. per ton). One only had to calculate how much the average household burnt in a week then multiply that by the number of houses in a town of village to calculate the requirements during the winter months. Much of this arrived in the local goods yard in either the private owners' wagons of the coal merchants or the colliery companies.

The principal types of farming in the area were arable, sheep farming and milk production, whilst in the south-east area around Wimborne and in the neighbourhood of Bournemouth a considerable area was devoted to market-garden crops and soft fruit. The main livestock markets along the line were at Ringwood, Wimborne and Dorchester, with traffic from Sturminster Newton and Blandford via the Somerset & Dorset line, whilst over the years traffic diminished from the smaller markets such as Wareham.

Prior to World War I and the gradual introduction of motor transport, the railways were well organized in the transportation of cattle both to and from markets. Wimborne and Dorchester were the two largest in the area, Wimborne's adjoined the railway station, a siding with loading facilities running almost into the site. Dorchester was but a few hundred yards from both the GWR and LSWR stations, whilst Ringwood market was originally at the other end of the town.

Agricultural traffic was varied ranging from farm supplies to produce and the transportation of livestock. At the top end of the market was the movement of horses those of high value being conveyed in horse boxes attached to passenger trains, whereas other livestock often referred to as cattle travelled in cattle wagons usually by goods train. The working of cattle traffic was dependent on the market of the day, the railway not knowing the requirements until after the sales, then there was the need to move the livestock as quickly as possible either by booked goods services or a special if required.

Milk was an important traffic to the railway, special arrangements being made for its transportation ranging from complete milk trains to smaller amounts carried on other services. In the days before bulk transport local farmers brought their milk to the local station by horse and cart for transportation to the dairy of their choice. A town the size of Southampton handled 3,000 gallons a day in 1906. During that period milk was carried in 17 gallon churns; interestingly the farmer was not charged by the churn, but only for the amount in each churn.

Traffic carried to and from weekly markets was always varied according to demand, this again applied to the annual livestock sales which required special arrangements. One such event was the annual Dorchester sheep fair held in May, where for the 1914 event 50 empty cattle wagons plus two brake vans were held at Dorchester, a further 50 at Wareham and 20 at Hamworthy Junction which would be brought to Dorchester as required. On the morning of the sale a sheep special was also run from Swanage and Corfe Castle to Dorchester arriving at 7.36 am. The problem was that nobody knew their destination until after the sale resulting in ad hoc arrangements. Two sheep specials to Eastleigh were arranged to travel via the Old Road with stops at Wimborne and Ringwood, and a third was expected to convey traffic for the London Brighton & South Coast Railway (LBSCR), with traffic detached at Wareham for the Swanage branch.

Although the Blandford Great Ewe Fair took place on the Somerset & Dorset Railway, the LSWR provided special arrangements for cattle specials from Wimborne after the show. Again there were ad hoc arrangements involving Bournemouth providing two engines and Wimborne guards and brake vans to work the specials forward, this could be either by the Old Road or via Bournemouth and Sway according to the requirements of the day, with the specials working either to Eastleigh and beyond or Portsmouth and beyond.

Another event that required similar arrangements was the Wimborne Horse Fair as it was not until 4.00 pm the previous day that the decision was taken to run a special from Dorchester or not. It has to be assumed that if a special was not required any traffic was conveyed on the normal services, in which case Bournemouth had to provide an engine for shunting purposes at Wimborne.

The various annual agricultural shows held on or near LSWR territory also generated a large amount of extra traffic. Dorchester was again the venue for the Bath & West & Southern Counties Society show between 27th May and 1st June, 1908, and before the extensive use of motor transport the railways played a major part. Both the GWR and LSWR provided additional facilities at their respective stations, the latter improving the triple loading dock which had been constructed for the 1887 show near Culliford Bridge. By March improvements were being carried out at Chalk Sidings, from where much infill for the Holes Bay curve had been taken. The existing sidings were lengthened to their upmost extent and two additional sidings added, it being intended to use the sidings for shunting and making up of goods trains, leaving the goods yard clear for other traffic. At Dorchester Junction the removal of chalk from the cutting sides for infill at the new Melcombe Regis station at Weymouth allowed the GWR to install a siding each side of the junction.

Such was the amount of traffic to be handled that both companies would not accept coal or coke wagons between 11th May and 8th June inclusive. A steam crane was used to handle much of the heavy equipment being unloaded and later reloaded at the loading docks near Culliford Bridge. Special cheap fares were offered from many LSWR stations during the period of the show. The entire railway operation, planned with military precision, was a credit to Mr A. Pearce who had only recently been appointed station master at Dorchester. The following week the Royal Counties Agricultural Societies show was held at Southampton, the entire elaborate process having to be repeated again.

June 1911 saw the Southern Counties Show visit Weymouth. The *Southern Times* reported that, 'Densely packed railway excursions from all parts of Dorsetshire and neighbouring counties have materially have swelled the attendance at the show today'.

A further example was the Royal Counties show held at Portsmouth from 10th to 14th June, 1914. Cheap fares were offered throughout the event allowing travel by normal services with a number of excursions running from Dorset and Hampshire. On the 12th, included in these was a special off the Somerset & Dorset, exchanging engines and guard at Wimborne whence a non-stop run was made to Southampton. An excursion departing Weymouth at 8.08 am stopped at all stations via the Old Road to Brockenhurst where it was joined by a special from Bournemouth West travelling via the Direct Line with the combined train leaving Brockenhurst at 10.15 am. The following day only the Bournemouth-Portsmouth excursion ran, leaving passengers from Dorset and the Old Road to travel via normal services.

The emergence of the 20th century saw an increase in Royal Train journeys both for official and private visits. The unveiling of the Queen Victoria statue at Weymouth by her youngest daughter Beatrice, Princess Henry of Battenburg on 20th October, 1902, required a special train from Southampton West consisting of two guard's vans, a composite first, a second class carriage, and a Royal saloon which arrived at 12.30 pm, five minutes ahead of time at an elaborately decorated station. Having been suitably wined and dined and done her duty HRH returned to the station arriving back at Southampton West at 4.53 pm. A further visit to Weymouth by Princess Henry took place on 16th November, 1910 when she opened a Naval bazaar and Nelson victory exhibition, having travelled from Ringwood in a special train supplied by the LSWR.

There had over the years been a number of private visits to gentry in the Wimborne area. However, a private visit in December 1905 became a public event as King Edward VII reviewed detachments of the volunteers who had assembled from all over Dorset; this in itself involved a considerable amount of additional traffic at the station. The Royal Train travelled via the Old Road and the account of the event in the *Southern Times* gave a very clear description of the train and the officials that were involved in its movement: '... the special had left Waterloo punctually at 1 pm and ran through Wimborne station some minutes before time. By the time it had backed on to the up line and pulled up at the platform it was nearly 3.30 pm the time fixed for the arrival'. The Royal Train hauled by a 4-4-2 radial tank No. 421 consisted of a saloon, a palace saloon, with a luggage composite at one end and a guard's van at the other end.

HM King George V, having spent several days with the fleet watching early Naval aviation tactics, landed at Weymouth harbour on Saturday 11th May, 1912. He proceeded to the arrival side of Weymouth station which was suitably decorated for the occasion; adjacent to the entrance was the band of the LSWR Institute Eastleigh, who played the National Anthem upon his arrival. Following the customary shaking of the hands of various officials, he boarded the LSWR Royal Train which, according to the *Southern Times*, consisted of a kitchen car, a first class coach, palace saloon, and a corridor coach hauled by 'L12' class 4-4-0 No. 425. Departing at 10.05 am the train arrived at Walton-on-Thames at 1.00 pm where His Majesty alighted for an afternoon at Kempton Races.

The Royal Train conveying HM King George V from Weymouth to Walton-on-Thames on 11th May, 1912. Photographed approaching Walton-on-Thames this view shows the simplicity of the Royal Train at that period, hauled by Drummond 'L12' class 4-4-0. No. 425 followed by a kitchen car, first class coach, palace saloon and a corridor coach. No. 425 entered traffic in December 1904 and was withdrawn in August 1951 having travelled a recorded 1,500,143 miles. *Author's Collection*

The efficiency of the LSWR in handling troop movements at small stations is demonstrated above, an unidentified Adams '445' class 4-4-0 stands on the up line at Wool with a troop special during 1911. The train appears to have arrived from the Dorchester direction with the troops preparing to march off over the board walk at the east end of the station. Note the rake of horse boxes standing in the down platform. Owing to the locomotive still retaining the square look-out windows in the cab front it reduces the likely locomotive to a choice of five: Nos. 445, 450, 452, 453, or 456.

Author's Collection

The proximity of several naval dockyards and many military camps resulted in the LSWR perfecting the running of both naval and army specials. In particular the mass movement of troops and volunteers (the Territorial Army from 1908) to their annual summer camps, many of which were situated in the Hampshire-Dorset area, including those at Lyndhurst, Beaulieu, Sway, Wareham, Swanage, Bovington and Lulworth. With the exception of Wareham these were small wayside stations which were suddenly overwhelmed by the amount of traffic resulting in extra staff having to be brought in to assist with the traffic. Although not all troops travelled by train, during August 1901 a large number of troops in the Swanage area had marched from Winchester.

The movement of troop specials during the period were numerous and only examples can be given to demonstrate the amount of traffic handled. On 2nd August, 1902 the LSWR conveyed the Weymouth detachment of the Dorset Volunteers to their summer camp on Salisbury Plain, being joined at Dorchester by the Dorchester detachment; there was then a delay caused by the late arrival of the Bridport detachment, having to march over from the GWR station. The following year the 2nd battalion of the Dorset Regiment, then stationed at the Verne, Portland, carried out exercises at Bovington, where they held their athletic sports day. The LSWR ran a special train to and from Portland to Wool to enable families and friends to visit.

Wool station was a focal point for camps at Lulworth and Bovington. On 13th July, 1907 the 6th Battalion Royal Fusiliers (Royal City of London Militia), who had held their summer camp at Bovington, departed in two special trains leaving at 5.55 am and 6.30 am conveying 18 officers and 660 men. The following year on 27th June, 1908 the 6th battalion of the Royal Fusiliers, having completed a month's training, departed in two special trains, later in the morning the 2nd Kings Liverpool Regiment left with 10 horses, 60 cycles and 10 tons of baggage by special train for Gosport.

However, their numbers were small compared with around the 3,000 troops of the Royal Warwickshire Territorial Brigade camp at West Lulworth early the following month. On the morning of Saturday August 2nd a train arrived bringing an advance party of eight officers, 185 men and 21 troop horses. This was followed by eight specials on Sunday: the first to arrive at 7.15 am consisting of LNWR stock brought 12 officers and 270 men and a Maxim gun, the second at 7.45 am carried 11 officers 350 men, four horses a Maxim gun and a wagon. The remaining six specials came in quick succession, at 11.23 am 13 officers, 345 men and 12 horses, followed half an hour later by a train containing 14 officers and 500 men. Then in less than 30 minutes two further trains arrived, the first containing 12 officers and 400 men, the second 12 officers and 421 men. At 3.06 pm 10 officers and 350 men arrived, the final train arriving at 3.37 pm brought approximately the same number. The following Sunday the brigade marched to Wool station and departed in a number of special trains to Ludgershall to continue training.

During the same period a further 5,000 troops were camped in the vicinity of Swanage having arrived in 24 special trains, these also departing on the Sunday and the following Tuesday. Also between 8th August and 8th September there was also a major army exercise involving 3,000 troops in the Holmsley area,

Troop manoeuvres and Territorial Army camps in the New Forest were common during the summer months in the years before World War I. Photographed at Sway station in August 1905 are a contingent of the 1st Bucks Rifle Volunteers; note the train and additional engine in the background.   *G.A. Pryer Collection*

With elaborate decoration 'T9' class 4-4-0 No. 773 stands with Kitchener's special train outside Southampton West on 12th July, 1902 after his return from the Boer War. In front of the engine are, *from left to right*, inspector Wilkinson, inspector Moore and driver James.

R.K. Blencowe Collection

again a number of special trains would have been required to handle this traffic. At the same time there were also a large number of Territorials camped in the vicinity of Weymouth.

A number of brigades and regiments carried out their training in the Wool area during 1911, by mid-July already five brigades and regiments had arrived and departed before the 15th when two trains brought the Hampshire Territorial Force consisting of 3,111 officers and men, they departing early in the morning of the 29th. Later the same day the South Western Infantry Brigade arrived, followed on 6th August by 3,077 officers and men of the South Midlands Brigade.

During 1913 a total of 2,142 officers and men of the 4th, 5th, 6th and 7th Hants Territorial Battalions arrived at Blandford on Saturday 26th July in seven trains between 10.20 am and 6.50 pm. It was a major undertaking having to work these trains off the LSWR in between the heavy Saturday traffic of the Somerset & Dorset Railway. Another movement on the LSWR that day was B Company of the 4th Battalion Dorset Regiment who travelled to Exmouth.

The 3rd August saw seven specials run from Bristol conveying the Gloucesters and Worcesters to Swanage for their annual camp, with three train loads returning and a further three train loads arriving the following Sunday, with the entire force departing on Sunday 17th.

During 1914 there were extensive manoeuvres, on Sunday 17th May the Hampshire Carabineers travelled from Aldershot to Verwood, with reversal of the train at West Moors. Later in the summer the LSWR were involved in the mobilisation of Territorials in three districts of Hampshire, Wiltshire and Dorset,

On Sunday 2nd August it was planned to send 24 trains carrying the 1st London Division Territorial Force from London to Wareham and Wool, nine of these specials travelling to Wool. It was a well-planned complex operation, the first train arriving at Wareham at 11.20 am and the last at 8.15 pm, with a number of the specials routed via the Old Road both outward and as returning empty stock workings with locomotives taking water at Ringwood.

However, as the first trains arrived war was declared. Other trains *en route* were stopped and returned to London, with stock having to be sent to return the men, horses and equipment that had already arrived.

The responsibility for the smooth handling of all this extra traffic rested with the station master of the station concerned. A typical example of the period was Stephen Hooker, the station master at Wool who had commenced his career as a junior clerk at Woolston in 1876. Moving up he was a clerk at Bournemouth East between July 1881 and 1895. In February of that year he was appointed station master at Wool with a free house for £95 per annum, his salary raised to £100 in July 1911. January 1916 saw him appointed station master at Liphook on £115 from where he retired in 1925. When he died aged 81 in September 1942 he left a son, four grandsons, and a son-in-law to continue the railway tradition. His eldest son, J.E. Hooker, had predeceased him having been station master at Windsor.

Important national events required both the mass movement of service personnel and the public. The Coronation of King Edward VII on 26th June, 1902, and the following fleet review at Spithead, required many special trains converging on London, Southampton and Portsmouth. Included in the arrangements were trains to convey troops for ceremonial duties. A battery of the Royal Horse artillery travelled by special train from Dorchester on 19th June, their guns and lumbers loaded aboard trucks placed at the end of the up platform ahead of which were coaches to convey the troops. The horses were loaded into 12 covered cattle trucks placed in the cattle dock siding. The *Southern Times* reported that into each truck eight chestnuts were boxed side by side, tethered to the bars in front. The trucks were afterwards shunted onto the front of the train before its departure at 8.30 am.

Unfortunately, owing to the King's illness the Coronation and other festivities were cancelled at the last moment, and apart from dispersing the assembled servicemen and visitors many of the planned specials were not required, although a number were run to view the assembled fleet. The revised date for the Coronation and fleet review in August again involved a vast amount of planning and extra traffic but was not on so large a scale as the previous planned event.

The same procedures were repeated in 1911 for the Coronation of King George V, again normal services were either altered or suspended.

In addition to these special workings, there were the regular movements of troops to and from overseas duties at Southampton Docks, often travelling via Southampton West to gain access to other lines via the Andover and Redbridge line, or to barracks at Dorchester and Portland. As an example on 9th March, 1914 the 2nd Battalion of the Royal Welch Fusiliers were transported to Portland and two companies to Dorchester.

As the 'Golden Age' approached its abrupt end in 1914, it is necessary to conclude two schemes mentioned earlier in this chapter. The Redbridge curve was never built despite extensions of time to the original Act in both 1911 and 1913, the Board deciding in June 1917 to allow the powers to lapse. Despite two world wars when it would have proved strategically useful, it was never proceeded with. Also the South Western & Isle of Wight Junction Railway had carried out trial borings during 1914 and obtained a further Act with extensions of time. However, World War I stopped further progress, and little further action was taken although the plan remained an option for a number of years.

Times were also changing for the railway delivery van with its much-loved horse, the motor age having arrived. In June 1911 it was reported that the five motor vehicles in use at Bournemouth Central for parcels and luggage delivery were insufficient to perform the work and it was recommended that a further motor van be purchased at a cost of £448, less 1¼ per cent discount for cash. Four months later in view of their satisfactory service and an increase in the company's earnings, it was recommended that four similar vehicles, but with four cylinder engines instead of two, be obtained for use at Bournemouth West, also one for goods and parcels work at Parkstone and one for Southampton. The cost of the vehicles would be £463 totalling £2,778, less 1¼ per cent for cash. Their introduction allowed the withdrawal of four horses and vans at Bournemouth West and one from Parkstone. Within weeks the question of a garage for the vehicles arose, a recommendation being made that the disused motorbus garage at Totton be removed and re-erected at Bournemouth West. At the end of 1913 when it was decided to purchase two more vans for the Bournemouth stations the price had dropped to £440.

As the railway moved into a further chapter of its history, a number of the older staff who had seen and assisted in its evolution over the years went into retirement. Charles Henry Staines retired in July 1913 after serving as station master at Totton for 36 years of his 45 years' service. In his early days as a clerk at Redbridge he gave Henry Holmes, later to become the superintendent of the line, his first lessons in railway work. Well respected, Mr Staines was presented with a number of gifts to mark the occasion, a gold watch chain subscribed for by 70 to 80 of his friends, a solid leather suitcase, an inscribed oak tantalus, a set of metal trays, a purse of money and a cheque for £75.

Early in 1914 Horatio W. Pine, station master at Lyndhurst Road since 1883, took retirement surviving until November 1940, when he passed away aged 87. April 1914 saw A.F. Gibson, station master at Moreton, who had been appointed at an annual salary of £90 early in 1905, transferred to Downton.

The railway itself had reached a high point to which it was never to return. The fastest expresses between Waterloo and Bournemouth took two hours to cover the 108 miles, other services were also of good quality and they were also at that time the undisputed carrier of goods. The experience the LSWR had gained and perfected, in particular with the mass movement of Territorial Army forces to their annual summer camps, was to be tested in the coming years as the lights went out all over Europe and the 'Golden Age' was extinguished, never to return.

The presence of the Somerset & Dorset Railway is recorded at Broadstone during 1914 with '2P' class superheated 4-4-0 No. 68 in the Somerset & Dorset Railway Prussian blue livery approaching with an up through train for the Midland Railway. The immaculate condition of the engine and the presence of a locomotive inspector on the footplate would suggest the photograph was taken shortly after the engine's construction in April 1921 at a cost of £8,130. No. 40325 (its BR number) was withdrawn in October 1951.
Kelland Collection/Bournemouth Railway Trust

Somerset & Dorset Railway Johnson-designed small 4-4-0 No. 45 stands at Bournemouth West before departure with an up train photographed after August 1909, at which date the larger Deeley pattern boiler and improved cab were fitted. No. 45 was constructed at Derby in February 1897 and withdrawn from service in February 1932. *Author's Collection*

Until the introduction of 4-4-0 tender locomotives in 1891 the Somerset & Dorset used 0-4-4 tanks for their passenger services, after which they were relegated to local services. Vulcan Foundry-built No. 55 of 1885 vintage approaches Broadstone with an up local train of modest length around 1920. *Kelland Collection/Bournemouth Railway Trust*

Chapter Two

World War One

The outbreak of World War I had an instant impact on the railways of Britain, particularly those in the South that were to carry the burden of traffic *en route* to the French coast. The Government, under the powers of the Regulation of the Forces Act of 1871, had taken over control of the railways from 4th August, 1914 with the Railway Executive Committee taking overall control. Herbert Walker of the LSWR became its Chairman, and all competition ceased as the railways set about their wartime role.

All excursions and cheap tickets were suspended and trains became crowded as men went to join the forces, there being sad farewells at many stations. At Poole on 3rd August around 60 Royal Navy reservists were given a civic send off as they boarded the 1.43 pm train to travel to Portsmouth. Later there were further distressing scenes at Wareham and other country stations as horses requisitioned by the Government from local farms were loaded into cattle wagons on the first stage of their journey to France.

Southampton was one of the main ports of embarkation where between 9th and 14th August, 1914, 130,000 troops, 38,000 horses, 344 guns, 1,574 lumbers, 277 motor vehicles, and 1,802 motorcycles passed through the port. On the Southampton & Dorchester line traffic increased considerably as various military establishments were opened in the district. Coal trains to bunker the ships based at Southampton and Portsmouth came from South Wales to join the Southampton & Dorchester line at Redbridge. A large number of special trains were run, often at very short notice; of greatest importance were train loads of ammunition for the forces destined for Southampton, Portsmouth and Portland. Soon the number of casualties resulted in the running of numerous ambulance trains.

It became necessary to provide additional sidings and other facilities to cater for War Department needs. The New Forest, previously a summer training ground, quickly became the site for a number of training camps and later military hospitals and convalescent homes. All these establishments relied heavily on the railway. In one operation requiring 80 trains the 7th division of the British Expeditionary Force, who were held in reserve in their camp at Racecourse Hill, Lyndhurst, were moved on the first part of the journey to Zeebrugge.

There had been a long association between the military at Wareham, Swanage and Lulworth, Territorial Army summer camps having been held in the area for many years. Wareham camp immediately became 'permanent' and extended to cover sites on both sides of the Worgret Road. This created a regular traffic as troops of various regiments moved on and off the camp - at times there were as many as 7,000 troops stationed there, creating not only considerable business for the railway but also for Wareham's tradespeople. An ordnance depot was established adjacent to Wareham station during 1915, a siding connecting with the up bay line being brought into use on 25th April. Army training camps had also been established at Swanage increasing traffic over the Swanage branch and at Wareham.

ANZAC troops from one of the camps in the area wait to entrain at New Milton station during World War I.   *G.A. Pryer Collection*

German prisoners of war captured in the early days of the battle of the Somme being marched to Southampton West station. In the background can be seen the Corporation electricity generating station and in the centre foreground the remains of the down platform of the pre-1895 Blechynden station.   *G.A. Pryer Collection*

Further down the line at Wool, a wayside station that normally came to life only briefly during the summer camp period suddenly became one of the busiest on the line. On 14th September, 1914 four trains brought 4,000 men from the Manchester area, who then marched to Bovington where they established a tented camp. The resulting increase in traffic caused an instruction to be issued in late 1914 that certain fast trains were to stop at Wool as required. These troops, plus other contingents based at Lulworth, increased traffic to such an extent that in January 1915 it was agreed to erect a footbridge at Wool station at an estimated cost of £250. In July it was decided that, in view of the increased road traffic of the district, Burton crossing (west of Wool) be provided with signals interlocked with the gates. Further up the line Worgret Junction was given an up main outer home signal to facilitate acceptance of trains.

The transportation of prisoners of war created other traffic movements; one such camp had opened at Dorchester shortly after the war commenced. However, within a period there were transfers to other camps and new arrivals, in mid-December 1914 there was a mass exodus with prisoners departing in special trains from both the GWR and LSWR stations, those from the latter destined to internment on the Isle of Wight. This was followed by the arrival at the LSWR station of 500 prisoners by special train from Frimley, numerous movements of this type taking place throughout the hostilities. At the same time there were troops moving from Dorchester by train when the Dorset Reserve Territorial Battalion departed for Southampton by two special trains within an hour of each other, to be followed by a further train from Bridport being transferred to the LSWR line at Dorchester Junction. The above movements are just a sample of many that took place across the system during hostilities.

There was also the need to supply troops based at camps in Hampshire and Dorset with food supplies. In the days before ready meals and a lack of modern refrigeration systems fresh supplies had to be delivered at regular intervals, meat being conveyed daily from cold stores at Southampton Docks in insulated meat vans to Wareham, Corfe Castle, Swanage, Wool, Dorchester, Weymouth and Portland.

As the war escalated a number of establishments, sidings and other facilities were provided along the Southampton & Dorchester line. By far the largest Government project in the area was located at Holton Heath; a desolate tract of country between Hamworthy Junction and Wareham, where the authorities decided to construct a large factory for the manufacture of cordite. Within weeks of the outbreak of the war, Winston Churchill had realised that the only way to ensure a constant and reliable supply of this invaluable war material was to set up such a factory and a committee was formed to investigate possible sites. They visited Holton Heath towards the end of 1914 and seem to have been instantly convinced that they had found the right spot. It was ideal for their purpose in many ways, perhaps its most obvious asset being ready access to both rail and water transport. It was also suitably isolated from any concentration of buildings and the site itself was fairly level, although it had near its centre a low hill which facilitated the construction of a reservoir and nitro-glycerine plant. At that time it was usual to make this substance in a factory built on a gentle slope so that it could flow from process to process in

An undated photograph during World War I shows German prisoners of war having arrived at Dorchester station before being marched to the POW camp. Apart from the removal of the canopy over the entrance door very few alterations appear to have taken place to the exterior of the station in later years. *Author's Collection*

Holton Heath station looking towards Poole: constructed during World War I for the transportation of workmen to the adjacent cordite factory, the blast proof shelters were a later addition. Although the cordite factory has now been demolished the station remains open as an unstaffed halt serving the replacement industrial estate and surrounding area. *Author*

lead gutters by gravity. The site was quickly leased from the owner, Sir John Lees of Lytchett Minster, construction work being put in hand without delay. The contract for construction of the factory and associated works was awarded to Messrs Topham, Jones & Railton.

In December 1914, to assist with the construction traffic the LSWR loaned the contractor two vintage saddle tank engines, No. 457 *Clausentum* and No. 458 *Ironside*, which had formerly belonged to the Southampton Docks Company. A large workforce was drafted in to prepare the site and erect the many large buildings - and in March 1915 two 'C14' class engines that had previously been withdrawn from traffic, Nos. 741, and 744, were returned to service. Coupled to trailers, they operated a service for workmen between Bournemouth West and the site, where a temporary platform was provided on the down side to the west of the later Holton Heath station.

In those days before the general use of the motor lorry even goods moved over a short distance went by rail. Records show wagons of special glazed bricks being carried from Sharp Jones pottery siding at Branksome to Holton Heath. Commencing on 3rd September, 1915 extra freight trains were worked by the Hamworthy Junction shunting engine when required departing from Hamworthy Junction at 8.15 am, 10 minutes being allowed to shunt at Holton Heath before arriving at Wareham at 8.39 am. A booked freight also departed from Hamworthy Junction at 1.45 pm terminating at Wareham, the return workings of these trains being at 8.50 am and 2.16 pm both stopping at Sandford siding to attach ballast wagons for Holton Heath.

A new signal box known as 'Holton' had opened on the down side of the main line on 10th May, 1915, its 16-lever Stevens frame (of which four levers were spare) controlling access to the works reception sidings. This was followed by a station with two 400 ft platforms on the main lines officially opened on 3rd April, 1916, but the down platform was ready in March and workmen made some use of it from that date. When first opened it handled only traffic connected with the cordite factory, the station being staffed from 8.00 am until 8.00 pm on weekdays and at train times on Sundays.

Those employed in the construction of the plant were issued with tickets by the contractor, being LSWR workmen's weekly tickets overprinted 'Topham, Jones & Railton'. Initially the hundreds of Admiralty workers necessary to operate the plant on a three-shift system who had to travel by rail from Poole, Bournemouth, Christchurch, Wareham, Swanage and elsewhere were issued with free quarterly season tickets. However, as there was virtually no local population and almost everybody employed at the Holton Heath factory incurred some travel expenses, this resulted in all workers regardless of the mode of transport being paid a weekly travel allowance of two shillings.

The main complex of the factory itself was completed during January 1916, and to facilitate transport of some of the output by water a pier was constructed at Rockley, about halfway between Hamworthy Junction and Holton Heath stations. Work on this started in August 1916, Topham, Jones & Railton being provided with a siding on the down side of the line, 2,100 yards west of Hamworthy Junction, for delivering materials to the site. The siding was brought into use on 17th August, the points being worked by a one-lever

The only known photograph of Lake Halt on the Hamworthy branch opened during World War I for the conveyance of workmen to the nearby wartime ship yard by workmen's train. In the background Brownsea Island can be seen, today the area surrounding the former halt is surrounded by housing in Lake Road, Rockley Road and Lulworth Close.

Transport & Travel Monthly

An Ordnance Survey map of the 1920s showing the World War I shipyard on the Wareham Channel at Hamworthy and railway sidings. Lake Halt is shown adjacent to where the Hamworthy branch passed over Lake Road. Today the shipyard has been replaced by a yacht marina, the Royal Marines boat base, and housing development. Likewise housing development in Lulworth Close near the former halt has also replaced other sidings and industrial premises.

Ordnance Survey

ground frame controlled from Hamworthy Junction box by Sykes lock and plunger with cabin door control. On completion, the pier was connected to the internal rail system of Holton Heath factory by a standard gauge line which crossed the main line on a skew bridge consisting of a steel span resting on brick abutments (still known today as 'Admiralty Bridge'), the contractor's siding and ground frame being removed on 1st April, 1917.

On the Hamworthy branch at a point about halfway between Hamworthy Junction and Hamworthy Quay, an establishment on the banks of the Wareham Channel known officially as 'Auxiliary Shipyard No. 62' was opened in 1917 for the construction of 1,000 ton concrete barges. The operators of the yard, Messrs Hill, Richards & Co., applied to the LSWR in late 1917 for permission to erect a platform on the branch 73 chains from Hamworthy Junction for the use of their workmen, and it was agreed that this could be done subject to an undertaking on behalf of Hill, Richards to construct the platform to the satisfaction of the LSWR engineer. It was to be not less than 500 ft long and the costs of any staff considered necessary to ensure safe working were to be borne by the shipyard owner, who also had to arrange lighting at their own expense. Known as 'Lake Halt' and situated on the south side of Dukes bridge, it opened in September 1918 for the use of shipyard personnel only. As the Hamworthy branch was then only open for freight traffic, special trains had to be run from Bournemouth to serve it. To save the very considerable cost of interlocking alterations at Hamworthy Junction signal box, facing point locks operated by levers on the ground were fitted as required to allow passenger trains to pass over the line. In November the same year a siding was laid on the site of the former up line between Hamworthy Goods and a point south of Lake Halt, where it passed through a gate to enter the shipyard which continued to be managed on behalf of the Government by Messrs Hill, Richards & Company.

The Hamworthy branch was very busy during the war as Southampton was virtually closed to commercial shipping, much of its traffic being dealt with at other ports - including Poole. In 1915 a total of 129,243 barrels of Channel Island potatoes were transferred from ships into railway wagons at Hamworthy Quay, this level being reached each season for the duration of the war. Even after the return of peace there was a great deal of activity. For instance, between the end of May and the end of August 1919, the quay had handled 33 shiploads of potatoes requiring 1,437 railway trucks, whilst another 11,029 wagons were needed to clear cargoes of tomatoes, apples, and general merchandise between August and November. Furthermore, this heavy traffic was handled at a wharf designed for the loading of china clay, with sidings at right angles to the quay wall to facilitate tipping. This gave rise to double handling, the off-loaded cargos being stacked on the quay wall before being wheeled along to the wagon doors on sack trucks: the layout was not just awkward, it was also very restricted! There were only four sidings serving that part of the quay, of which two - with a total capacity of 20 wagons - were available for shipping traffic. Of the other two, one passed through a shed used as a clay store and the other was reserved for coal wagons to bunker ships. Such was the congestion that wagons loaded with ammunition awaiting shipment were often stabled in the Kinson Pottery siding at Hamworthy Junction awaiting acceptance.

With Southampton West still alongside the water, this photograph taken on 5th June, 1917 shows the commencement of the construction of the train ferry terminal line. It was also the beginning of a process of land reclamation that was to continue for a number of years. The low-sided wagons in view are a mixed collection from various railway companies including, Midland, Lancashire & Yorkshire, North British, North Staffordshire, Hull & Barnsley and Cheshire Lines Committee, all in use as 'common user' wagons for the war effort.

The Royal Engineers Library, Chatham

On 17th August, 1917 construction work on the line to the train ferry terminal had proceeded past the Pirelli factory (*right*). Looking north the chimney in the centre background is that of the Southampton Corporation power station, Southampton West station is to the left.

The Royal Engineers Library, Chatham

Giving details of all the Government traffic handled at Southampton during the war would overwhelm this book, and as the new Western Docks did not exist at that time much of the traffic only traversed the Southampton & Dorchester line between Northam Junction and Redbridge. However, in April 1917 it was decided to construct a train ferry terminal about 100 yards west of Royal Pier, resulting in a branch line being laid from the west end of the down side of Southampton West station. Some 40,000 tons of stone debris were brought from Easton on the Portland branch by special trains commencing on 11th May, 1917 to form an embankment, followed by a wooden-piled pier with double track and train ferry bridge and link span at the end. The work was executed with the sort of speed that only seems achievable in wartime, being completed by late autumn 1917, allowing an advanced sailing to Dieppe on 13th December, an additional berth being added during mid-1918. Other work completed shortly afterwards included a double track link to the Royal Pier and Town Quay for military barge traffic.

Other facilities included seven sidings on the down side at Southampton West on land adjoining the Corporation power station, and a marshalling yard adjoining the Pirelli factory which had 12 loop sidings to accommodate 500 wagons and eight additional sidings holding 200 wagons. There was a fuel oil storage facility and engine shed to accommodate the War Department and Inland Waterways & Dock Board engines that worked the sidings, the inward and outward trains being worked by the LSWR.

Traffic ceased in March 1919; although the facility was short-lived it is recorded that eight locomotives, 42 carriages, and 6,753 goods wagons went to France by this route and 272 locomotives and 1,250 wagons were returned. After closure there was then the spectacle of various Government departments putting their heads in the sand over reparation to the owners of part of the land and Southampton Corporation. The link span was removed in September 1923, and the spur from Southampton West was last used in 1929 for spoil trains during the construction of the Western Docks, likewise the remains of the pier were put to use for unloading materials brought in by sea.

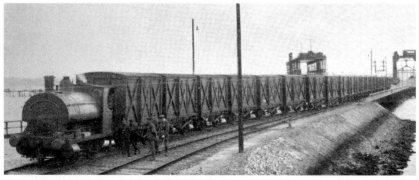

An unidentified Peckett 0-4-0 saddle tank photographed with a train of WD vans at the end of the ferry link span. Behind the vans can be seen the high framework of the deck lift of Train Ferry No. 4.   *Southern Railway Magazine*

Southampton photographed from a seaplane shortly after World War I, to the left the train ferry pier with train ferry No. TF 4 to the right and the cruiser HMS *Hermione* laid up on the left. Royal Pier is to the centre right with Town Quay behind, in the background the River Itchen lies beyond the city. *Author's Collection*

The urgent requirement for timber caused the War Department Timber Committee to request a siding at Woodfidley - one of the loneliest spots in the New Forest; this came into use on 20th June, 1916. The points, which trailed into the down line, were operated from Woodfidley signal box, two levers being added to the locking frame to accommodate the additional signalling. This siding was short-lived, being removed in July 1917. Another siding for the Timber Committee was provided on the up side at Lyndhurst Road during 1917, but in this case no signal alterations were necessary as it connected into the existing up siding by hand points. However, the cost of this siding – the provision of which created the need for a new entrance to the goods yard - was estimated at £1,082.

Timber was also being felled north-east of Wareham by Mr L. Basso, a Weymouth contractor. In October 1918 Basso sought permission to load timber and pit prop traffic at Sandford Pottery Siding; the pottery company having no objections, it was agreed that each wagon so forwarded would be charged at one shilling over and above the Wareham rate. However, in the event Basso either continued with his previous arrangements or at the end of hostilities terminated his contract, for in March 1919 it was reported that he no longer wished to pursue the matter.

A further siding to deal with timber traffic was at Whitley Ridge, on the up side between Brockenhurst and Woodfidley signal box, opening in January 1919 for the use of the Canadian Forestry Corps. It was operated from a ground frame released by Brockenhurst East box and was taken out of use on 12th December, 1922.

At Ringwood additional siding accommodation for War Department hay storage was provided during 1917 whilst at Wool a siding was laid for the Ministry of Munitions, and in the December it was agreed that a 10 ton crane and roadway be provided here. A new siding for Government traffic was provided at Brockenhurst in the latter part of 1918.

Worgret Camp has already been mentioned, but it had no rail connection until 20th November, 1918 (just days after the war ended). On that date a new ground-level signal box known as 'Worgret Siding', together with a siding into the camp and a crossover, was brought into use. The box contained an 8-lever 'knee' frame and was opened only when required to shunt traffic to the camp. It lasted until 22nd June, 1923, the siding's purpose in later years being a site for the scrapping of tanks; today two loading docks survive in the undergrowth.

Worgret army camp, Wareham viewed from the north looking across Wareham Common. The railway between Wareham station and Worgret Junction runs in the fenced cutting in the foreground. *Author's Collection*

A brace of Somerset & Dorset Railway '4F' class 0-6-0s head northwards from Holes Bay Junction with a through train for Bath and beyond. To the left can be seen the earthworks of Longfleet Military sidings brought into use in June 1918 and abolished in July 1922.

G. Bailey Collection

The 1934 Ordnance Survey map showing the Bovington camp branch between Wool station and Bovington Camp (closed in 1928 but not dismantled until 1936).

Reproduced from the 1934 Ordnance Survey Map

Between Wareham and Holton Heath a military siding was opened in 1918, the points, which trailed into the up line immediately on the Wareham side of Keysworth crossing, being controlled from a ground frame released from Wareham signal box. This siding connected with the existing Sandford gravel pit and Pottery sidings, but was taken out of use on 5th July, 1921. Its purpose is now obscure, for earthworks in the fields suggest that it ran in the direction of Holton Heath factory which already had a fully comprehensive internal rail system by 1918.

Another development of 1918 was the Royal Naval Airship station at Woodsford, near Warmwell. This occupied a large area of flat land on the up side of the line between Woodsford No. 38 and 37 crossings, and in May of that year a siding was laid in to serve it. The points, trailing in the up line, were operated from Woodsford Crossing signal box, which was adjacent to No. 38 crossing. Later the same year a halt with wooden platforms 500 ft in length was opened at No. 37 crossing. It was available only to forces personnel so an official closure date in not recorded, but it appears to have gone out of use in 1923 – although the siding remained in use until 24th March, 1928.

Two sidings for military traffic, known as 'Longfleet Sidings', were laid in parallel to the Broadstone line at Holes Bay Junction (west of Poole) on 30th June, 1918, a Hudswell, Clarke 0-4-0 saddle tank, No. 336 of 1889 vintage, being hired by the War Department from Sharp, Jones' pottery at Branksome for shunting purposes. For almost two years the points leading to these sidings were not directly controlled from any lever frame - despite their close proximity to Holes Bay Junction box - but were barred over as required and secured by clip and scotch. They were belatedly connected to the signal box on 20th March, 1920, shortly, after which the site was vacated by the War Department and taken over by Messrs Hill, Richards & Co. and the Waller Housing Corporation; traffic included ashes from Holton Heath and pebbles from West Bay. This arrangement did not last long and the sidings were abolished in July 1922.

Bovington Camp became permanent during 1915, the tents replaced by lines of wooden huts so typical of army camps of that period. It was a move that was to settle the future of Bovington to this day. In June 1916 the Heavy Branch Machine Gun Corps were transferred from Thetford, Norfolk; the men underwent gunnery training at Lulworth whilst encamped at both Bovington and Worgret Heath near Wareham, adding further to the already heavy traffic handled at Wool and Wareham stations. The introduction of the tank into warfare led to the opening of a tank training camp at Bovington later that year, the first machines arriving at Wool station by rail and were driven the short distance to the camp. In 1917 it was reported that 300 tanks were on site (all having arrived at Wool by rail) this resulted in the decision to construct a branch railway to the camp. The LSWR for their part had to make alterations at Wool to accommodate the branch approving plans for new sidings and connections for the branch, the cost of which exclusive of fillings, sleepers and crossing timbers was estimated at £2,776 which would be borne by the War department. A letter sent to the Board of Trade by the LSWR on 26th October, 1918, referring to alterations made to sidings and connections at Wool, stated that work would be carried out on 3rd November, and it was necessary to make use of the connection in question immediately it was placed in its new position.

Wool—Bovington Military Camp Line.

The Line between Wool and Bovington Camp is worked by this Company's Engine and Staff, and used only for the conveyance of Goods Traffic.

The distance from Wool Station to Bovington Camp is 2 miles 15 chains, and the Camp Line connects with the Military Siding on the Up Line side at the east end of Wool Station. A gate, which is kept normally padlocked across the Camp Line, is provided at the Company's boundary at Wool Station and the key of the padlock will be held by the Station Master at Wool.

Two public roads cross the Railway, one at Wool Bridge Crossing, 20 chains distant from Wool Station, and the other at Lytchett Crossing, 46 chains distant from Wool Station. Gates are provided at these crossings to fence the public roadways, and will be kept normally padlocked across the Railway, the keys being held by the Station Master at Wool. There are also two occupation crossings on the Line, one situate between Wool Station and the River Frome Bridge, and the other a short distance the Bovington side of Lytchett level crossing. At Wool Bridge crossing there is a siding connection with the Bovington Camp Line, the points of which are facing for Trains from the direction of Bovington. These points must be kept normally set for the siding and padlocked in that position, in order to form a catch for any vehicles running back from the direction of Bovington.

At Bovington Camp there are several sidings, which have facing connections with the Main Camp Line for Trains from the direction of Wool, and these are provided with dead-ends and serve the military sheds, unloading docks, etc. There is also a run-round loop, which must be kept clear for shunting operations. The sidings mentioned are provided with catch points to prevent vehicles running out on to the Main Camp Line, and the points will be padlocked in the throw-off position and the keys held by the Railway Company's Staff.

When shunting operations are being carried out at Bovington Camp the Engine must always be at the Wool end of the vehicles.

The gradients on the line are as shewn hereunder :—

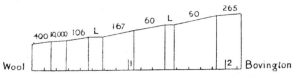

The load of Trains on the Camp Line must not exceed 15 ordinary Goods Wagons and Van, or 4 Military Tanks and Van A heavy Brake Van must be provided at the rear of each Train, accompanied by a man in charge, and the speed of Trains running over the Line must not exceed 15 miles per hour. Before a Train leaves Bovington for Wool the men in charge must apply such number of wagon brakes as may be necessary to supplement the brake power of the Train and safely control it on the falling gradients.

The following engines only may be permitted to work over the Camp Line :—029, 083, 0101, 0151, 0152, 0153, 0154, 0155, 0160, 0162, 0163, 0167, 0302, 0303, 0307, 0310, 0311, 0312, 0336, 0337, 0338, 0341, 0345, 0347, 0369, 0370, 0371, 0380, 0381, 0384, 0397, 0400, 0433, 0436, 0439, 0440, 0441, 0442, 0445 to 0456 inclusive, 0460 to 0472 inclusive, 0147, 177 to 236 inclusive, 473 to 478 inclusive, 496, 506, 509, 515, 526; 160ᴀ, 162ᴀ, 273ᴀ, 277ᴀ, 278ᴀ, 285ᴀ, 286ᴀ, 287ᴀ, 288ᴀ, 289ᴀ, 337ᴀ, 347ᴀ, 351ᴀ, 370ᴀ.

The Guard of the Train scheduled to perform the work on the Camp Line will take charge of the movements over the Camp Line, assisted by another man to be provided from Wool.

The Line is worked as a siding, as it is not provided with signalling of any kind, and the crossing gates are not provided with lamps or targets. The movement of traffic over the Line must be confined to the hours of daylight, and not more than one Engine, or two Engines coupled, in steam, must be permitted on the Line at one time.

The Station Master at Wool must previously arrange with the permanent way foreman on the spot for men to be provided at the public road level crossings before referred to, and hand them the necessary keys of the padlocks securing the gates. He must also provide them with the key of the padlock of the points at the siding at Wool Bridge, in order that those points may be released. In addition to this, he must arrange for the gate in the Company's boundary at Wool Station to be unlocked and opened.

Whistle Boards are provided on the Camp Line as under :—

One Board on Down Side of Line, 350 yards the Wool Side of Wool Bridge Crossing.
One Board on Up Side of Line, 430 yards the Bovington Side of Wool Bridge Crossing.
One Board on Down Side of Line, 350 yards the Wool Side of Lytchett Crossing.
One Board on Up Side of Line, 450 yards the Bovington side of Lytchett Crossing.

Drivers on approaching these Boards must sound the Engine Whistle to acquaint the men at the gates of the approach of the Train. They must be prepared to stop dead before reaching the crossings should they find that the gates have not been placed clear of the line for the passage of the Train.

After the passage of Trains proceeding in the direction of Bovington the men at the crossings must again place the gates across the Line and secure them in that position, whilst the man at Wool Bridge Crossing must also reset the points of the siding, to act as a catch, and secure them in that position. In good time before the return Train from Bovington is due to leave, the men must again take up their positions at the gates, in order to open them and correctly set the points of the siding at Wool Bridge for the passage of the Train

The keys of the several gates and point locks must be promptly returned to the Station Master at Wool after use.

The men appointed for duty at the gates must provide themselves with hand flags and exhibit a green flag to the Driver when the crossing is clear for the passage of the Train and a red flag when it is necessary for the Train to be brought to a stand.

When nearing Wool Station the Driver must sound the Engine Whistle, so that the gate in the Company's fence can be placed clear of the Line, and must be prepared to bring the Train to a stand should this not be done and a hand signal is not received from the Staff at the Station to draw into the Military Siding.

The traffic conveyed to Bovington is confined to truck loads only, and the Station Master at Wool must arrange for the member of his Staff who accompanies the Train to Bovington Camp to do what is necessary there in the way of getting consignment notes, signatures for traffic, etc., and also to see that the traffic is properly loaded, sheeted and roped.

Working instructions concerning the Bovington Camp branch from the 1921 *Appendix to the Rules and Regulations and to the Working Time tables of the London and South Western Railway.*

The single-track branch line 2 miles 15 chains in length was constructed by the Military Works Company of the Royal Engineers consisting of around 100 men assisted by German prisoners of war. Little is recorded of the line's building, the work was under the supervision of Captain A.R. Finlayson RE who had affiliations with the London & North Western Railway. Many LNWR features were adopted in the construction of the line including LNWR-style mileposts, gradient and other notice boards. The track was standard LSWR standard bullhead rail and fittings. A five-ton crane, 30 ballast wagons and three unspecified contractor's locomotives were employed during the construction period. Although work on the line did not commence until October 1918 progress must have been brisk, as Finlayson is recorded as stating that in January 1919 tanks were being moved over the partly-completed railway employing a heavier engine to work the trains which were limited to four loaded Rectank wagons.

There is no record of the date the line was completed, Finlayson stated that the LSWR took over the working and maintenance of the line on 7th August, 1919, although it was not until 19th November that the LSWR issued instructions for working the Wool and Bovington Military Camp line, which was army-owned.

Apart from two short sections on the level, the line was on a continuous rising gradient with two sections of 1 in 60. It curved away from the up sidings in Wool goods yard through a gate and then on an embankment with an 8 chain radius curve. It then crossed the marshy water meadows before reaching a 50 ft steel girder bridge with a centre support to cross the River Frome,. There followed a gated level crossing over the main road, shortly after which it curved north through Blindman's Wood in a shallow cutting. Curving north-west the line then ran on a 14 ft-high embankment before turning west towards the tank depot and workshops where a number of sidings were laid out including two each capable of holding 12 Rectank wagons, loading docks for end loading were also provided.

A poor quality view of a train photographed during the construction of the Bovington branch. The locomotive is considered to be one of the Hunslet 0-4-0 saddle tanks used during the period. *Courtesy Bovington Tank Museum*

The open countryside of the area is demonstrated in this view looking down the branch from Bovington towards Wool during the line's construction.   *Courtesy Bovington Tank Museum*

A siding was also provided into the Board of Trade timber mills situated near the level crossing of the Wool-Bovington road. A considerable amount of traffic was derived from the mills, otherwise traffic was purely of a military nature, which after the end of hostilities consisted mainly of badly damaged tanks returning from the Continent together with general military stores, although there was a lively outwards traffic in scrap metal and captured enemy tanks that were sent for exhibition to a number of provincial towns as war trophies! The number of damaged tanks scrapped at Bovington was such that trainloads of salvaged metal were being dispatched for a number of years.

German prisoners of war walking along the line whilst working in the vicinity of Bovington.   *Courtesy Bovington Tank Museum*

A Rectank wagon loaded with a Mk V tank stands in a siding near the Bovington tank maintenance shed, which was then under construction, is shown in the background.

Courtesy Bovington Tank Museum

A photograph of a lance corporal sitting on a sponson trailer near the workshop sidings at Bovington Camp showing an unidentified LSWR Adams 4-4-0 in the background shunting a G. Bryer Ash private owner's coal wagon.

Courtesy Bovington Tank Museum

An unidentified saddle tank locomotive, thought to be WD Hunslet 0-4-0 No. 521 (1891) which was recorded as being at Bovington in April 1919, either hauling or propelling four Rectank wagons loaded with two male and two female Mk IV tanks. Female tanks were equipped with two machine guns to each sponson whereas male tanks had a 57 mm (six pounder) each side. *Courtesy Bovington Tank Museum*

Although not directly connected to the Southampton & Dorchester line, mention must be made of the Blandford Camp Railway that opened on 12th January, 1919. The camp had been constructed as a depot for the Royal Naval Division before their departure to the Dardanelles, after which it became the records office of the RAF with a personnel centre and recruitment wing. This activity involved the employment of many civilian staff, many of them female and coming from around Bournemouth and Poole. As soon as the branch was opened a special train was run for their benefit, starting from Poole and running through to the camp station - a reversal being necessary at Blandford station.

It would be impossible to give details of many of the special train workings during the war period. However, the following two illustrate railway working at the time. Wimborne, a station that had declined in importance, again found itself very busy as the Old Road regained some of its former status. From 15th November, 1915 a special goods off the Somerset & Dorset line commenced to run through from Wimborne to Ringwood complete with Somerset & Dorset engine and crew, although the LSWR provided a pilot driver and pilot guard. Leaving Wimborne at 3.15 am the train was made up to a full load and arrived at Ringwood at 3.40 am, the engine and guard's van then proceeding to Poole to work a return goods up the Somerset & Dorset.

There was also a goods departing Eastleigh at 7.35 am arriving at Ringwood at 8.32 am, the engine then would then shunt at Ringwood until 5.50 pm when it worked a special goods to Portsmouth. The 6.00 am goods from Dorchester to Eastleigh via the Old Road carried wagons off the previous night's GWR Bristol-Weymouth goods transferred at Dorchester for stations *en route*. The return working at 12.40 pm had strict instructions to collect empty coal wagons for South Wales (Stephenson Clarke & Co. excepted) and Great Western wagons for the Great Western line via Dorchester, and must run on time to enable the wagons to be transferred to the 6.30 pm up Great Western goods.

Another interesting fact is that although many troop trains were run during the war on occasions troops actually marched considerable distances. In May 1915 a battalion from Wareham camp did just that: a postcard home from a soldier stated, 'Dear Mother, we are moving from here to Winchester, we are having to march there'.

Throughout all this activity with a depleted work force the railways attempted to carry on their normal service. Added to the problems of war were those created by nature: a violent gale combined with high tides on 5th November, 1916 caused the down line to be washed out across Poole Park embankment, Holes Bay curve, and a section west of Rockley viaduct, with single line working over all three sections until track repairs were carried out. The severity of the conditions also caused damage to the Lymington branch and the suspension of the Portsmouth-Ryde steamer service.

It seems strange that, in the midst of all this urgent activity, the LSWR should turn its attention towards comparatively trivial matters of everyday operation, yet they did precisely that. Platform tickets had first been introduced at Waterloo in 1913, but it was not until 1917 that a campaign to 'close' stations and enforce the purchase of platform tickets was pursued throughout the system, £30 10s. was the estimated cost to introduce platform ticket arrangements and a porter's bell for public use at Wareham, with £27 being spent at Ringwood and £58 at Dorchester to this end. In March 1918 it was reported that at Totton, where the only entrance to the platform was through the booking hall, £1 a week was being raised in platform ticket revenue! Such a paltry sum would be beneath the notice of top management today, but at the time it paid almost half the wages of one of the station staff, so was well worth collecting.

During the mobilisation period in August 1914 there had been a reduction in the train service with it returning to normal for a period afterwards. This was later followed by a steady decline until the drastic reduction in train services and introduction of reduced speeds from January 1917. These reductions were not only necessary to save coal and ease the staff shortage on the railways, but also to provide pathways for the many troop and supply trains then being run at short notice. A further casualty of war was the closure of Meyrick Park Halt from 1st November, 1917. However, the LSWR managed to retain a number of restaurant car services, it still being possible to take refreshments on certain Bournemouth trains in 1918!

Second class travel was abolished from 22nd July, 1918, over the years improvements in third class accommodation having narrowed the distinction between these two classes. Thus second class that had once been the preserve of those whose claim to gentility was not matched by the appropriate income to afford first class was falling into decline. At this distance in time and in view of the war it appears odd that this situation had taken so long to resolve, the neighbouring GWR having removed second class over a period of time and completing the process by September 1910. Second class compartments were re-classed as thirds, and as less accommodation had to be provided it was claimed to save 33,252 carriage miles per week, although there was a loss of revenue - a pre-war third class journey costing 19s. 7d. cost 21s. 6d. second class.

The perennial problem of level crossing gates again surfaced during 1917, on 19th September when the 2.40 pm passenger train from Bournemouth West to

Brockenhurst passed the Crow Crossing up home signal in the on position and entered the Crow Crossing-Holmsley section before the 11.20 am special goods from Dorchester to Eastleigh had cleared Holmsley. The Crow Crossing signalman sent the 'Train running away on right line' signal to Holmsley, the passenger train arriving at 3.36 pm, one minute after the goods train had left. The excuse of heavy rain and steam from the engine did not impress authority, the guard receiving a caution and the driver being reduced in grade.

On 16th October at 2.23 pm the 10.45 am goods from Ringwood to Dorchester ran through the level crossing gates at Lytchett crossing and struck a four-wheeled wagon loaded with pit props that was passing over the crossing, overturning the vehicle but fortunately neither the men in charge or the horses were injured.

A little-known result of the war was a shortage of calcium carbonate (carbide) which resulted in several stations reverting to oil lighting, including Brockenhurst - although in that case the large lamps in the down sidings were allowed to remain carbide consumers. Then, as if the war had not created enough problems for the railway, other external forces conspired to add their burden - such as the timber yard fire adjacent to Branksome signal box, which broke out on 6th November, 1918. The flames spread quickly, destroying the roof and west side of the wooden superstructure of the box.

The following year was to see industrial unrest. During the war railwaymen had received a war bonus, but this was to be stopped from the 1st January, 1920 resulting in a large reduction in pay ranging from 1s. to 16s. per week. The strike began on 26th September, 1919, but was brought to a conclusion on 5th October. Although the strike was national the response was varied, it being reported that services were operating from Weymouth to Bournemouth but the company could not guarantee connections further along the line.

July 1921 saw the sad case of Charles Rattey, station master at Hamworthy Goods for the previous 13 years and a railwayman with 41 years' service, being brought before Poole magistrates on eight charges of embezzlement and falsification of accounts amounting to £129. After a lengthy hearing during which he pleaded guilty to four charges he was bound over under the First Offenders Act to the sum of £10. However, the real punishment was having lost his employment, pension and good name.

By the end of World War I there was a marked change in social attitudes and the pattern of life in general. Also the railways had to contend with a serious challenge from road transport. Before 1914 the motor vehicle had been little more than a novelty, but during the war it was not only been improved to the point where it was robust and reliable but it was cheaply mass-produced. People now took trips to places of interest by charabanc with the same enthusiasm their forebears had exhibited for the railway excursion. In 1921 the *Southern Times* commented on visitors to the 21st annual Dorset Constabulary Sports at Dorchester arriving by both train and motor charabanc. Furthermore, the motor bus was becoming popular and causing the railways grave concern, although competition from trams in urban areas was nothing new. Before the war the trams that ran between Christchurch and Poole through Bournemouth had captured a vast amount of local trade, but the country bus was another matter altogether as it robbed the railways of more lucrative fares.

With an unidentified Drummond locomotive, at the head four medium 'C' type tanks built by Messrs Foster of Lincoln and a Mk V tank loaded on Rectanks stand in the down sidings at Wool. It is reputed that these tanks were being moved into position in case of disturbances during the wave of strikes and industrial unrest involving miners, transport and other workers of 1919. *Courtesy Bovington Tank Museum*

Bournemouth & District Motor Services began to operate between Bournemouth Square and Ringwood railway station via Ferndown on 19th July, 1919, thus taking the first step in a process that offered the public a viable alternative to the trains with a more direct route and convenient stopping points. Although Ferndown at the time was not the vast expanse of housing that it is today, its nearest railway stations were Wimborne and West Moors - both a good two miles distant - and a train decanted its passengers at either Bournemouth West or Bournemouth Central, both of which were fairly remote from the town centre. It goes without saying that the buses were an instant success!

By February 1920 Bournemouth & District had started to operate from Southampton and the same month a daily service of three buses each way commenced from Lymington via Brockenhurst, Lyndhurst, Lyndhurst Road Station, and Totton to Southampton. Whilst this did link Lyndhurst with its distinctly isolated station, it is doubtful if many people transferred to or from trains there when having business in Southampton as it was more convenient (and cheaper) to stay on the bus! In May that year a service was started in conjunction with Wilts & Dorset Motor Services from Bournemouth Square to Salisbury via Christchurch, Ringwood and Fordingbridge, whilst at the same time a service from Poole to Wimborne and Blandford was added to the bus company's sphere of activity. On 27th July, 1920 the name of the undertaking was changed from 'Bournemouth & District' to 'Hants & Dorset Motor Services', and henceforth they became the railway's main competitor in the country east of Wareham.

To the west, the Weymouth Motor Company started a daily service between Weymouth and Bournemouth via Dorchester on 15th November, 1920, and Messrs Road Motors commenced a regular bus service between Portland and Weymouth on 26th October, 1921 with several journeys extended to Dorchester. In July 1922 the National Omnibus & Transport Company commenced a summer-only service from Weymouth to Dorchester, Wool, Wareham, Corfe Castle and Swanage, with a vehicle garaged overnight in Swanage for the morning journey to Weymouth.

The sudden upsurge in bus services was having a direct effect on railway traffic receipts, at the same time another opponent was slowly developing, the long distance motor coach. Royal Blue of Bournemouth commenced a daily service between Bournemouth and London during the 1919 and that year's rail strike made it very popular and it continued in the 1920 summer season, the fare being 15s. single 25s. return. Other operators became involved and Southampton was also served, beginning what was to become a very large and complex operation in competition to the railways.

The slow decline of Wimborne as a railway town that had started in the opening years of the 20th century recommenced once the additional traffic thrust upon it by war subsided. Economies were deemed necessary, the first of which was the withdrawal on 11th July, 1920 of the few remaining Somerset & Dorset passenger trains that had continued to use the original route between Corfe Mullen Junction and Wimborne.

Alterations in the Dorchester area were also contemplated in 1920 when it was decided to close Chalk Siding signal box. Mansfield siding, which was opposite this box, was placed under the control of a ground frame released from Dorchester box whilst the Chalk sidings themselves, which were situated on the up side to the east, were removed on 17th February, 1921, together with the crossover, and the signal box was abolished a week later on 24th February.

This was followed by the removal of the wartime connection to Keysworth Admiralty siding on 5th July, 1921. The connections at Southampton West leading to the sidings and the train ferry were removed during early 1922, and Whitley Ridge siding between Brockenhurst and Beaulieu was taken out of use on 12th September, 1922. The same year had seen the provision of a private siding at Bournemouth Central goods yard for the exclusive use of the Stonecrete Manufacturing Company.

The railways began to return to peacetime operation, although shortages of materials and other factors did little to assist. The Bournemouth-Birkenhead service had been restored in May 1919, and the Bournemouth-Newcastle service as far as Sheffield in July 1921 and completely restored in the October. The return of advertisements for cheap day trips, day excursions and period excursions by both the LSWR and GWR began to appear during 1921.

Theatrical traffic was still being carried by rail. On Sunday 19th March, 1922 three theatrical companies travelled in the district: the 'Pedlars Pie' Co. from Bournemouth Central to Southampton on the 5.53 pm with 10 passengers and a 21 ft truck; 'The Night of Folly' Co. from Weymouth at 2.30 pm with 15 passengers and a 21 ft covered truck for Brighton; and the 'All Put' Co. from Salisbury to Weymouth with a 21 ft covered truck and 22½ passengers.

However, the biggest drama was being played out in Parliament. Although the war was over, Government control of the railways continued until 15th August, 1921, and it was clear that the companies could not be returned to pre-war days. The railways had been run into the ground and the 120 individual railway companies stood little chance of recovering with a Victorian system and business values.

During 1918 the Coalition Government hinted at support for nationalisation. Indeed, the matter had been simmering for a number of years with the formation of the Railway Nationalisation League in 1895. With the support of the railway unions it became Labour Party policy followed by the formation of

At the head of an up train in the Hamworthy area is Adams 'T3' class 4-4-0 No. 561. Fitted with a Drummond chimney but retaining an Adams boiler the locomotive is in LSWR livery, not being painted in Maunsell green until October 1924. Built at Nine Elms in February 1893, No. 561 was withdrawn in October 1930. *G. Bailey Collection*

the Railway Nationalisation Society in 1908. It was also the view of a number of industrialists and traders who considered that the railways should act as a public corporation rather than a profit-making business.

The *Railway Gazette* during 1919 had publishing a number of serious schemes on nationalisation, a matter that was openly discussed by ministers, although rejected through public opinion, which as the *Economist* put it, 'were concerned about being at the mercy of bureaucratic bunglers'. In the event the Government decided against nationalisation by reforming the companies into four groups as a result of the Railways Act, which came into force on 1st January, 1923.

The new companies, the Great Western Railway, the Southern Railway, the London Midland & Scottish Railway and the London & North Eastern Railway were and are often referred to as 'The Big Four'. The GWR was the least affected by this upheaval as it retained its pre-Grouping name and much of its old identity. The London & South Western Railway became part of the newly-formed Southern Railway (SR) along with the London Brighton & South Coast and the South Eastern & Chatham (SECR) railways. The Somerset & Dorset Railway Joint Committee became the joint responsibility of the Southern Railway and the London Midland & Scottish Railway (LMS).

One man who was to be spared the upheaval of the new order was Sidney Harry Smith, station master of Dorchester, who retired on the 31st December, 1922. He had commenced his career as junior clerk at Downton in 1878 moving to Gosport the following year, in February 1884 he was appointed station master at Nursling, advancing to Stockbridge in February 1892. In September 1898 he was appointed to Wimborne at £100 per annum, this had risen to £145 by April 1911 when he was appointed to Dorchester where he was receiving £155 by the August. July 1914 saw this raised to £165 and to £180 in July 1917. To give an idea of the very rapid inflation of the time, in August 1919 he was receiving £360. In retirement, his years of service were rewarded with a pension which he enjoyed until he passed away in December 1943 aged 84.

Construction of the present Rockley viaduct taking place during 1923, looking east the previous structure stands on the left. The new girder sides under construction in the background will later be brought forward onto the new piers. *Railtrack*

Heading an up train, Adams 'X2' class No. 584 crosses the completed Rockley viaduct. Constructed at Nine Elms in April 1891, No. 584 was withdrawn in September 1933.
G. Bailey Collection

Chapter Three

Between the Wars
Under Southern Railway Ownership

The first year of Southern Railway ownership was to be a year of changes and cuts! On 4th January, 1923 the signal box at Woodsford Crossing was abolished as a block post, the box being retained as a ground frame to operate the crossing gates and the existing up and down home and distant signals. The points leading to the Admiralty airship station siding (near Moreton) were worked by a single-lever ground frame controlled by an Annett's key in Woodsford Crossing cabin.

Another wartime requirement, Worgret Siding signal box and its associated connections were abolished on 22nd June, and on 13th September the siding on the up side at Wareham leading into the ordnance depot was removed as were Longfleet military sidings (Holes Bay Junction) on 14th September; here the private siding agreement was terminated in July 1922. Latterly the Longfleet site had been occupied by Hill Richards & Company and the Waller Housing Corporation.

The former Somerset & Dorset engine shed at Wimborne closed on the 22nd January. The Post Office was also looking for savings: the daytime Travelling Post Office (TPO) train was reintroduced on 6th October, 1923, but only ran between Waterloo and Bournemouth and not through to Dorchester as in pre-war days.

On the civil engineering side the construction of new sidings between Northam Junction and Mount Pleasant crossing involved the construction of a new signal box at Northam Junction, opening on 8th July, 1923. Situated on the north side of the up line from Southampton West it replaced the previous box situated across the tracks on the south side. Rockley viaduct (west of Hamworthy Junction) was also reconstructed during 1923, the contract being undertaken by the Horsley Bridge & Engineering Company of Tipton (Staffs) for £14,400.

The following year a new gasworks was opened at Poole alongside the main line to the east of the station, sidings serving it being brought into use on 13th April. The lever frame in Poole East box was extended accordingly and a covered ground frame was provided to operate the Parkstone end of the sidings. Holton Heath station also opened for public traffic in July 1924, doubtless as a result of motor bus competition along the nearby Wareham-Poole road.

During this period some matters left over from the war years received attention. The Admiralty siding to Woodsford airship station was reviewed. It had been provided at Government expense and the Admiralty apparently wished to retain the facility. The SR recommended a formal agreement to the affect that the Admiralty would pay the company - as from 25th December, 1923 – the sum of £1 per annum as rent for the occupation of railway land by the platforms, siding etc., plus the cost of maintaining the siding, signalling, platforms, sleeper crossing, fencing and lighting. Traffic rates applicable to Moreton would apply, plus an additional 5s. 3d. for every loaded wagon worked to and from the siding. However, it would appear little use was made of this arrangement, for the halt went out of use in the early 1920s and the siding was abolished on 24th March, 1928, the ground frame being removed.

More complex were the arrangements that had been made at Hamworthy Quay, which reflected the quickly changing trading conditions at the period. In

June 1921 the LSWR had signed an agreement with James Smith who occupied a yard in which the Steam Boat Quay siding terminated, but two other parties now became involved - namely the Machinery & Trading Company and the Steel Breaking & Dismantling Company - who both wished to use their own steam cranes on the siding for the purpose of loading material from old warships which were being broken up at the site. This was agreed subject to certain conditions, for company records show that in December 1922 the LSWR had approved use of the siding by the Machinery & Trading Corporation Ltd who were sub-tenants of the Stanlee Shipbreaking & Salvage Company Ltd and lessees of the Poole Harbour Commissioners. However, by July 1926 the old lease had expired and the Commissioners granted a new lease of the wharf to Southern Roadways Ltd with a request to the SR that the siding be reassigned to the new tenants. In October 1927 the siding was referred to as the 'Poole Harbour Commissioners' Siding' when Messrs Southern Roadways applied for permission to use a Muir Hill NC-type locomotive upon it, to which the company had no objection subject to a suitable supplemental agreement.

Meanwhile, improvements to motive power depots were not being overlooked. In October 1923 it was agreed to replace the 50 ft turntable at Dorchester with one of 55 ft displaced from Exmouth Junction shed, but this does not seem to have happened as the 1934 Appendix document lists the Dorchester turntable as '49 ft 6 ins.'. The lack of space at Bournemouth engine shed was eased in July 1920 when £245 was authorized for the extension of three of the shed roads through the back of the building on to open ground towards Beechy Road bridge. Two years later the antiquated coal stage was improved with the provision of a Cowans Sheldon electrically-operated coaling crane. The 25 ton engine-lifting hoist was replaced by a new 50 ton structure ordered in March 1926 from the Chatteris Engineering Company. This massive piece of equipment, with its winding drum housed in a shed-like structure on top, was far too lofty to stand beneath the fitting shop roof in the manner of its predecessors, so a section of the roof had to be removed. As the new hoist was able to move along on a short section of rail a considerable length of the building was laid open to the sky - and as the fitting shop was in any case without walls on its southern side working conditions were far from pleasant during the winter months!

Various ideas had been discussed for improving facilities in the Bournemouth area, but in April 1925 it was decided that a fresh scheme be prepared, the contents of which make interesting reading! It was proposed to provide Bournemouth Central station with four through platform lines without disturbing the existing roof and exterior supporting walls, but necessitating the demolition of the up platform buildings. The down platform and down bay would remain undisturbed, with the down middle road being upgraded to a passenger line and furnished with a platform face on one side of an island. The other face of this new platform would have been served by the up line, slewed over to a new position close to the up side curtain wall of the station but still beneath the overall roof, whilst a new through up loop line and side platform - upon which the new station offices would stand - would be provided on the site of the station forecourt. All the through platforms were to be 800 ft in length (capable of accommodating 12-coach trains), and a horse loading dock would be provided at the west end of the new up platform. The work

With an interesting selection of stock Adams 'X2' class 4-4-0 No. 596 heads into Hamworthy Junction off Holes Bay curve with a down train. Note the two LSWR tanks standing in the down sidings. No. 596 is painted in early Southern Railway livery which took place in November 1924. One of a class of 20 locomotives No. 596 was constructed in May 1892 and withdrawn from service in May 1931. *G. Bailey Collection*

would also include some re-arrangement of the buildings on the down platform, including provision of a large parcel office. However, this bold scheme was prepared on the assumption that the motive power depot would be moved away from the environs of the station, and there were indeed plans to relocate it on a site within the triangle at Branksome with access for locomotives from both Branksome and Bournemouth West Junction, the existing coal sidings being removed to a new facility provided nearer to Bournemouth West station, but none of these schemes were proceeded with.

To make allowance for expanding long-distance passenger business - especially that from the Midlands and North via the Somerset & Dorset line - it was desirable to enlarge Bournemouth West station by constructing three additional platforms on the goods yard site and providing a new goods yard on land already acquired by the company on the down side between Bournemouth West Junction and the station. The Civil Engineer was instructed to prepare the necessary plans which were to include modern offices and public facilities at the West station. It was also proposed that land be purchased on the down side of the main line between Iford and Pokesdown for the laying out of a mileage yard and a nest of marshalling sidings, together with the reconstruction of Pokesdown station.

At the time there were no proper facilities in the area for the cleaning of carriages, so it was further decided to prepare a scheme for providing a modern four- road carriage shed capable of holding 12-coach trains, with two outside roads and space for up to three additional sidings at a later date, adjacent to the new goods yard site between Bournemouth West Junction and Bournemouth West.

Poole yard was becoming congested and the siding accommodation at that place came up for review. It was thought that any additional sidings that could be squeezed into the existing goods yard would be suitable only for down line traffic, so the company took steps to purchase an area of vacant land at Holes Bay Junction (in fact, the site occupied by the War Department during the war) where marshalling sidings for up trains could be provided. This new yard was to be connected to the existing goods sidings by a shunting line.

Another grandiose scheme of 1925 involved New Milton, where development of the area was proceeding apace and the anticipated growth of rail traffic called for urgent measures. Indeed, the Southern Railway Board foresaw the time - in the near future - when quadrupling of the line through New Milton station would become necessary, and to allow for this some additional land should be acquired on the down side to allow the goods facilities to be moved further south.

The capital expenditure involved in these schemes was truly enormous, so it is perhaps not surprising that none of them had made much progress by October 1926 (the year of the General Strike with its consequent effect on revenue). But there was still much talk; the proposed mileage yard between Iford and Pokesdown was to include two long refuge sidings plus several storage sidings and various other connections. It was also decided that if the main line between Christchurch and Boscombe was quadrupled and the stations at Christchurch, Pokesdown, and Boscombe rearranged there would be no necessity to widen the section between Boscombe and Bournemouth Central - which was just as well, for that area was already closely developed and the line occupied a narrow strip of land between the houses, often flanked by brick retaining walls. Quadrupling of this section would have been a very costly exercise!

Bournemouth Central goods yard was becoming inadequate for the traffic being handled, and it was proposed to concentrate the coal traffic on Boscombe to provide more space for general merchandise.

Further east, at Brockenhurst, there was also need for improvements. The 1925 report spoke of plans that had been prepared 'during the past twenty years' for modernising the station - including the provision of a separate single line running parallel to the down main for Lymington branch trains. A marshalling yard was also envisaged at the west end of the station on the down side, the sidings to be of sufficient length to hold 60-wagon trains and having a capacity of not less than 300 wagons. An up loop line would also be provided from a point immediately on the Brockenhurst side of the footbridge at Lymington Junction which would allow Ringwood line trains, goods, and stopping main line trains the use of a separate 'Slow Line' thence to Brockenhurst station. Many of these facilities were to appear in later years, but not as parts of an overall project.

Towards the western end of the line, Wool station came under notice for the inadequacy of the station buildings. The traffic that grew during the war with the construction of permanent military establishments in the district remained afterwards. The small cottage-style station, designed for the traffic generated by a village, was simply not up to the task. It was decided that a scheme of 'general improvements' should be prepared for consideration, but as the land available was restricted a residence for the station master should be provided in the form of a flat above the station offices.

Interesting though this report is very little direct action resulted from it, what was eventually done falling far short of what was envisaged. No doubt the huge costs involved brought about a major rethink!

The LSWR - and even the new and larger Southern Railway - served a part of Britain generally lacking in heavy industry, and there is no doubt that Southampton Docks was the jewel in their crown! Then in 1920 came the promise of even more freight traffic from the Solent area when the Anglo Gulf West Indies Petroleum Corporation

Ltd (AGWI) selected a site at Fawley, on the south shore of Southampton Water, for its new refinery. Surprisingly, in view of the heavy nature of the project construction was carried out without the aid of a contractor's railway from the main line, most heavy equipment being brought by sea to the site. However, delivering the finished product to inland customers was another matter. Initially it was intended to build a pipeline across the New Forest to a railhead at either Lyndhurst Road or Beaulieu Road stations - the latter emerging as the preferred location as it was well removed from any concentration of houses and there was ample space to lay out a large depot.

This idea was soon replaced by plans to construct a railway to the refinery, either from Totton or from one of the other two main line stations named, eventually the former being selected. Thus was formed the Totton, Hythe & Fawley Light Railway Company, with AGWI Petroleum holding most of the shares. In this case the term 'Light Railway' was something of a legal nicety, which allowed some economies of construction and operation, such as ungated level crossings, and minimalist signalling in exchange for a severe speed limit, but some really heavy traffic was destined to pass along it! It had nothing in common with earlier proposals for railways into this area of Hampshire, which had been seen as passenger lines to open up the district.

The Light Railway Order was confirmed on 26th January, 1922 and the proprietors lost no time in transferring the powers to the LSWR. On 4th October, 1923 Sir Robert McAlpine & Company Ltd was awarded the contract and construction commenced immediately, the 9 mile 31 chain branch opening for traffic on the 20th July, 1925.

The Fawley branch ran parallel to the main line from Brokenford to a point some 300 yards west of Totton station, where a connection was made with the main line. The points and signals of the junction were controlled from Eling Crossing signal box (renamed 'Eling Junction' in recognition of its new role) and a 16-lever covered ground frame was provided to control connections between the branch and extended goods yard. Although the passenger service was light and aimed principally at the refinery employees, oil traffic soon began to flow from the branch.

The *Southern Railway Magazine* stated that on 23rd June, 1930 one train load of 26 loaded tank wagons left the branch followed by a special freight equal to 45 loaded wagons to clear the traffic, and the next day two trains were also required including a 43 wagon load of 319 tons of petroleum pitch worked by a special train from Totton to Basingstoke. The passenger service was sparse, five years later it consisted of three trains to Fawley and four return workings. The refinery had also undergone a number of changes during that time: in 1924 it had been purchased by the British Mexican Petroleum Company, who sold petrol under the name of Redline. The following year the Standard Oil Company of New Jersey acquired the business taking the name the Anglo American Oil Company for the British operation and sold petrol under the brand name of Pratt's, this was changed to the now familiar Esso in 1935.

Returning to the Old Road, which despite the ever expanding competing bus services still handled a variety of traffic, during 1925 an average of 75 passenger and goods trains passed through Broadstone Junction per day, over one-third of these being Somerset & Dorset movements, whilst at West Moors nine down trains daily came off the Salisbury line, seven passenger and two goods, there being six passenger, two goods and one milk train in the up direction.

By this time the principal passenger services over the Old Road operated between Brockenhurst and Bournemouth West, with a few trains to and from other destinations passing along the line. Apart from seasonal extras the only reminder of its former main line status was the 12.28 pm Weymouth-Waterloo, by then the only through train using the old route. The first two down trains of the day started from Wimborne, being the 6.50 am and the 7.58 am followed by the 7.23 am Salisbury-Bournemouth West calling at Wimborne at 8.40 am. Very little passenger traffic by then travelled over the section between Broadstone Junction and Hamworthy Junction, passengers having to travel to Poole and change, one exception being the first down train of the day, the 7.52 am Eastleigh-Weymouth.

The first up train was the 6.30 am Bournemouth West-Reading GWR. A further through train was the 9.49 am from Swanage connecting at Wimborne with the 10.10 am Bournemouth West-Salisbury service. Later in the day the 5.03 pm Wimborne-Brockenhurst service made a connection with the 4.25 pm Bournemouth West-Salisbury, as did the 8.05 pm Wimborne-Brockenhurst connecting with the 7.30 pm Bournemouth West-Salisbury. The last two up trains of the day, the 9.30 and 10.50 pm from Bournemouth West terminated at Wimborne, where the stock was berthed to form the early morning services.

On the direct line via Sway, services had not returned to their pre-1914 peak, London expresses still lacked that pre-war two hour timing. The fastest timing from Waterloo to Bournemouth Central took 2 hours 15 minutes on the 12.30, 4.30 and 6.30 pm Waterloo-Weymouth services, which after Bournemouth Central only stopped at Poole, Wareham and Dorchester reaching Weymouth in 3 hours 26 minutes.

Other services were more pedestrian: the 5.40 am from Waterloo took 3 hours 6 minutes to Bournemouth with stops at Brockenhurst and Boscombe, finally arriving at Weymouth at 10.12 am having stopped at Branksome, Parkstone, Poole Wareham, Wool and Dorchester. The 8.30 am from Waterloo after Southampton West only stopped at Brockenhurst taking 2 hours 46 minutes for the journey to Bournemouth Central and arrived at Weymouth at 12.28 pm having stopped at Poole, Wareham, Dorchester and Upwey Junction, being the only Waterloo train to do so, Upwey like the other intermediate stations on the line was only served by the Bournemouth stopping trains. Fast up trains to Waterloo left Weymouth at 7.35, 9.17 am, 1.23 and 5.25 pm calling only at Dorchester, Wareham, Poole, Bournemouth Central and Southampton West.

The Hurn branch, which by this time was in terminal decline offered a service of six trains between Bournemouth and Ringwood and five return journeys with an extra late train in each direction on Thursdays and Saturdays. Goods traffic on the branch, being light, was usually worked as a mixed train between Christchurch and Ringwood, any additional traffic being handled by the Christchurch shunting engine.

The LSWR Appendix for 1925 stated:

> Avon Lodge, Private Halt and Siding is a private halt for the use of Lord Egmont, the owner of Avon Castle, his family, friends, tenants and persons having business with him, and also certain duly authorised residents in the neighbourhood.

Trains will call at Avon Lodge halt if necessary on notice being given to the guard at the previous stopping station, and, in the case of passengers joining the train, on the up or down distant signal, worked from the adjacent level crossing cabin, being maintained in the danger position, which must be taken as an indication that the train is required to stop at the halt.

The instruction also revealed that the crossing keeper both collected and issued tickets, and gave instructions for the private siding which was to be used only for traffic to and from Lord Egmont, his tenants and persons authorized by him.

Incidents with crossing gates still occurred, one such took place on 4th February, 1925 when the 6.00 am Brockenhurst-Ringwood goods train ran into and smashed one of the gates at No. 14 crossing. The crossing keeper admitted to oversleeping, in consequence of which he arrived for duty just as the train was approaching, but some speedy action on his part succeeded in getting three of the gates open before the engine struck. At night when there was no booked traffic the gates were maintained open for the roadway and, owing to a misunderstanding by the staff, it had become the practice to extinguish the lamps on the gates after the passage of the last train each day.

Two further incidents that could have had far more serious consequences took place the following year within three days of each other - both involved special coal trains from Dorchester to Eastleigh. The first happened on 18th September, 1926, when the engine collided with a permanent way trolley loaded with sleepers at Holmsley station and the second, on 21st September, the train hit a similar trolley loaded with ballast between Brockenhurst and Woodfidley. Both incidents happened in daylight, and investigations revealed that the hand signalmen were not protecting the trolleys at the required distance.

During the first few years of the Southern Railway there were a number of changes of station master and the opportunity to transfer men to and from both the former LBSCR and SECR areas. In January 1923 Mr W.J. Liley who had been station master at Brockenhurst for the past five years moved to Dorchester, to be replaced by Francis Uriah Sansom who was a third generation station master, his grandfather Uriah was station master at Moreton 1850-1882 (*see Vol. 1 p.149*). F.U. Sansom had commenced his career as a clerk at Weybridge in 1891 under his father who was station master; following various moves he was appointed relief station master in 1906 and after appointments at Milford and Witney was appointed to Amesbury in December 1914 before promotion to Brockenhurst on £335 per annum This had risen to £350 by early 1926 when he moved to take charge of both Barnstaple Junction and Town stations, followed by a move to Eastleigh in mid-1931. He followed into his father's footsteps at Woking in April 1933 from where he retired in October 1936.

On 9th December, 1924 William Tinsley, station master at Broadstone since 1921, died aged 49. His father had been station master at both Wool and Wareham in the 1890s. The following year Charles George Stretch, station master of Lyndhurst Road since 1914 and only just retired, was hurrying to catch a train at the station when he collapsed and died on 17th July, 1925. He was one of six brothers, four of whom were station masters on the LSWR. Death also denied Mr A. Fenwick a long retirement as he passed away in November 1927, just 13 months after retiring from the post of station master at Ringwood, a position he had held since May 1918.

Ashley Heath Halt opened on 1st April, 1927 to serve a developing area west of Ringwood. Viewed towards Ringwood, on the right past the down platform stands crossing cottage No. 18 with the gates and the signal box beyond. The latter was named Woolsbridge Crossing signal box until 1st April, 1927 when, with the opening of the halt, it was renamed Ashley Heath and reduced to a ground frame. *G.A. Pryer Collection*

Hurn after the removal of the loading dock siding and loop, photographed between August 1927 and September 1935. Viewed from the up home signal looking towards Ringwood the roof of the signal box is just visible in the bottom right-hand corner. Opposite it is the crossing cottage, with the station beyond. The goods siding is in the distance and to the right of it there are two railway cottages. *R. Smith Collection*

T.W. Watkins, station master at Holmsley since 1900, retired in May 1926, his place being taken by W. Swetman who came from Ashey on the Isle of Wight. The same year saw Mr T.F. Wright move to Egham after supervising West Moors since August 1916, his replacement being Mr F.W. Reeves from Portsmouth Arms.

Economy measures were undertaken in January 1927 when Mr J.J. Hibbard, the station master at Beaulieu Road, was transferred to Sheffield Park and the station placed under the supervision of the Lyndhurst Road station master. Likewise in April 1928 Mr W. Swetman, the Holmsley station master, was transferred to Penshurst when the station was placed under the supervision of Ringwood, saving £250 per annum on the salaries account.

In May 1926 the railways had become embroiled in the General Strike, the repercussions of which were to have a lasting impact - the more so because the continuing coal strike (until November) not only robbed the railways of one of their staple traffics but also created a shortage of locomotive coal. The fledgling road transport industry was quick to take advantage of this situation, and when industrial peace was restored it was found that a number of traders now supported road transport and some traffic was lost forever. This, together with wage rises and industrial unrest both within and outside the industry, was to sweep away many of the earlier practices together with much of the rivalry that had existed between the companies as they struggled to come to terms with the modern world.

There followed a period of retrenchment. Economies and reductions had to be made, although new works continued where they were seen as a long-term benefit to working. Despite the rather gloomy picture, certain types of business - especially long-distance and holiday passenger traffic - was still booming.

Typical economies of the time were implemented at Redbridge and Holmsley, where Sunday traffic was so light that the Traffic Committee decided to close these stations on the Sabbath from the start of the winter timetable on 21st September, 1926. On the other hand a new halt called 'Ashley Heath', situated at Woolsbridge crossing between Ringwood and West Moors, was opened on 1st April, 1927. With two platforms, each 347 ft long, it served the area around the main Verwood to Ringwood road that was starting to develop. At the same time Woolsbridge Crossing signal box was abolished as a Block post and renamed Ashley Heath ground frame and at the same time a siding was added on the down side adjacent to the halt.

Hurn was also simplified on 9th August, 1927: the signal box which also controlled a level crossing at the south end of the station was reduced to a ground frame, and the passing loop and cattle dock siding removed, as was the ground frame at the Ringwood end of the station.

In the rapidly changing post-war world the railways no longer enjoyed their former monopoly; the motor lorry, bus and the charabanc which later developed into the long-distance motor coach, were all serious challengers. A bus war between various bus operators offering services between Lyndhurst and Southampton again came to the fore during 1927 and its impact was felt by the railway. The three contestants, Hants & Dorset, J.T. Cousin, and C.A. Croucher engaged in a price war over the fare of 1s. 6d. single and 2s. which

Hurn station looking towards Christchurch. The down loop had been removed on 9th August, 1927, with the 15-lever signal box being retained as a gate box only. *Author's Collection*

Avon Lodge Halt looking north with a push-pull train waiting to depart for Bournemouth. The train is formed from half a former LSWR block set converted to push-pull operation. The lever to operate the wire & pulley control system is visible in the centre window, and the pulleys for the wire on the end of the roof. To the left is the hut containing the 10-lever ground frame controlling the crossing and private siding. *Kevin Robertson Collection*

Hants & Dorset managed to reduce from Lyndhurst to Southampton to 6*d*. return and Lyndhurst-Totton to 5*d*., it being said that at one stage the independent drivers had to bargain with the passengers over the price of the day! By November 1928 it had reached a point where Croucher's 'Yellow Bus' could sustain the service no longer and sold out to Hants & Dorset, with an agreement that the Lyndhurst-Southampton return fare could not rise above 1*s*. This was honoured for 22 years!

On the other hand there were services that complemented the railway, one example being Messrs Pink & Stretch of the station yard Lyndhurst Road station. During that period they operated six journeys daily from Lyndhurst to both Lyndhurst Road and Brockenhurst stations, the fare for either service being 6*d*.

At the western end of the line Hants & Dorset commenced a service between Bournemouth and Wareham in April 1923, with a cheap fare of 1*s*. 9*d*. single, 3*s*. return, whilst the National Transport & Omnibus Company operated its Weymouth-Swanage service daily in 1924 and at the same time introduced a summer service between Swanage and Lulworth Cove via Wareham and Wool. The following year National acquired both the Weymouth Motor Company and Road Motors thus consolidating their position in Dorset.

During this time railway companies (the GWR in particular) realised that they had no legal powers to do something they had done for years - namely operate bus services! The Southern Railway (Road Transport) Act of 1928 granted the SR the right but, in common with the other railways, they were fearful of opposition from within the (by then) well-established bus operators and decided to attack the problem by acquiring large shareholdings in them, instead of running competing services of their own. A year later the Southern Railway bought shares in Hants & Dorset Motor Services at £2 5*s*. each.

Photographed outside the Fox & Hounds public house in Lyndhurst is this Bean 14-seat bus registration No. OU 5134. Registered to Messrs Pink & Stretch in April 1930, motor bus proprietors of Lyndhurst, they ran a service from Lyndhurst to both Lyndhurst Road and Brockenhurst stations. Competition was fierce with other operators including Hants & Dorset Motor Services who were offered the business of Stretch & Pink in January 1934 but declined the offer, the Stretch & Pink service ending shortly afterwards. *Author's Collection*

Matters were more complex at Weymouth, from where the National Omnibus & Transport Company ran services eastwards to Bournemouth, Wareham and Swanage. In 1929 this concern was split into three companies - Eastern, Western, and Southern National - the latter being formed that July with the Southern Railway taking 50 per cent of the shares. At Weymouth there was further complication in that the GWR and SR jointly operated a local service between Radipole Spa Hotel and Wyke Regis Hotel. This continued until 31st December, 1933, after which the service was absorbed by Southern National. Two additional routes begun in 1930 were Weymouth-Wool-Lulworth Cove, and Bovington Camp-Wool-Lulworth Cove; although the latter no doubt acted as a railway feeder, the other connecting routes abstracted potential passengers from the railway.

Adding further to the railway's potential loss of revenue was the opening of the chain ferry across the mouth of Poole Harbour at Sandbanks in April 1927. This reduced the distance from Poole and Bournemouth to Swanage considerably, unfortunately at the expense of the railway upon which a similar journey usually involved a change of trains at Wareham. However, it was Hants & Dorset which operated the regular bus service via the ferry, so these substantial shareholdings in the bus companies gave the railways a measure of control over their potential rivals and, at the same time, allowed them a share of the profits.

Despite the more relaxed attitude to Sunday trading during the 1920s, paddle steamers still did not run on a Sunday from Bournemouth, Poole or Weymouth, although they did from Southampton. This rule was broken in July 1922 when Sunday trips began running from Weymouth and Poole. The Poole steamers were well patronised, soon resulting in special trains commencing at Christchurch running to Poole station. However, traditions died hard and it was not until 1928 and 1929 respectively that Sunday steamers sailed from Bournemouth and Swanage piers.

Returning now to matters directly connected to the railway, there were a number of economies and improvements. On 25th March, 1928 a new 30-lever signal box was opened at Wareham, replacing the 40-lever Wareham West box that stood at the Worgret Junction end of the station, East box at the level crossing, and the 12-lever ground frame at the east end of the layout. On 4th November of the same year the military branch between Wool station and Bovington Camp was closed, although the track was not dismantled until 1936.

The 1st April, 1928 had also seen the closure of the Somerset & Dorset Wimborne Loop signal box at the start of the original route of the Somerset & Dorset. In view of the sparse traffic passing over this section it is not surprising that the services of this additional signalman were considered superfluous - but it is amazing that so much expense was incurred in the process! There was considerable rearrangement of the layout at Wimborne Junction, a new connection between the double and single lines being provided closer to the main line where the conventional junction layout remained.

Mr W.J. Liley, the Dorchester station master for the past five years, retired in 1928 and was superseded by Mr P.J. Collins. The annual salary of this post was £350, which seems paltry today but - representing almost £7 per week - was a handsome income in the 1920s and, with the exception of Bournemouth and Southampton, made it the best paid position on the line. Mr A.J. Hardy at Poole, who was also responsible for the Harbour Tramway and Hamworthy Junction, received only £320 a year until his appointment to Southampton West in April 1928.

It seems that the railways were still rather conservative in their attitudes, for whilst most businesses had welcomed the telephone from its inception as a means of improving contact with their customers, they were slow to do so. Indeed, it was 1927 and 1928 respectively before Wareham and Lyndhurst Road stations were connected to the GPO system.

The Hamworthy Goods branch was still a good source of income. In 1929 Messrs Doulton & Company requested the provision of a private siding on the down side of the line at 116 miles 37 chains to serve its clay field, for which the annual output was estimated to be 20,000 tons, the siding and associated ground frame costing £544 coming into use on 29th October that year. However, in July 1931 Messrs Doulton requested the siding be lengthened by one truck's length at a cost of £26, but quickly having second thoughts requested it be extended by three wagon lengths at a cost of £57.

During that period negotiatons had been proceeding between the railway company, Poole Harbour Commissioners and Poole Corporation in connection with the reclamation of land and its development for wharfage purposes to the south of the existing 'Steam Boat Quay'. Thus by 1935 a considerable area had been reclaimed and a new quay added to the end of the previous structure.

Savings were made at Ringwood with the reduction of the East signal box to a ground frame on the 20th January, 1929, whilst various sidings were removed and other layout alterations made in both October 1928 and October 1930. The latter involved alterations to the level crossing at the west end of the station which had spanned four tracks, as a result of which the gates had failed to meet each other when open for road traffic. This had allowed stray New Forest ponies and other animals to wander onto the railway line and a constant watch had to be kept by staff. By reducing the length of the up siding and lifting the Christchurch bay approach line the gates could be moved inwards to fully protect the running lines. A new connection leading from the branch to the down line west of the station allowed branch trains to use the main platforms and thereafter the former branch bay became a short siding entered from the east end. Other alterations included the removal of the turntable situated on the down side, which with a length of only 42 ft was of limited use.

The same year an application was received from Messrs Webb Major for alterations to be carried out at its private siding at Moreton, which connected with a line to the firm's sand and gravel pits. The siding was situated on the down side behind the platform and was connected to the line from the pits via a wagon turntable. To enable the working of the line and siding to be more efficient it was requested that the turntable be eliminated. As the rail charges from the firm's traffic frequently exceeded several hundred pounds per month, and in view of the fact that persistent efforts had been made by road hauliers to obtain the traffic, it was recommended by the Traffic Committee that the alterations be proceeded with. During the previous year the goods yard at Moreton was simplified, the wagon turntable and siding leading from it into the brickyard being removed.

Part of the up platform at Bournemouth Central under reconstruction during May 1925. Standing in the bay platform is Urie 'H15' class 4-6-0 No. 331. Originally built as one of Drummond's unsuccessful 'F13' class she was reconstructed in November 1924 and performed sterling work until withdrawn in March 1961 having covered 1,149,690 recorded miles.   *Author's Collection*

For some considerable time improvements had been taking place in the Bournemouth area. At Bournemouth Central work had commenced on abolishing the down bay platform at the west end of the station in December 1927 and the removal of a siding and short loading dock at the east end took place in March 1928 to allow the down platform to be extended towards Holdenhurst Road bridge. This, plus the extension at the Branksome end, gave a total platform length of 1,748 ft - the third longest in the country. Various other alterations to the track layout gave the station both up and down through roads in the centre and a scissors crossover between the down through and the down platform roads enabled the newly-extended platform to be worked as two platforms - a very useful facility as many down trains divided at the station. Owing to the position of the engine shed the up platform could not be lengthened and until the end of steam traction the procedure was for the portion from Bournemouth West to run into the station first and then be drawn back by the station pilot into a siding alongside the engine shed. Then the Weymouth portion would arrive in the platform, and the Bournemouth West portion would be propelled out to couple onto the rear. Usually the engine of the Weymouth section took the train forward, having worked to Weymouth earlier with the rear portion of a down train, the leading part of which had gone to Bournemouth West behind the engine that had brought it from Waterloo. To work the new layout the two original signal boxes (one at each end of the station) were replaced on 8th July, 1928 by a new 60-lever box, elevated above the station canopy towards the western end of the down platform. At the end of May 1930 approval was given for the construction of a carriage shed on the approaches to Bournemouth West (a scheme originally proposed five years earlier), and for reasons never explained Broadstone Junction was again renamed in July 1929 as plain 'Broadstone' - although it continued to be a junction station.

Thus as we come to the end of the 1920s many improvements and some rationalisation had taken place as the Southern Railway moved forward in a changing world. Although the motor lorry was beginning to handle short haul traffic, when the Bath & West show visited Dorchester between 22nd and 26th May, 1928 it created much additional traffic, six special trains being required, and additional horse box traffic was dispatched by ordinary services.

The Royal Train was in frequent use for various visits including a visit by King George V to Lulworth Gunnery Ranges on 24th April, 1928, the Royal Train travelling to and from Wool station via the Direct Line.

Special trains were still the preferred means of transport for moving large numbers of people. On 21st June, 1928, 1,000 elementary school children from the Bournemouth area were conveyed by special train to Southampton where they visited the SS *Mauretania*. Despite the advancement of the charabanc rail travel was still preferred for the longer distance outing, resulting in a varied programme of special trains, excursions and cheap fares during the period. The most important event of the period was the Wembley Exhibition during 1924, a follow on being that all future FA Cup Finals and other important matches would be played there thus ensuring an excursion market.

A perusal of the local press and the handbills displayed at stations offered a vast variety of interesting attractions. One such was the annual Tidworth searchlight tattoo with cheap fares from all stations with a special return train from Tidworth at midnight giving Dorchester and Weymouth spectators a good day out for 4s. 6d. and 5s. respectively. Although times were changing, a check on motor vehicles revealed only 1,471 passed over the level crossing at Wool between 10.00 am and 7.00 pm on Easter Monday 1929.

Pokesdown station was completely rebuilt in 1930, the island platform of 1886 reached from the Christchurch Road bridge by a long flight of steps, giving way to new 750 ft side platforms served by loop lines. These were brought into use on 15th June, after which the island platform was demolished and two through lines laid across the site. The new platforms were both accessed by steps from a covered footbridge linking them to the new office building fronting onto Christchurch Road and by lifts to cater for parcels and luggage. The station frontage was of brick and stone in the latest style of the SR and incorporated some small shops - and at the time it was the smartest station on the line. Doubtless this was intended as the first stage in the proposed quadrupling from Christchurch to Boscombe, but nothing else was done in that direction. To handle this new layout a 22-lever signal box, situated at the west end of the up platform, was opened on the 27th April.

Incidentally, the new arrangements at Pokesdown somewhat flew in the face of current trends where the emphasis was on economy and manpower reduction, for although the signal box could switch out it could only do so for the through lines and it had to be manned - even at times of light traffic - whenever trains were booked to call at the station!

Wimborne looking north-east with an unidentified 'M7' class 0-4-4 tank running into the station with a down train during the late 1920s or early 1930s; the engine still retains fittings for wire-operated push-pull working. To the right is the goods shed which replaced the earlier structure destroyed by fire, alongside which an ancient coach body.   *R.K. Blencowe Collection*

Drummond 'T9' class 4-4-0 No. 113 speeds through Ringwood with the summer 1.56 pm Swanage-Waterloo (Saturday only) service on 18th September, 1926. A number of Swanage and Weymouth extras were routed over the Old Road to avoid the Bournemouth area.
                                                                              R.J. Harvey Collection

Drummond 'T9' class No. 288 running between Wool and Wareham with an up train consisting of an LSWR four-coach set with vans in tow on 22nd July, 1932.   *Author's Collection*

Drummond 'T9' class 4-4-0 No. 733 runs into Wareham station with a Weymouth-Southampton semi-fast in September 1933. Of note are the lower quadrant signals and the overhead electric wires supplying power to the converted gas lamps.   *G. Beale Collection*

The use of breakdown cranes for other work is clearly illustrated in these views taken in Wool station yard during the summer of 1931 involving the Salisbury crane. The top view shows a Mk V heavy tank in the foreground, whilst in the lower the crane is lifting a medium C tank onto a wagon.

Southern Railway Magazine

Reconstruction of Pokesdown station taking place during early 1930 with the original island platform and its buildings and signal box still in use. The new down platform and retaining wall are under construction and the new up platform is well advanced in the foreground.
John Alsop Collection

Work at a further stage showing the completed up and down platforms with the original island platform removed. A certain amount of work still remains to be completed; a number of workmen are attending to the catch point protecting the new up through road from the up platform line.
Dr J. Boudreau Collection

Photographed during the eleven weeks of 1931 when the 'Bournemouth Belle' ran through to Weymouth, 'Lord Nelson' class 4-6-0 No. 862 *Lord Collingwood* runs into Dorchester with the Weymouth portion on 16th September, 1931.   *Author's Collection*

Creekmoor Halt reincarnated in concrete from its original timber construction. Today the trackbed forms the Broadstone bypass, Broadstone Way, and the level crossing at the end of the platform is today the point where a pelican crossing and a set of bus-activated traffic signals allows buses to cross the bypass between Creekmoor Lane and York Road. *Author's Collection*

On 19th June, 1933 a halt was opened at Creekmoor, immediately to the north of Sykes' Pottery siding on the line between Broadstone and Holes Bay Junction. The wooden structure with two 60 ft platforms was intended to serve an area in the northern part of Poole that was about to be developed. This event demonstrated the gulf then existing between the commercial practices of the different transport undertakings. Whereas the Hants & Dorset Bus Company regularly took out full page advertisements complete with timetables in the local Press to publicise their services, the railway had not only ceased to do so many years before but even failed to do so for this new facility. No doubt handbills were distributed at the local stations, but this was very much a case of 'preaching to the converted'.

The perennial problem of level crossings again came under scrutiny between the wars, but it seemed that little scope existed for hastening the removal of these costly and increasingly dangerous locations - although Brokenford, a minor crossing between Totton and Ashurst, was successfully abolished in the early 1920s. Improvements and realignments of the A35 Southampton-Bournemouth trunk road allowed the closure of Totton crossing on 19th November, 1930 and Lyndhurst Road in August 1932, both being replaced by overbridges. The endless difficulties caused by the two level crossings in the centre of Poole continued to bedevil both the railway and road users alike as the years passed. In 1924 Poole Council considered a scheme for building a bridge over the line at the White House Laundry site (later Kingland Crescent), but procrastination set in. In 1936 the scheme was still being discussed, by which time a central bus station had also become a pressing need which also involved the Kingland Crescent site. Two years later some progress could be reported, but the outbreak of World War II precluded any work taking place.

At 5.54 am on the morning of 8th October, 1932 an accident took place that could have caused the loss of life. An 'M7' class 0-4-4 tank, thought to be No. 255, was heading the 5.54 am Salisbury-Weymouth newspaper train which, approaching Dorchester, ran into three wagons that had become derailed at the catch points 506 yds in rear of the outer home signal.

The impact forced the first wagon over the engine knocking off the chimney, the second went under the engine causing it to turn onto its left side coming to rest at an angle against the cutting side only four yards from Wareham Road bridge, the third wagon breaking away, ran back 400 yds. By a miracle none of the crew suffered any serious injury.

Both lines were blocked until 8.00 am when single line working was put into operation between Dorchester and Moreton over the up line, this remaining until 8.00 am the following morning. The services of the Bournemouth breakdown crane were required to recover the three vehicles of the newspaper train and the locomotive. At the subsequent inquiry it was revealed that the wagons had been shunted onto the down line the previous night (Friday) and forgotten. The shunter having not pinned down the brakes resulted in the wagons gravitating down the 1 in 113 gradient in the prevailing high wind.

By the 1930s traffic over the section of line between Hamworthy Junction and Broadstone was extremely light, in recognition of which it was reduced to single

The commencement of the reconstruction work at Southampton West during 1933/34. The steam crane is unloading materials onto the down platform, which became an island platform with the completed works.   *R. Blencowe Collection*

Southampton West station showing the construction of the foundations and other work for the new down side buildings during 1934. In the background the clock tower of the then new Southampton Civic Centre is prominent on the skyline.   *R. Blencowe Collection*

track on 11th December, 1932. The former up line was retained and the electric key token system introduced, with the intermediate signal box at Lytchett Crossing being downgraded to ground frame status. Just four years later the company was considering the closure of this section, as by then it was carrying only one passenger train per day plus a couple of freight movements. However, eventually it was decided to be a step too far and remained as a useful diversionary line.

Further economies were made with the closure of Beaulieu Road signal box on 2nd July, 1933 and Parkstone signal box a week later on the 9th. In both these instances traffic capacity was maintained by the installation of Intermediate Block Sections (intermediate signals) controlled from the signal boxes in rear. In November 1929 the Engineer was asked to quote for demolishing Holes Bay Junction signal box and removing the crossover, a job he costed at £239 3s. 11d. However, it was not until 28th October, 1934 that this box was closed and control of the junction was transferred to Poole West box, which was extended by 11 ft to accommodate the additional levers. The original 27-lever Stevens' frame was retained with altered locking and made up to 51 levers, the work - which included electrical point machines for the junction and a considerable amount of track circuiting - was carried out by the Westinghouse Brake and Signal Company, which supplied levers and segments of Stevens' pattern for the occasion.

In June the same year Towngate Street Crossing ground frame, at the other end of Poole station and tucked between the footbridge and the crossing gates on the up side, was replaced by a 9-lever structure on the down side to the east of the gates.

Whilst there is no denying that the improvements wrought at Bournemouth Central and Pokesdown were necessary, Southampton West was a far more urgent case! It had seen few changes over the years - and was a little too close to Southampton Water at times, such as when high tides brought flooding to the tracks through the platforms. Furthermore, the existing facilities were being worked to saturation point, it being estimated in 1923 that the level crossing gates at the east end of the station were swung 292 times daily on average, and that every year some three million passengers were handled together with 97,000 parcels and 1,000 milk churns every week - not bad for a station with only two through platforms and a bay! Minor improvements were carried out in May 1927 when the up platform was extended 300 ft at the western end.

Further developments commenced with the provision of several sidings and ground frames between Southampton West and Millbrook in connection with the reclamation of 400 acres of foreshore from a point near Southampton Town Quay to beyond Millbrook for the construction of a new dock complex and trading estate, to be known as the New Docks (renamed Western Docks in 1965).

Also included in the scheme was the a major enlargement of Southampton West station, to provide four platforms each 900 ft long with a 470 ft bay platform on the down side. Platform canopies provided protection from the weather, 550 ft, 530 ft and 600 ft respectively on the up, island and down platforms.

The completed rebuilding of Southampton West which was renamed Southampton Central. In the background is the rail-connected Corporation power station and to the right the extent of the reclaimed land, a complete contrast to when the River Test lapped the old down platform. *G.A. Pryer Collection*

Work on the latter started in late 1933. The original up platform and offices - complete with the imposing clock tower - would remain, whilst the down platform was rebuilt as an island with the former down line becoming the up through line. The new face of this island (No. 3) served a new down through line and a new down platform (No. 4), complete with booking office and other facilities, served the new down local line. A down bay platform was provided at the west end.

An integral part of the scheme was a new road from Four-Posts Hill, north of the station and spanning the railway by a bridge over the west end of the platforms. A spur of the road curved east to pass the new downside buildings before linking up with Western Road. The other spur continued south to the site of the later-developed Docks Estate.

These improvements allowed Blechynden Street level crossing to be abolished on 25th June, 1934 but the pedestrian footbridge was retained with an additional span across the two new down lines. On 2nd June, 1935 the signal box was replaced by a new structure 'Southampton Central', situated on the up side at the west of the station, containing a 75-lever Westinghouse 'A2' frame. On 7th July the station also became 'Southampton Central'.

At last Southampton had a station befitting its position as the leading ocean liner port in the United Kingdom. The finished article contrasted the best architectural styles of the 1890s on the up side with the 'Odeon'-style adopted by the Southern Railway and so characteristic of the period on the down side. The latter facilities, built largely of concrete, provided a spacious booking hall 36 ft by 30 ft and ticket office, a refreshment room, enquiry office, parcel and left luggage office and staff accommodation. In the booking hall, situated between the two barriers leading onto the platform, was an attractive indicator display featuring a plan of the docks and the positions of shipping arriving and departing for the day. The *Southern Railway Magazine* described the new buildings as:

A new note in British Station architecture will be struck in the design of the buildings on the Down Side, which together with the roofing and the footbridge, will be of concrete, the whole being planned as an architectural unit in accordance with the latest Continental station construction.

The nature of the sub-soil was not without its difficulties, between four and five hundred concrete piles having to be sunk to support the new platforms, buildings, and footbridges.

The new layout provided quadruple track between the east end of Southampton Central station and Millbrook, with the up and down through lines in the centre and local lines on the outside, and made it necessary to completely remodel Millbrook station as well. The original up platform was demolished and the level crossing closed on 1st May, 1935, the down platform being reconstructed as an island containing the station offices which were reached from a ramped footbridge. A new signal box with a 70-lever Westinghouse 'A2' frame was built between the up and down through lines at the west end of the station, this coming into use on 2nd June, 1935 when the original box was closed. There was also a double-track junction leading to the New Docks.

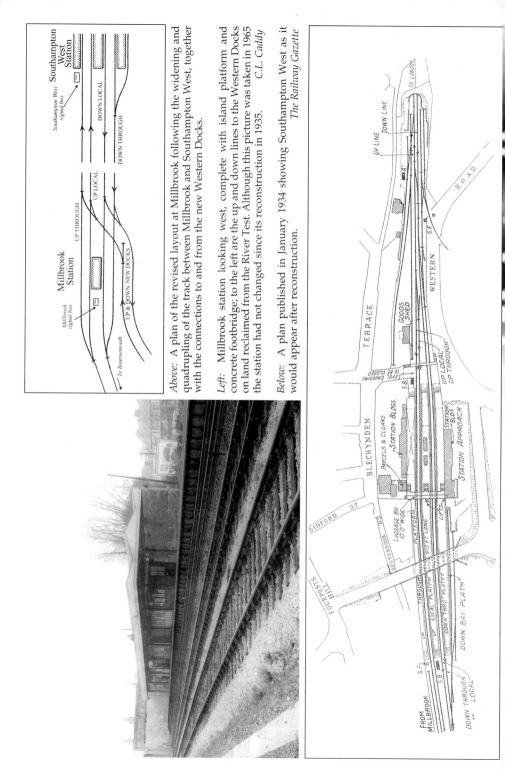

Millbrook Station

Southampton West Station

UP THROUGH
UP LOCAL
DOWN LOCAL
DOWN THROUGH

Millbrook signal box

Southampton West signal box

To Bournemouth

UP & DOWN NEW DOCKS

Above: A plan of the revised layout at Millbrook following the widening and quadrupling of the track between Millbrook and Southampton West, together with the connections to and from the new Western Docks.

Left: Millbrook station looking west, complete with island platform and concrete footbridge; to the left are the up and down lines to the Western Docks on land reclaimed from the River Test. Although this picture was taken in 1965 the station had not changed since its reconstruction in 1935. *C.L. Caddy*

Below: A plan published in January 1934 showing Southampton West as it would appear after reconstruction.
The Railway Gazette

The new dock works, estimated to have cost £10 million, stretched from Mayflower Park at the end of Town Quay to the extreme west of Millbrook. The first vessel to use the still unfinished work was the famous liner *Mauretania* (1907) which steamed in on 19th October, 1932. When completed, the works provided 1,200 ft of deep-water quays and a graving dock 1,200 ft long (the King George V Dry Dock) and all was virtually complete on 19th January, 1934 when the *Majestic* (1914) became the first liner to enter it. It was the beginning of a new era for Southampton, and the reclaimed land situated between the docks and the Southampton to Dorchester railway soon became a vast trading estate.

Having completed the major engineering works at Southampton the company turned its attention to Brockenhurst, where some long-considered improvements were made during 1936. Both platforms were considerably lengthened at the west end and the former down bay extended eastwards to form a down loop. At the same time a new range of buildings was erected on the down side - again in the 'Odeon'-style - and some extensions made to the buildings on the up platform. The old Brockenhurst West box was replaced on 5th April, 1936 by a new one containing a 40-lever Westinghouse 'A2' frame, but as though to emphasize the point that - despite all the new works - 'economy' was still the watchword, the old East box of 1888 vintage was made to suffice with a few levers added! 'East' and 'West' boxes became 'A' and 'B' respectively to conform with standard SR practice on 3rd April, 1939.

With the nameboard proclaiming 'Brockenhurst, Junction for Lymington and the Isle of Wight', 'King Arthur' class 4-6-0 No. 782 *Sir Brian* runs in on a down Bournemouth express before the down bay platform was converted into a down loop during 1936.

SOUTHERN-IMAGES

The last day of service over the Hurn branch was 28th September, 1935. 'M7' class 0-4-4 tank No. 21 approaches Christchurch waterworks with a train from Ringwood shortly before closure. Note the use of concrete posts in the fencing of the line, with the Christchurch waterworks filter beds in the background.   *Mark Yarwood/Great Western Trust Collection*

A rear view of the same train as it passes Christchurch waterworks, to the left is a wooden ganger's hut with a substantial brick chimney, and a foot crossing between the camera and the train. Today the public footpath has been diverted as extensions to the filter beds now cover the track formation, whilst urban development has taken the land to the right.

Mark Yarwood/Great Western Trust Collection

Whilst expansion and improvements had been taking place at the eastern end of the line, further west the picture was rather more dismal. The fate of the original railway to Bournemouth, the Hurn branch which had long been a rural backwater, was now signed, sealed and delivered. Since the opening of the Direct Line in 1888 it had carried few passengers and because of its sharp curves and generally light construction was of little use as a diversionary route for main line traffic. Hurn had already been plucked of most of its facilities in 1927 and in August the following year the branch bay at Ringwood had been abolished, so what remained was very basic. It is perhaps surprising that the line survived as long as it did, but services were eventually withdrawn after the last train ran on Saturday 28th September, 1935. Unlike such occasions in later years, the closure attracted little attention either locally or in the railway press. Ironically, that same year Hurn was the first station in the area to have camping coaches provided for the summer season. However, with the closure of the branch the two coaches were removed at the end of the season never to return. Track on the branch was removed in July 1937, except for a long headshunt at Christchurch, which was used for stabling coaching stock.

During the 1930s there were also reductions in the facilities at Wimborne with the final closure of the original section of the Somerset & Dorset line between Wimborne Junction and Corfe Mullen to freight traffic on 17th June, 1933, allowing the closure of Wimborne Junction signal box the following day. The line was lifted as far as Carter's siding, which was thereafter reached from the Corfe Mullen end. The remaining track in the disused engine shed sidings was soon lifted and the turntable, last used on 6th July, 1931, was also removed. However, two sidings remained on the former engine shed site to serve a coal yard, known as 'Canford Sidings', access to which was controlled by a two-lever ground frame released electrically from Broadstone signal box.

Traffic at Wimborne had been suffering from the impact of regular bus services into Poole and Bournemouth and the station was the subject of a 1929 scheme to replace the conventional booking office with a passimeter-style entrance at a cost of £127 8s. 9d. However, the idea was not pursued and the station began to exhibit a neglected air, but on a tour of inspection in 1936 the officers declined to spend any money on improvements 'in view of the small traffic using it' (a sad comment on what had once been the busiest station in Dorset) and seem to have settled for little more than a routine repaint! Some simplifications to the layout were, however, carried out. The West ground frame was abolished on 26th March, 1933 and the up bay platform was reduced to a siding, whilst the Gas Works siding was taken out of use on 10th March, 1936 and the down bay platform converted to a siding on 10th April, 1938; it had been difficult and dangerous to work with a very narrow platform face.

It would seem that whilst making their inspection of Wimborne the traffic officers were offended by the sight of a number of wooden 'shanties' in the goods yard. Instructions were issued that every effort should be made to remove them after finding the 'residents' (probably coal merchants' staff) alternative accommodation.

The 1930s brought another bout of crossing incidents including one at Stoke crossing where the gates were always locked against road traffic. At 8.12 am on

Hurn station on the last day of services, 28th September, 1935, looking towards Christchurch with 'M7 'class 0-4-4 No. 21 standing in the platform with a Ringwood-bound train. No. 21 had been constructed at Nine Elms works in January 1904, fitted with push-pull equipment in July 1930 she was withdrawn in March 1964.   *Mark Yarwood/Great Western Trust Collection*

Avon Lodge Halt viewed from a carriage of a Ringwood-Bournemouth train on the last day of service, 28th September, 1935.   *Mark Yarwood/Great Western Trust Collection*

18th August, 1935 an empty troop train from Wareham to Weymouth ran through and smashed one of the gates. It transpired that the crossing keeper had opened the western pair of gates to permit a car to cross and left them open for a motor lorry. Forgetting about the booked special, he went to the toilet attached to his cottage from where he could not hear the relay bell.

Woodsford (No. 38) crossing was the scene of two run-throughs, the first on 21st August, 1937 involved 'Schools' class 4-4-0 No. 933 *Kings Canterbury* hauling the 6.30 pm Waterloo-Weymouth service. The down side gates were smashed and the up side ones put out of action whilst two windows in the crossing cottage were broken by flying debris, the locomotive vacuum brake and steam heating pipes were broken, the front buffer beam lamp irons were bent and the head lamps damaged. At the subsequent inquiry crossing keeper Day stated that after the 'is line clear' signal was passed to Moreton, he let a car over the crossing but then failed to close the gates against the road. He then stated that he went back into the cabin and sat down thinking he had closed the gates and lowered the signals, despite the fact that the levers and repeaters in the cabin showed the opposite. The first he knew anything was amiss was when he heard the noise of the impact. Day stated he had not heard the 'train entering section' signal, for this oversight he received a reprimand, as did the driver for not pulling up in the 944 yards between the distant signal and the gates.

The following year Day was again on duty on 5th October when the overnight goods from Nine Elms to Dorchester crashed through the gates. However, a repetitive job with long hours and lack of sleep can cause mistakes to be made, as the report clearly shows:

> Day attends to the gates as required from 6 pm to 10 am. Day was not able to retire until between 1.30 and 2 am owing to the cars (mostly RAF officers returning from Dorchester to Warmwell aerodrome, passing over the crossing) and was called out to let a car over at 2.40 am. He was then able to sleep until 6.25 am when a car went over. The gates were thereupon closed across the road until after the passing of the 7.05 am train from Dorchester to Broadstone, when Day opened them for a lorry, but did not afterwards replace them against the roadway.

Day stated that he did not hear the bells for the freight, but it was considered that he did not realise that the train had not passed (as the train was nearly an hour late) and he was not listening for them. Upon hearing the train approaching Day rushed out but was too late to open the gates; he admitted that he was not working the gates in accordance with the instructions exhibited at the crossing. This incident resulted in Day receiving two days' suspension and removal from Woodsford, whilst the driver who had failed to stop was suspended for one day.

On the Dorchester to Weymouth section, where many matters were discussed by the Joint Committee, they looked at the costs of running both Dorchester stations. At the requests of both General Managers the traffic officers examined the question of providing a joint station at Dorchester Junction, and whilst this was practicable from an engineering point of view, any economy resulting therefrom would not justify the considerable expense involved. Moreover the location of the proposed station would be undesirable, and the scheme was not recommended. The first economy took place from 3rd October, 1932 when the

Bournemouth Central looking east viewed from the top of the mechanical hoist situated in the engine shed complex. Works materials and a cement mixer in the left foreground suggest that modernisation work has commenced.
Author's Collection

A view taken from the east end clearly showing the fitting shop and mechanical hoist with the engine shed to the left. These two views clearly demonstrate the cramped conditions for a depot of such importance.
Author's Collection

retirement of Mr C.A. Drew, the GWR station master, allowed Mr S. Wood (who for the past two years had been the Southern station master) to take control of both stations effecting a saving of £368 per annum.

Further economies were made from 1st January, 1936 when GWR goods shed traffic was transferred to the Southern goods shed along with the GWR goods clerical staff, although both stations continued to handle yard traffic. Combined with a small saving in staff, the goods cartage arrangements were reorganized. The Southern Railway employed a cartage agent, Mr Rimmer, who was paid £700 per annum; the GWR carried out its own cartage using one 4/5 ton lorry, a two ton lorry and a single horse and cart. By dispensing with the cartage agent and allowing the GWR to supply all the cartage vehicles, which under the new arrangements consisted of one 4/5 ton lorry, one 2 ton lorry, one 3 ton mechanical horse and two trailers, and three single horse teams with two spare carts, it was estimated that £267 would be saved on the cartage account.

Bournemouth Central station may have been remodelled but the cramped conditions of the engine shed still had to be addressed and, with the Branksome scheme finally laid to rest, it was decided in 1935 to improve the existing site. The shed building would be lengthened to cover the open yard at the rear and increased to the full four roads of the existing building, a new turntable and a water softening plant installed, the yard rearranged and better staff facilities provided.

Work commenced without delay after authorization was given that December; the coaling facilities had been modernised and the 65 ft vacuum-operated turntable installed by the commencement of the 1936 summer service. However, the shed extension - consisting of pre-cast concrete beams covered with corrugated asbestos sheeting - was not constructed until the following winter and was completed by the end of the summer of 1937 with the water softening plant following the next year. The shed remained operational during the entire reconstruction process.

Other minor improvements carried out during that period included a replacement footbridge at Redbridge station. The new structure (of concrete), which came into use on 7th September, 1937, also provided pedestrian access for workmen employed at the adjacent sleeper works who had previously been obliged to use the level crossing adjacent to the signal box.

More staff costs were saved from 10th April, 1938, when the signal box at Uddens Crossing (between West Moors and Ringwood) was abolished as a block post and placed under the care of a crossing keeper.

At Dorchester the original train shed of 1847 was finally demolished in 1938 and the station tidied up, but having invested heavily further up the line, Dorchester was a low priority as the report of 18 months earlier shows:

The question of improving Dorchester has been considered on many occasions, but owing to the serious expense involved it has from time to time been deferred. It is fully admitted, however, that the conditions at this station are very antiquated and require improvement, but from an analysis of the traffic dealt with, and the absence of any indication that there is likely to be a material increase in the future, it was considered that the expense of reconstructing the station could not be justified.

It was therefore decided that the station and general layout should remain as at present, and that a scheme embodying the following improvements, together with a general modernisation should be prepared for consideration.

A view of the rear of Bournemouth shed before the 1937 extension with Beechey Road bridge in the background. Locomotives on view from the left are: 'G6' class 0-6-0 No. 275, 'A12' class 0-4-2 No. 624, 'M7' class 0-4-4T No. 21, 'T1' class 0-4-4T Nos. 364 and 73. *Author's Collection*

Viewed from the same position on 21st June, 1937 'T9' class 4-4-0 No. 728 approaches under Beechey Road bridge with the 12.25 pm Weymouth-Bournemouth Central service. In the background construction is taking place of the extension to the engine shed using pre-cast concrete beams that will later be clad with asbestos sheeting. *Author's Collection*

The roof of the old carriage shed to be dismantled, the old disused platform to be cleared away. The present roofing of the Up platform which is supported on columns along the centre of the platform to be removed, and replaced by modern roofing carried on cantilevers from the station wall. The station offices on the up platform be rearranged and the parcel office enlarged.

The goods shed suffered from a lack of floor space, so it was decided that the four loading bays be filled in and canopies fitted over the doorways of the three of them that were not already so provided.

The question of closing the engine shed was again raised, with the engines being moved to Weymouth. The General Manager expressed a desire that the matter be reviewed; however, it was decided the existing arrangements were more satisfactory. Although for traffic purposes the engines would have been better situated at Weymouth where a majority of trains either terminated or commenced, space and operational considerations would have been a problem. The Southern shed there was not only small but lacked a turntable, so tender engines would have needed to run to the GWR shed for turning - and that company would have certainly made a substantial charge for the facility - whilst stabling SR engines at the GWR shed was attended by numerous problems, not the least of which was that Southern interests would have taken second place!

Unfortunately, other events were to overshadow any future plans. Weymouth's Brunel station of 1857 was still doing service; despite improvements during the 1880s and additional sidings laid during the past 30 years the platform facilities were woefully inadequate. In February 1938 the GWR announced that Weymouth station was to be rebuilt. The work would be carried out in stages, firstly with improvements to siding accommodation, followed by alterations and extensions to platforms, then the construction of new station buildings. That work would commence in the next few months and its anticipated completion was no later than the end of December 1940.

Preliminary work commenced within months, the SR shed was closed on 2nd January, 1939 and demolished to clear part of the site for the new station, work on which was due to commence at the end of the summer service. Unfortunately, the worsening international situation and the outbreak of war caused any further progress to be halted for a further 17 years.

There were a number of changes of station master during the 1930s, including Mr P.G. Collins who moved from Dorchester to Eastbourne during 1930 to be replaced by Mr H.M. Wood. The following year Mr G. Longhurst moved from Broadstone to Barnham and Mr J.J. Hibbard returned from exile at Sheffield Park to take charge of Broadstone although his stay was brief, another exile, Mr W. Swetman coming from Penshurst to replace him in 1932 until his own retirement four years later.

In 1932 Mr C. McGarvey who had been station master at Ringwood since 1926 moved to Sherborne, his place being taken by Mr P.H. Corrick from Grateley. Mr H.W. Hayward, station master at Wimborne since 1930, transferred to Fareham in 1933, his replacement being W.J. Gard who had previously had control over the stations on the Meon Valley line.

The standing of a station master in the local community was often displayed upon his departure or promotion, such as when Robert Newton Parsons who had joined the LSWR in June 1885 and served at Moreton as station master since February 1921 took retirement in May 1937. The occasion was marked with a presentation, held at the Plaza cinema, Dorchester, of a gold watch and chain together with an illuminated address by the Mayor of Dorchester Miss Winifrede Mardsen. The station master's wife could also be an asset to the community: at Moreton Mrs Parsons taught the local children dancing, singing and recitations, she organized shows and they would present plays, Mrs Parsons making all the costumes. She also took them on the local bus to visit other villages to broaden their local knowledge.

Although the above might paint a picture of delightful village life, there were difficulties that the town dweller did not have to contend with; until just before World War II there was no running water at Moreton. Water for the station and the adjoining station cottages was like that of a majority of crossing cottages along the line - supplied in cans delivered by train. In a bizarre twist when the well at the 'Frampton Arms' ran dry, water was delivered in barrels by train from Strong's brewery at Romsey.

The 1930s also saw changes in the cartage of milk; whereas local farmers had brought it to Moreton station twice a day in carts and loaded it onto trains, a lorry from Parkstone collected it directly from the farms. This was beginning to take place across the country, and it was not only milk traffic that was being lost, agricultural traffic in general was in decline as motor lorries and the services they provided demonstrated greater flexibility in the transportation of many items including grain and cattle feed.

Excursion traffic was still important during the 1930s. On 15th April, 1931 a visit to Fry's chocolate factory at Somerdale, including a charabanc tour of Bristol, was on offer from either Wimborne or Broadstone at 5s. 9d. And on 6th September these two stations offered excursions to Bristol, Newport or Cardiff at 4s., 6s. and 6s. 6d. Other excursions during June and July offered Exeter, Dawlish, Teignmouth, Newton Abbot, Torquay or Paignton as destinations, but as the departure from Broadstone was not until 11.00 am, allowing for reversal at Templecombe and Exeter, the stay in Devon was brief.

In addition during the 1930s there were regular Sunday excursions from Portland, Weymouth, and other stations to Poole, Bournemouth, Southampton, Fareham and Portsmouth, the latter destination being popular with naval personnel and their families.

Regularly featured during the 1930s were excursions to Southampton to view the various liners, the floating dock and Southampton Docks. The fare from stations between Easton and Upwey was 6s. from Dorchester and Swanage 3s. 3d. and from Corfe Castle and Wareham 3s. For an additional 2s. one could enjoy a paddle steamer trip in the Solent, or for 1s. a 16 mile motor bus tour of Southampton. On 14th May, 1931 the RMS *Aquitania* was on view and on 29th August RMS *Berengaria*, such was the choice, later to be joined by the *Queen Mary*. On 12th July, 1939 the new RMS *Mauretania* was the focal point and a week later the RMS *Empress of Britain*, although by this time the fare had risen to 8s. from Weymouth and 7s. 6d. from Dorchester or Moreton.

Other marine attractions offered by the SR were paddle steamer cruises from Portsmouth to Southampton and Bournemouth with the option of train travel for either the outward or inward journey. There were also a number of combined rail and sea excursions offered with other paddle steamer operators, and in the event of a Red Funnel steamer being unable to embark passengers at Bournemouth on a return sailing to Southampton passengers were entitled to return to Southampton by train on production of the return half of the boat ticket and payment of 1s.

Touring exhibition trains had also been popular during the inter-war years: in December 1934 the Fry's Chocolate train visited Southampton West attracting 5,800 visitors and a further 8,800 at Bournemouth. The following year on 11th and 12th May the HMV gramophone show train visited Bournemouth West.

The Coronation of King George V1 on 12th June, 1937 again provided the railway with much extra traffic both for the Coronation in London and the Fleet review at Spithead. On Whit Sunday 18th May, an excursion was run from Weymouth to Portsmouth and other stations to Portsmouth to view the assembled fleet, the fare of 8s. 6d. including a steamer trip around the fleet.

There were also a number of special chartered trains: on 18th April, 1931 No. 861 *Lord Anson* hauled a seven-coach special from Waterloo to Beaulieu conveying guests to the wedding of Clodach Pamela Bowes-Lyon to Lord Malcolm Avendale Douglas-Hamilton at Beaulieu. Whilst on 3rd June, 1937 many of the 700 invited guests to celebrate the centenary of Eldridge Pope the Dorchester brewers attended the gathering, arriving on a special train that ran from Eastleigh.

LMS '4F' class 0-6-0 No. 4166 runs into Bournemouth West with an excursion from the Midlands via the Somerset & Dorset line on Easter Monday 2nd April, 1934. The running of excursions often stretched the resources of the traffic department. The first coach with its arc roof and centre guard's look-out is of interest.

Mark Yarwood/Great Western Trust Collection

'G6' class 0-6-0 No. 262 shunts wagons in one of the two private sidings serving the Eldridge Pope brewery at Dorchester during 1937.   *Author's Collection*

A Bournemouth via Wimborne push-pull train consisting of set No. 352 (formerly half of an LSWR four-coach bogie block set converted during 1915) waits to depart from Ringwood station. On the extreme right buffer stops protect the remains of the former Christchurch bay platform line, the signalling arrangements indicate that the photograph was taken between 1931 and 1938.   *Author's Collection*

A number of guaranteed excursions still ran, the 1935 working timetable giving details of those operated by Restall's between Waterloo and Weymouth. The circus train also made a re-appearance, in 1933, when Bertram Mills decided to move its entire circus by rail with Dorchester being one of the venues that season. As the winter quarters were at Ascot the SR provided a majority of the wagons. A second train was added the following year and by 1939 it consisted of four trains when Dorchester was the venue from 27th-29th July before proceeding to Bournemouth for a 10 day visit. At the end of August, with war imminent, the railway requested the return of the trains.

Whereas Bertram Mills circus train was a regular feature there were occasional one-off movements such as on 1st December, 1935 when a special train, consisting of two trucks of scenery, two bogie 'Covcars' with wild animals, six horse boxes two corridor coaches and a brake van, moved Sanger's Circus to Brighton.

The Royal Counties Show was held at Bournemouth in both 1933 and 1938, the latter held between 1st and 4th June. Not allowing for extra passenger traffic, 342 truckloads of implement traffic were unloaded at Bournemouth Central goods yard, whilst 357 trucks were loaded at the conclusion of the show, and four cattle specials dispatched. Almost as an omen for 10 years hence, the showground office occupied by all four companies had a large board above with the words 'BRITISH RAILWAYS'!

Looking back over the years following the World War I, the railways had achieved a great deal - despite their rundown condition at the end of World War I hostilities and the competition from road transport. Sensible economies and forward planning by men who understood the industry had allowed the Southampton & Dorchester network to come through almost unscathed, such losses as the original S&D route from Wimborne to Corfe Mullen and the line through Hurn being of little significance as both had been supplanted by lines of superior alignment.

A pre-war view as former Somerset & Dorset Armstrong 0-6-0 No. 57 constructed in 1922, later LMS '4F' class 0-6-0 No. 4557, waits to depart from Bournemouth West with an S&D train. Note the Whitaker automatic tablet exchanger fitted to the front tender hand rail; in the shadows stands an 'M7' class 0-4-4 tank waiting to depart with a train for the Old Road.   *Dr J. Boudreau Collection*

'H15' class 4-6-0 No. 490 passing through Christchurch station with a Waterloo-Bournemouth train on Sunday 10th July, 1937. To the right of the locomotive stands Christchurch West ground frame which controlled the crossover at the Bournemouth end of the station.

Author's Collection

GWR '2251' class 0-6-0 No. 2277 heads through Broadstone on 9th July, 1939 with a Taunton-Bournemouth West excursion that had joined the Somerset & Dorset line at Highbridge. It then travelled over the original Somerset Central line to Evercreech Junction before proceeding southwards onto the former Dorset Central near Bruton. Almost a re-enactment of the route taken by trains in the early days. Ironically, No. 2277 was transferred to the Somerset & Dorset line in her final years before withdrawal in December 1963.　　　*Author's Collection*

The gains were many. Train services had improved, the introduction of the 'Bournemouth Limited' in 1929 and the all Pullman 'Bournemouth Belle' in 1931 bringing much prestige to the line. The centenary of the opening of the complete London & Southampton Railway took place on 10th June, 1939. A hundred years before it then took the 'fast train' three hours to complete the journey between Nine Elms and Southampton Terminus. On the centenary day in 1939 'King Arthur' class 4-6-0 No. 779 *Sir Colgrevance* with 12 Pullman cars weighing 466 tons ran from Waterloo to Southampton Central in 84 minutes and a further 35½ minutes to Bournemouth West. Whilst the 'Bournemouth Limited' managed Waterloo to Bournemouth non-stop in 116 minutes with a further 55 minutes and three intermediate stops before reaching Weymouth.

Many other services were of an improved standard. The Southern was the 'Holiday Line': on a weekday during the summer of 1939 there were 13 down trains between Waterloo and Bournemouth, on a Saturday there were 26 and between 7.25 am and 5.15 pm 22 up trains, with a further five in the evening including the mail train. The modernisation of Bournemouth, Pokesdown, Brockenhurst, Millbrook and Southampton Central stations with the construction of the New Docks all proved successful - the latter being fully equipped to play a vital role in the forthcoming years of conflict.

Having worked a Wolverhampton-Bournemouth Central through train and then berthed the empty stock at Hamworthy Junction, GWR 'Saint' class 4-6-0 No. 2916 *Saint Benedict* stands in the down sidings at Broadstone on Saturday 7th August, 1937. No. 2916 is waiting to return light engine to Bournemouth Central shed and in the process of using the Hamworthy Junction-Broadstone Junction-Holes Bay Junction triangle to turn.

Author's Collection

Drummond 'L11' class 4-4-0 No. 157 stands at Southampton Central with a Wolverhampton-Bournemouth train during 1939. Although only a four-coach train of GWR stock, two of the coaches are of clerestory design a number of which remained in service until after World War II. *Author's Collection*

Within two weeks World War II would shatter this typical railway scene as Drummond 'T9' class 4-4-0 No. 718 approaches Broadstone with the 10.07 am Bournemouth West-Salisbury train on 21st August, 1939. To the extreme left workmen attend to a minor earth slip in the cutting. No. 718 gave the railways good service, constructed in September 1899 she was not withdrawn until March 1961. *Author's Collection*

Chapter Four

World War Two
and its Aftermath

Unlike World War I the situation in Europe had been deteriorating over a long period, and as it became clear to the railway companies, the military and other authorities that action would have to be taken in case of war many plans were devised and a number of schemes already put in place. It was to be a different war than the one fought just 20 years before. With the advances of the aeroplane and other military technology it would be brought to the doorsteps of every person in the British Isles with air raids causing mass destruction to both railways and other infrastructure.

At Warmwell, not far from the site of the former Woodsford Royal Naval airship station, RAF Warmwell was established in May 1937, later to become a fighter base; although not directly rail connected much of its traffic for both goods and personnel was handled at Moreton. Two sidings were laid opposite Doulton's siding at 116 m. 37 ch. on the Hamworthy Goods branch and brought into use on 4th July, 1938 for the use of the Air Ministry. Aviation spirit and petrol was piped to storage tanks for use with flying boats, which were later transferred from Southampton to Poole Harbour, this becoming their base for the duration. The following year work commenced on the construction of an ordnance factory at Creekmoor alongside the Poole-Broadstone line.

Although Territorial Army camps were a regular feature in the New Forest during the summer months, 1939 saw them on a much larger scale than previously. It is estimated that during that August 30,000 troops were camped in the Burley, Beaulieu and East Boldre area requiring the running of many troop specials.

As the situation deteriated the railways were brought under Government control on 1st September, 1939. With the fear of massive air attacks on large cities, plans were drawn up and quickly brought into action and children from Southampton were moved by train to New Milton, West Moors and other locations in the surrounding countryside. With the sudden loss of holidaymakers, train services were cut, restaurant cars taken off and the 'Bournemouth Belle' withdrawn. Blackout and air raid precautions were introduced as was an overall speed restriction of 60 mph and an extension of journey times; also for a short period there was a drastic reduction of services.

On 18th October two withdrawn LBSCR 'I2' class 4-4-2 tanks Nos. 2013 and 2019 were towed from Eastleigh and placed over a pit in Bournemouth shed. Covered in sandbags they served as an air raid shelter until January 1941 when concrete shelters were provided, the two engines later being transferred to the Longmoor Military Railway. To assist with the extra traffic a train control office was constructed at Southampton Central in a ground level concrete bunker on the up side near the entrance to Southampton tunnel.

Traffic quickly changed to troop trains and supplies for the dockyards at Portland and Portsmouth, Poole again became a naval base. The shipping of petrol from Hamworthy Quay to the British Expeditionary Force in France was taking place by late 1939, resulting in the section of the former up line, which had been retained as a siding into a shipyard, being provided with crossovers at 117 m. 3 ch. and 117 m. 25 ch. to form an additional run-round loop during February 1940. By April it was noted that two trains (each of 30 wagons) and one on alternate days were arriving at the quay. Carried in cans, the petrol was loaded into vessels using one crane belonging to Poole Harbour Commissioners plus runways from the truck sides to the decks of the vessels. Extra cranes had been obtained from Harwich Parkeston Quay and one had been erected and was almost ready to commence work when the fall of France changed the situation. To shunt this volatile cargo LMS diesel-mechanical shunter No. 7053 was sent to Hamworthy Quay. Historically interesting as a one-off of its type owned by the railway it was built by in 1934 by Messrs Hunslet (No. 1723). A SR Committee Minute of November 1939 stated that there was a problem with the LMS engine at Poole and any money spent on it should be charged to the War Department to whom it was on loan. It appears that the problems were overcome as the engine was observed shunting at Hamworthy during June 1940, and residing at Bournemouth engine shed during the July and August, later being acquired by the War Department and receiving number WD 23.

With Southampton a target for the *Luftwaffe* it had been decided at the time of the Munich crisis that flying boat services would be transferred to Poole harbour, this taking place on 1st September, 1939. As well as the civilian service operated by British Overseas Airways Corporation (BOAC) both the RAF and Royal Navy operated seaplane bases in the harbour at various times during the war. To serve the BOAC service a special train often containing a Pullman car was operated between London, Victoria and Poole, at times carrying VIPs on important missions.

During April 1940 two rail-mounted former World War I 12 inch Howitzer guns were stored in a siding at Ringwood. On 1st May Drummond 'K10' class 4-4-0 No. 393 hauled them to the Swanage branch and placed them on special sidings near Corfe Castle where they formed part of the area defence network.

Gradually the severe cuts in services were reduced. The 1st January, 1940 saw the restoration of the 8.20 am Bournemouth West-Waterloo with stops at Southampton Central and Winchester only, and the 1.30 pm Waterloo-Bournemouth West together with the 6.05 pm Bournemouth West to Waterloo on Fridays and Saturdays.

It would be impossible to mention all the troop specials that were run during this period. However, the transfer of the 5th Battalion of the West Kent Regiment from their training ground near Bridport to Southampton Docks during the morning of 5th April, 1940 deserves mention. The four trains were handed over the SR at Dorchester Junction, a further four trains being run on the 8th. On the same day there were trains from Chard Junction (2), Crewkerne, and Sherborne (2) joining the Southampton & Dorchester line at Redbridge.

Under conditions of great secrecy the Royal Train with Their Majesties King George VI and Queen Elizabeth travelled over the Old Road in the early hours of Tuesday 14th May, 1940, hauled by 'T9' class 4-4-0 No. 119. The seven-coach train consisting of Great Western stock travelled from London to Broadstone where LMS 'Black Five' 4-6-0 No. 5274 backed onto the rear and took the special over the

Royal occasion at Broadstone on 15th May, 1940: the empty stock of the GWR Royal Train having been brought from Blandford back to Broadstone behind 'Black Five' No. 5289 departs behind Drummond 'T9' No. 119 towards West Moors and Downton. Here Their Majesties will rejoin the train following their visit to Blandford Camp. *Author's Collection*

Somerset & Dorset to Blandford where it was stabled for the night. The next morning the train returned to Broadstone as empty stock hauled by 'Black Five' No. 5289. Here 'T9' class No. 119 was coupled onto the rear to work the train over the Old Road to West Moors then onto the Salisbury & Dorset line to Downton where the Royal party reboarded before returning to Waterloo via Salisbury.

Despite the war Bertram Mills circus commenced a tour during 1940 using only two trains, a visit being made to Southampton between 13th and 18th May after which they departed for Cheltenham and other venues. The deteriorating situation caused the show to be closed the following month.

The subsequent evacuation of Dunkirk and other ports resulted in many troop trains being run at short notice, some with unusual motive power. Many were bound for Bournemouth West, others to Wool, Dorchester, Weymouth and Portland, and at least 12 passed onto the Somerset & Dorset at Broadstone in the four days 28th-31st May.

With the fear of invasion, tank traps, pill boxes, and other defences appeared alongside various sections of the railways in southern England, and plans were drawn up to evacuate the south coast if necessary. Casualty evacuation trains were placed at various locations, two trains Nos. 301 and 302 being allocated to Bournemouth West. For reasons never explained, on 27th May, 1940 the up line between Ringwood and Holmsley was used for the berthing of wagons, single line working being put into operation over the down line between these two stations for the period whilst the up line was blocked. Air raids on Southampton Docks resulted in a number of vital records and other paperwork being transferred to the safety of Holmsley, a clerk travelling from Southampton daily to administer the necessary paperwork.

Damage to Southampton Central following dropping of two parachute mines on the station in the early hours of 22nd July, 1941. The extensive damage to both the up platform buildings and the island platform canopy is clearly illustrated. *B. Moody Collection*

The total destruction of a large section of the 1934 precast concrete buildings, including the ticket hall on the new down platform, after being hit by two parachute mines. *B. Moody Collection*

On 12th May a stencilled circular was sent to staff instructing them to remove level crossing gates in case of invasion in the forward area, the gates to be either tied back clear of both the track and the road or removed from their posts and laid alongside the line.

A further set of stencilled notices on 3rd August, 1940 gave instructions for the removal of stock and locomotives from both the Hamworthy Goods branch and Poole Quay in the event of invasion. It stated that on the Hamworthy branch all wagons loaded or empty were to be removed from the branch, including Hamworthy New Quay, the coal company's wharf, Dibble's Wharf, Doulton's siding and Air Ministry siding. The two steam locomotives of the Hamworthy Wharf & Coal Company could be utilised to haul a load within their capacity to Hamworthy Junction, and if not in steam should be hauled dead to the junction and immobilised. In the event of the number of wagons exceeding the siding capacity at Hamworthy Junction and Broadstone, the single line between Hamworthy Junction and Broadstone was to be utilised, traffic being worked via Poole. Upon completion of the withdrawal of stock the branch was to be crippled by the removal of point parts. Likewise the same arrangements applied to the Poole Harbour tramway, the stock being placed in Poole goods yard and point parts removed.

On a wry note the following circular to staff puts today's prices into context with those of 1940:

... the price of petroleum has again advanced ½d. per gallon and Station Masters and others concerned are reminded that particular care must be taken to avoid wastage and every effort must be made to see that economy is exercised in the use of petroleum.

With the exception of Southampton, the routes to Weymouth only received a minimum of air raid damage, and at Southampton despite the destruction inflicted upon the city and docks the main line survived. On 23rd November, 1940 the up side buildings at Southampton Central were damaged in an air raid, the line at St Mary's bridge between Southampton Tunnel Junction and the east end of Southampton tunnel was blocked on the 8th July, 1941. Down trains were diverted via Southampton Terminus and then over the Docks & Harbour Board lines to the Western Docks before regaining the main line at Millbrook to run back into Southampton Central, whilst up trains run back to Redbridge and travelled via Romsey and Chandlers Ford to Eastleigh.

The most severe damage was caused in the early hours of 22nd July, 1941 when parachute mines landed on and near Southampton Central station. The centre section of the new down side buildings containing the ticket office and booking hall was completely destroyed. The island platform canopy and the roof of the up side building were also severely damaged, a member of staff also being killed in the raid. Again whilst the lines were blocked traffic was diverted via the dock lines and Romsey.

Damage was done to Redbridge sleeper works during a raid on the 19th June, 1940 and an unexploded bomb alongside the line at Sterte west of Poole station caused delays to traffic on 9th January, 1941. On 21st March the 5.19 pm works train from Holton Heath to Christchurch was attacked just after it left Holton Heath. Six bombs straddled the train breaking windows and causing minor injuries to the many women workers on board. The driver managed to draw the train into the cutting short of Hamworthy Junction and then into the station where assistance was given to the injured. What would have appeared to have been an attack on the viaducts at Branksome took place on 27th March; missing the viaduct the bomb went into the canteen of the Bourne Valley gasworks situated below the railway. As it was dinner time the canteen was crowded and the delayed action bomb exploded killing 34 workers. The line at Ashley Heath crossing was blocked by bomb damage following a raid on 12th May, the following month severe damage was done to Southampton Central station - a further section of the down side building being almost destroyed.

The severe damage in the Southampton area not only affected the railways and with a view to reducing the pressure on associated bus companies during peak periods, the interavailable ticket arrangements were extended to cover the Southampton-Romsey and Southampton-Totton routes. During one week in August 1941 nearly 400 return tickets issued by Hants & Dorset Motor Services were exchanged at Southampton Central to cover the journey by rail to Totton. A further additional traffic was created by the number of former residents evacuated to other towns, resulting in running additional early morning and late afternoon trains to convey them to and from their employment.

Raids continued into 1942: on 28th November 'T9' class 4-4-0 No. 120 was working the 6.00 am Brockenhurst to Dorchester goods and was standing at the Wool down advanced starting signal when the train was attacked by enemy aircraft making two level attacks with 20 mm cannon fire. Driver H. Clarke sustained injury to the head and fireman D. Keegan injury to the leg and, after receiving first aid, were taken to the military hospital at Bovington. It was discovered when the engine was examined that holes had been shot in the tender sides and the outer firebox casing, whilst a lubricating pipe was broken and the cab look-out windows smashed, but the locomotive was able to work the train forward to Dorchester following the arrival of a relief crew.

Although air raids were a constant threat, aircraft could also cause other difficulties. On 27th March, 1942 a damaged Spitfire making for Holmsley made a forced landing on the track near Bagnum crossing (No. 14) which was situated just east of Crow crossing between Holmsley and Ringwood. Mrs Ventham, the daughter of the crossing keeper, upon hearing the crash seized a red flag and ran a distance of about 670 yds to warn the crew of an approaching train which was brought to a stand about 15 yds short of the plane. The incident occurred at 2.30 pm and the RAF recovery team had the line clear at 3.50 pm. Commended for her action by the divisional superintendent, Mrs Ventham received a cheque from the company in recognition of her actions.

The cottage at Burton crossing No. 35 and its occupants were not so lucky when it was destroyed with loss of life during an air raid on 15th May, 1944. A little to the west on Winfrith Heath and to the south of the line was a decoy airfield for RAF Warmwell, a situation that made this section of line vulnerable to attack.

Freight and troop trains off the Somerset & Dorset line added to the amount of traffic handled at Broadstone, Hamworthy Junction and Poole. At the latter station new goods reception roads were laid in September 1941 and brought into use with an extended goods yard on 9th October.

A number of signalling and other alterations were carried out during 1942 in preparation for extra traffic. In the April a number of changes were made to signalling at Bournemouth West. On 27th October a siding to hold 44 wagons was brought into use at Lyndhurst Road; controlled by ground frame B it was situated west of the station on the down side. June 1942 also saw the closure of the Somerset & Dorset engine shed at Branksome for the duration, locomotive servicing being transferred to Bournemouth Central.

By the end of 1942 Britain was turning to the offensive from the defensive. The build-up for the invasion of Europe was starting to take place, and the main part of the force was to depart from the Hampshire and Dorset coast, from Portsmouth, Southampton, Poole, Weymouth and Portland. In the New Forest area 12 airfields were constructed, this work alone requiring 20,000 men a majority of whom were brought in from outside the area.

At West Moors work on the construction of a vast 430 acre petroleum dump was commenced in 1939 for the use of the British forces. A connection with the main line east of the junction with the Salisbury line at West Moors came into use on 14th February, 1943 and work on the sidings complex was completed on 24th July, the layout consisting of 8.6 miles of track with 41 sets of points. By August 1943 the American 3877th Quartermaster Gas (i.e. petrol, oil and lubricants) Depot Q328 was in residence to store petrol for shipment to France. At its peak the depot stored about 75,000 tons in five gallon jerry cans.

To assist the flow of traffic into Southampton Western Docks, a new connection at the east end of Redbridge station, consisting of both up and down lines allowing traffic to arrive and depart from the west, was brought into use on 28th March, 1943. At Uddens Crossing on the Old Road where the signal box had previously been reduced to a ground frame, it was restored to a block post on 8th June with the opening of a Government siding on the down side. At Brockenhurst seven extra sidings were laid on the down side to handle extra traffic in October 1943; together with an existing siding they gave a capacity of 306 wagons. Also during 1943 the construction of a Military Port at Marchwood, complete with sidings served from the Fawley branch, involved the movement of additional traffic in the Southampton area.

There had for many years been through workings from the Brighton line and the GWR via Basingstoke of LBSCR and GWR locomotives respectively working on booked services and excursions. However, the necessities of war saw a number of engines used from both the Eastern and Central sections that had rarely appeared on the Southampton & Dorchester line before. From the outbreak of the war a weekly special goods was run from Portsmouth to Portland Dockyard this being hauled as far as Bournemouth by LBSCR 'C2X' class 0-6-0s; from here the train was taken forward by a 'Q' class 0-6-0.

During the evacuation of Dunkirk in 1940 many locomotives strayed far from their usual routes, two former SECR 'C' class 0-6-0s Nos. 1229 and 1585 being reported at Weymouth with French Navy personnel. On 11th March, 1941 former LBSCR Atlantic 4-4-0 No. 2422 appeared at Bournemouth with a troop special, and sister engine No. 2421 was at Dorchester on 17th July with a van train, both engines being on loan to Basingstoke shed. SECR 'D1' class 4-4-0s Nos. 1494 and 1739 were noted at Weymouth with troop specials of London & North Eastern

Railway (LNER) stock on 11th October, 1942, and LBSCR 'K' class 2-6-0 No. 2346 appeared at Weymouth on a van train for Portland on 9th December.

South Eastern 'D1' and 'E1' class 4-4-0s would often haul the BOAC flying boat specials between Victoria and Poole in place of the regular 'T9' class 4-4-0. And in mid-1942 whilst awaiting their return journey these locomotives would at times operate Bournemouth West-Salisbury, Weymouth-Andover Junction and other stopping services out of Bournemouth. Christmas Eve 1943 saw SECR 'D' class 4-4-0 No. 1734 shunting at Poole, and sister engine No. 1726 at Weymouth on the 17th May, 1944 with a troop train.

By January 1943 LMS '8F' class 2-8-0s that had been constructed at Eastleigh works were to be seen employed on freight trains between Eastleigh and Bournemouth. Later a number of both British War Department and United States Army Transportation Corps locomotives were to be seen both working trains or in store awaiting shipment overseas via Southampton.

Towards the end of the year the plans for the invasion were well advanced, the thick forest foliage being ideal to hide the vast amounts of equipment and large numbers of troops that were to be camped in the area ready for the move. They had to be backed up by supplies and more troops who were brought to the area over the Somerset & Dorset, the Andover & Redbridge, the former Midland & South Western Junction (MSWJ) and the Didcot, Newbury & Southampton, all lines that before the war had been rural backwaters.

Brockenhurst station became a dispersal point for many of the camps and airfields as troops and equipment arrived by the trainload. Holmsley, another rural backwater, also became an important railhead for troops and equipment; bombs were unloaded in the sidings to be transferred by road to Holmsley aerodrome. Opposite the station the Ministry of Supply operated a saw mill, the finished sawn timber and pit props being dispatched by rail.

The war brought additional traffic to Wimborne, the sidings on the site of the former Somerset & Dorset engine shed at Merley having been taken over by the military by late 1942 and were served by two trains daily. Wimborne also became the railhead for the transhipment of materials for the construction of Tarrant Rushton airfield and the military hospitals at St Leonards and Kingston Lacy. As D-Day approached large numbers of troops encamped in the area, arriving and departed from the station. Hamworthy Goods was also busy with its limited siding space, resulting in many wagons being retained at Hamworthy Junction until it was possible to work them down the branch. This caused friction between station master Charles Dominey at Hamworthy Goods and his counterpart Harry Brixton who also had little space at the Junction as a number of goods trains to and from Dorchester and the Swanage branch were remarshalled there.

As more troops and supplies moved into the area the preparations for D-Day became more intense. Many parts of the south coast had become a restricted area and it was not unusual for police to question passengers as to their reason for travelling. Security was tight, as special trains conveying the Allied commanders visited the south coast. On 12th-13th August, 1943 General Eisenhower aboard his special train 'Alive' travelled from Yeovil to Bournemouth West and then to Southampton Terminus.

On 11th February, 1944 three special trains travelled to Swanage when King George VI, Allied Commander Eisenhower, General Montgomery, and Prime Minister Winston Churchill watched rehearsals for the D-Day landings at Studland. The King also inspected the preparations for D-Day at Portland on 25th May, 1944, after which he joined the Royal Train at Dorchester before returning to Waterloo.

Poole Harbour had also become very busy, with naval shipping including Bolson's ship yard which was working around the clock constructing landing craft, the materials being brought in by rail. Traffic on the Hamworthy branch reached saturation point as the invasion drew near, in the weeks following D-Day petrol for the British forces was shipped out of both Hamworthy and Poole Quay.

At various periods during the war ambulance trains were kept ready at Bournemouth West usually in charge of LNER 'B12' class 4-6-0 locomotives, which owing to their high route availability and Westinghouse air brakes were suitable for the work. Full details of their duties are lost in time, however, trains Nos. 37 and 41 arrived at Bournemouth in March 1944, and train No. 36 was based at Templecombe. In June 1944 ambulance trains were reported working in the Bournemouth area and onto the Somerset & Dorset, and in January 1945 train No. 67 consisting of SR stock and train No. 72 of LNER stock were reported as based at Bournemouth. The two principal military hospitals in the area were at St Leonard's (West Moors) and Blandford, as well as many other large residences taken over by the authorities, one such being Moreton House from where wounded troops would be taken by ambulance to Wool station where ambulance trains would wait in the up siding.

Many normal services were cancelled during the invasion period to provide pathways for the specials involved in both the movement of troops and materials; for obvious reasons the full details of many of these have never been recorded. However, in August 1944 it was understood that a limited sleeping car service was available for certain service personnel on the Waterloo-Weymouth line and that two LNER sleeping cars had been borrowed for the purpose. The same report also stated that 20 USA 2-8-0s and 75 American bogie box cars were stored at West Moors petroleum depot and that shunting was being carried out by War Department locomotive No. 1973 that had arrived the previous month. This locomotive was an American-built Vulcan 0-6-0 tank. It was later purchased in April 1947 by the Southern Railway as USA class No. 72 for shunting within Southampton Docks. Withdrawn in 1967 as No. 30072, it is today preserved on the Keighley & Worth Valley Railway in Yorkshire.

The war years saw a number of station masters retire, their final years of service being anything but normal with the pressures of work thrust upon them. Mr T. Bishop, originally a clerk from Bournemouth, became station master at Lyndhurst Road in 1933, moving to Totton during 1937 and retiring during 1943. The following year there were several moves when Mr G. Fryer of Bournemouth Central moved to Salisbury to be replaced by Mr R. Prosser of Brockenhurst, his place being taken by Mr R.G. Nobbs of Swanage. Mr P.G. Collins, who had been station master of Southampton Central since 1934, retired on 1st September, 1944.

Many station masters and staff received awards for their services during the war years. One such man was Charles John Leach, the Dorchester station

'Merchant Navy' class No. 21C2 *Union Castle* on the turntable at Bournemouth Central shed. The photograph is reputed to have been taken on the first visit of the locomotive during trials on 7th June, 1941. Note the works grey livery and the nameplate covered prior to the naming ceremony which took place at Victoria on 4th July. *G.O.P. Pearce/C.L. Caddy Collection*

Drummond 'L12' class 4-4-0 No. 429 backs stock out of Bournemouth West up to the carriage sidings on 21st March, 1943. Constructed at Nine Elms works in February 1905, No. 429 was withdrawn from service in September 1951. *G.O.P. Pearce/C.L. Caddy Collection*

master, who was awarded the BEM in the 1945 New Year's Honours list. He came to Dorchester in December 1942 from Devonport where he had served during the bombing of Plymouth during 1941. It was for his work at Plymouth at that time and the subsequent work at Dorchester before D-Day that he received the award. He had served at Dorchester early in his career as a goods clerk between 1902-1904 when he also played goal for Dorchester Saturday Football Club. Retiring from the railway on 24th March, 1945, he became landlord of the Swan Inn, Fordington.

His successor at Dorchester was Stanley A. Smith, formerly station master at Winchester City. S.A. Smith was the son of Henry James Smith, chief clerk at Dorchester from 1882 and station master from 1893 until his death aged only 38 in October 1898.

As the war came to an end a private siding was installed to serve the Wellworthy Factory at Ringwood, being brought into use on 21st February, 1945. On 6th May the wagon turntable and siding serving Webb Majors sand pit on the down side at Moreton was taken out of use. A further private siding closure took place on 25th August, 1946 when Mintey's siding at Ringwood was rendered redundant. At that time the Old Road was still busy, correspondence concerning crossing No. 16 at Ringwood in April 1945 stating that the gates were operated about 165 times during the working day.

The railways in the area had escaped much serious damage in the latter part of the war, unfortunately three other incidents on the line were to prove fatal. Peace had not been declared when on 23rd April, 1945 disaster overtook 'Lord Nelson' class 4-6-0 No. 854 *Howard of Effingham* when firebox failure, resulting in a rush of steam and water out through the firehole door, threw the fireman, Victor Perry of Bournemouth, onto the back of the tender. Fortunately, the driver escaped much of the blast and, although scalded, was able to stop the train. American doctors who were travelling on the train attended the severely scalded fireman who later died of his injuries. In just over an hour the crippled engine had been removed from the train and with a relief engine the train continued on its journey. At the subsequent inquiry it was revealed that the firebox crown had collapsed due to a lack of water in the boiler and a fusible plug failed to operate to save the firebox. However, as the train had only travelled 11 miles and there had been a full glass of water at Bournemouth Central, and the firebox had only been renewed the previous December, the occurrence was, to say the least, unusual.

On 25th June, 1946 a serious accident could well have become a disaster. Just after 1.30 pm the Brockenhurst-Hamworthy goods stopped at Branksome down home signal where the first six wagons were uncoupled and shunted into Branksome goods yard. As the engine was returning to the remaining 31 wagons, mostly loaded with coal, they commenced running away 'wrong line' back towards Bournemouth Central. At that moment the 1.30 pm Bournemouth West-Brighton train crossed the path of the runaways at Gas Works Junction, fortunately the rear of the train cleared the junction just ahead of the oncoming wagons. However, a short distance before Thwaites bridge the wagons collided with an 'N15' class 4-6-0 proceeding tender first towards Bournemouth West. The impact of the collision forced the guard's van over the top of the first two wagons resulting in the death of the guard.

General photographs of the railway during the war years are by the nature of events rare. However, on 15th September, 1941 LMS '2P' class 4-4-0 No. 628 was also photographed backing stock out of Bournemouth West towards the carriage sidings.

G.O.P. Pearce/C.L. Caddy Collection

Right: A very poor quality image of the scene at Thwaites Bridge near Gas Works Junction, Branksome on 25th June, 1946 shortly after wagons of a Brockenhurst-Hamworthy Junction freight ran away wrong- road and collided with an unidentified 'King Arthur', resulting in the death of the guard of the goods train.
Bournemouth Echo

At about 2.45 pm the remaining 29 wagons were pulled back to Branksome yard and single line working instigated just before 4 pm. At the subsequent inquiry it was stated that the shunter had failed to carry out rules and the special local instruction in regard to the pinning down of wagon brakes.

A third fatal accident took place on Monday 21st October, 1946 when an explosion wrecked the buffet on the up platform of Brockenhurst station. So severe was the blast that it blew the wall out of the building and damaged two coaches of the 9.20 am Weymouth-Waterloo train that was just about to depart. One coach receiving the full blast had many broken windows and damaged bodywork. The two damaged coaches of the train were removed to a siding and the train departed 25 minutes late.

Including passengers on the train, 14 people were injured, 11 being admitted to hospital, one, the buffet cellarman, later died of his injuries. The inquest revealed that owing to there being no mains gas supply a gas cylinder was placed in the cellar to operate the tea urn. The buffet was leased to Frederick Hotels Ltd who employed a district cellar man based at Southampton to carry out various duties including change the gas bottles. The previous week the staff had complained of a smell of gas in the cellar and of a hissing noise from the bottle; it appears that the cellarman had attended to the matter on the Saturday. However, on the Monday morning there was still a smell of gas in the buffet which the cellarman told the staff he would attend to; shortly afterwards there was the explosion, caused by the rising of the gas upon coming in contact with the flame on the tea urn in the buffet.

Added to the railways' problems immediately after the war was a coal shortage, a matter the Government responded to by arranging for the railway companies to convert a number of locomotives to oil burning. Beset by technical difficulties and troubles in obtaining materials resulted in the scheme getting off to a slow start.

The *Railway Gazette* at the end of December 1945 reported that the Southern Railway had converted 31 locomotives of passenger and mixed traffic type, and that these were operating between Southampton-Bournemouth, Bournemouth-Eastleigh, Portsmouth-Salisbury, Eastleigh-Andover and Southampton-Romsey. Of the locomotives converted were a 'West Country' class 4-6-2, 13 'T9' class 4-4-0s, eight 'L11' class 4-4-0s and five 'N15' or 'King Arthur' class 4-6-0s, the latter were reported to perform well as oil burners. Of these locomotives 'N15' class No. 740 *Merlin* carried out a trial run with the 12.10 pm Bournemouth West-Eastleigh on 10th March, 1947 and was reported working Waterloo-Bournemouth services the following month.

Only complete fueling facilities were installed at Fratton, those at Eastleigh and other depots were of a temporary nature. Inter-departmental disputes between the various Government departments involved in the scheme developed into a Whitehall farce, after which a balance of payments crisis involving the purchase of imported oil saw the scheme discontinued by late 1948, so ending the trail of greasy thick black smoke across the countryside so often the tell-tale mark of an oil-burning locomotive.

The summer of 1946 was the first opportunity for many families to take a holiday since the beginning of the war. Although there had been a fare rise of just over 16 per cent since the beginning of the war, most trains were crowded. From 6th May through trains recommenced between Bournemouth, Newcastle,

Resplendent in Southern Railway malachite green Urie 'King Arthur' class 4-6-0 No. 740 *Merlin* waits to depart from Bournemouth Central with an up train on 17th May, 1947. A close examination of the tender shows the tank fitted whilst the engine was equipped for oil burning between December 1946 and October 1948. Constructed in April 1919 and after travelling a recorded 1,357,971 miles the locomotive was withdrawn in December 1955. *Merlin* ended her career when as a demonstration for the BBC television programme 'Saturday Night Out' she was derailed on the Longmoor Military Railway. *G.O.P. Pearce/B.L. Jackson Collection*

At Southampton Central civic dignities, including the Mayor of Southampton Reginald Stranger, greet the first down 'Bournemouth Belle' after the war on 7th October, 1946 hauled by 'Merchant Navy' class 4-6-2 No. 21C18 *British India Line*. This locomotive was the first of the class to be rebuilt in February1956 and was withdrawn in August 1964 remaining in Barry scrapyard until March 1980 when rescued for preservation, although at the time of writing still awaiting full restoration. *Author's Collection*

Birmingham, Sheffield, and Birkenhead. Both the Newcastle and Birkenhead through trains were quickly duplicated in early June by extra trains on Saturdays to Sheffield and Birmingham with corresponding down trains, the extra trains continuing until 28th September. Through carriages between Waterloo and Swanage were also introduced on two Saturday trains commencing from the 1st June, and by mid-August cheap day tickets were again available on Tuesdays, Wednesdays and Thursdays to Bournemouth from many stations in the area.

Seat reservations were again available on certain weekday trains between Bournemouth and Waterloo and the 'Bournemouth Belle' was reintroduced on the 7th October, 1946. Ten Pullman cars hauled by 'Merchant Navy' class Pacific No. 21C18 *British India Line* made the inaugural run which was greeted by the Mayor of Southampton Reginald Stranger, during the stop there, and then by the Mayor of Bournemouth Robert Old upon its arrival. Despite the austere times there were passengers from both Bournemouth and Southampton who could well afford the 3s. supplement to travel by Pullman and usually the cost of a meal. From the railway's point of view the use of the Pullmans slightly eased the shortage of rolling stock.

However, it was not only the railways that were returning to normality. The long distance coach industry had recommenced operations despite fuel rationing. Royal Blue, whose services had been suspended in 1942, commenced a limited service during April 1946, including six journeys each way daily between Bournemouth-Southampton and London.

Goods traffic was still heavy during that period with all goods yards and most sidings busy, and shunting horses were still employed on certain duties at Hamworthy Goods. During the same year Messrs Eldridge Pope, the Dorchester Brewers, who had had a private siding at Bournemouth Central goods yard for a number of years applied for it to be diverted and lengthened to a new store the firm was to construct on its property. Although less than 30 miles from its Dorchester brewery, the difficulties of road transport at that time, including the rationing of petrol and shortage of new vehicles, made railway transport a viable proposition.

There were still acute shortages, rationing and a make do and mend policy existed in many walks of life. The railways were suffering from five years of intensive use with only essential maintenance work carried out; a chronic shortage of serviceable wagons, coaching stock and other supplies did little to alleviate the situation. Work had begun on the backlog of maintenance and improvements required. Between 26th October and 2nd November, 1947 the track layout at the east end of Hamworthy Junction was remodelled. Included in this work was the removal of the direct connection from the Broadstone line to the new (1893) down line, after which down trains from Broadstone had to pass along the outer face of the down platform to gain access to the main line west of the station.

The whole railway system was still under Government control and the political mood of the time did little to encourage investment. It was the declared intention of the Labour Government to nationalise the majority of public utilities and associated industries, including the railways. The idea of nationalisation was not new, during the 1830s the Duke of Wellington publicly expressed his concern over 'monopoly and mismanagement' suggesting state ownership. In 1844 the President of the Board of Trade William Gladstone drew up a Bill that would

Still in wartime black livery 'Schools' class 4-4-0 No. 930 *Radley* waits to depart with an up train at Southampton Central. Around are reminders of the war: the damaged canopy of the island platform, the temporary repairs to the roof of the up side buildings and, behind the locomotive, one of the ubiquitous Nissen huts that appeared everywhere during the war years.

Author's Collection

A pre-June 1948 photograph of Urie 'H15' class 4-6-0 No. 521 in Southern Railway livery heads westwards from Millbrook with a substantial freight via Sway. The up and down line to the Western Docks are seen curving away in the right foreground. No. 521 was constructed in July 1924 and having covered a recorded 1,161,139 miles was amongst the last four members of the class withdrawn in December 1961.

Author's Collection

have imposed strict controls and the compulsory purchase by the state of strategic lines. However, in the free trade spirit of the age a diluted Bill only gave limited powers including for troops and police to be carried in times of unrest. Thereafter Government interference was restricted to regulations concerning safety and the enforcement of certain powers over passenger and freight rates.

Labour had first agreed a policy to nationalise the railways at their 1908 party conference, an idea they nurtured and advocated in their 1945 election manifesto along with other key services and industries.

Thus the Royal Assent was given on 6th August, 1947 to the Transport Bill, establishing the British Transport Commission for the purpose of setting up a publicly-owned system of inland transport, other than by air. The intention was to take-over on 1st January, 1948 the railways and canal undertakings (including the London Passenger Transport Board) specified in a schedule, which included all the main line railways and their joint committees, and the smaller railway undertakings, at that time under the control of the Railway Executive Committee. Privately-owned railway wagons were to be transferred to the Commission, with the exception of certain vehicles of special types designed for special traffics. The Commission would also acquire those road haulage undertakings engaged predominantly in long distance carriage for hire. Provision was made for area schemes to be prepared by he Commission for the co-ordination of passenger road transport. In this instance the fact that the railways already held a substantial share holding in all the major bus companies made matters simple following the remaining shareholders in both the Tilling and British Electric Traction groups capitulating and selling their shares to the Commission. Thus in the minds of many the stage was set for a panacea to Britain's transport system; unfortunately as the following chapters reveal there was to be no Utopia!

Before their decline a number of bus services served Wool station, where 1938 vintage Southern National Bristol L5G No. 277 ETT 943 with a Mumford B31R body waits for passengers. Photographed prior to November 1949 when the vehicle was fitted with a Beadle B35R body, it was withdrawn from service in 1957. The chassis frames were then incorporated into the rebuilding and lengthening of another vehicle. *R.K. Blencowe Collection*

Crowds gather on the up platform of Dorchester South station for the naming of 'West Country' class 4-6-2 No. 34042 *Dorchester* on 23rd September, 1948, by the Mayor of the Borough Mr H.G. Longman.   *Author's Collection*

Former London Brighton & South Coast Railway 'H2' class Atlantic 4-4-2 No. 32424 *Beachy Head* departs from Bournemouth Central with the Bournemouth-Brighton through train on 5th February, 1949. The engine is still in Southern Railway malachite green livery with 'SOUTHERN' still lettered on the tender, but the new British Railways number painted on the cab side.   *Author's Collection*

Chapter Five

Nationalisation

On 1st January, 1948 the nation's railways were taken into state ownership under the control of the British Transport Commission and its Railway Executive. Unfortunately - to the disadvantage of the rail system - there was much infighting between the Commission, the Executive, politicians and other interested parties - and the want of a workable Transport Policy brought about uncertainty.

For several years the new ownership had little impact on the railways - either for the casual observer or the customers - despite the appearance of new stationery and tickets bearing the legend 'British Railways'. Even this modest change was by no means universal, for existing stocks were used until exhausted - and for some of the less issued items it was many years before the old company name vanished completely. However, some experimental liveries for both locomotives and rolling stock were given an airing: on the Southern several sets of coaches appeared in 'plum and spilt milk', three 'Lord Nelson' class engines were decked out in apple green and six of the 'Merchant Navy' class 4-6-2s were given a deep blue livery.

The return to peacetime conditions was slow; at Poole the BOAC flying boat base closed at the end of March 1948, returning to Southampton. Ironically the service, which had survived the difficulties of war, was in rapid decline and within 10 years all British commercial flying boat operations had ceased.

In a country still struggling with rationing, shortages of various kinds and the general aftermath of war, the naming of a railway engine was an occasion to be savoured! In a ceremony held at the buffer stop end of the up platform at Dorchester on Thursday 23rd September, 1948 the Mayor of Dorchester, Mr H.G. Longman, named 'West Country' class 4-6-2 No. 34042 *Dorchester*. With a slight twist to the conventional ship launching ritual he said,

I name this engine 'Dorchester'. May she go forth on her journeys with all our good wishes, bearing the good name of our county town.

Three days later, on 26th September, 1949, Dorchester station was officially renamed 'Dorchester South'. At the same date the former GWR station was given the suffix 'West'.

February 1949 saw the unusual movement of an industrial locomotive along the main line when Peckett 0-4-0ST No. 920 *George Jennings*, belonging to the South Western Pottery of Parkstone, travelled under its own steam complete with a brake van and a British Railways driver on the footplate from Parkstone to Bevois Park yard, Southampton, for repairs at a Northam engineering works.

On 21st June a Royal Train conveying the Princess Elizabeth and the Duke of Edinburgh ran from Waterloo to Weymouth consisting of three-car sets Nos. 812 and 819 with Pullman car *Cecilia* hauled by 'Merchant Navy' class No. 35024 *East Asiatic Company* in the new blue livery.

Earlier in the year there had been several changes to locomotive workings. One of the most interesting was the 7.38 am Weymouth-Waterloo being hauled by a 'Merchant Navy' class locomotive. However, as the class was barred from

Assuming the headcode is set correctly, Drummond '700' class 0-6-0 No. 30350 heads towards Southampton Central with a passenger service off the Fawley branch. Painted during May 1948 in the early British Railways plain black livery with British Railways on the tender in Gill Sans lettering, No. 30350 was constructed in August 1897 and withdrawn from service in March 1962.
Author's Collection

Photographed on 20th August, 1952 'West Country' class 4-6-2 No. 34008 *Padstow* near Lytchett crossing on the single line section between Broadstone and Hamworthy Junction with a Waterloo-Dorchester all Pullman special including the 'Devon Belle' observation car. After the party detrained at Dorchester the stock continued to Weymouth for servicing and turning of the observation car.
B. Knowlman

entering Dorchester shed it precluded the previous arrangement of the engine staying overnight. Instead the engine ran light from Bournemouth shed to Wimborne where it took over the Weymouth paper train which had departed from Salisbury at 3.50 am. The summer service also saw the resumption of the pre-war practice of the through working of Western engines on excursions to Bournemouth. The year was rounded off by the naming of 'West Country' class No. 34091 *Weymouth* by the Mayor of Weymouth, Mr P. Burt, on 29th December.

The pre-war practice of running a relief Weymouth-Waterloo express via the Old Road was revived on Easter Monday 10th April, 1950 with 'Battle of Britain' class 4-6-2 No. 34056 *Croydon*. This followed upgrading of the line allowing the class, subject to a speed of 40 mph throughout and 15 mph over bridges Nos. 66 and 67 west of Ringwood. Previously the 'L12' class 4-4-0s were the largest engines permitted between Lymington Junction and West Moors.

The previous week the first of many subsequent changes of Regional boundaries took place when from 2nd April, 1950 the former GWR line between Dorchester Junction and Weymouth, the Portland branch and the Weymouth Harbour Tramway became the responsibility of the Southern Region. They also assumed control of the former GWR lines between Dorchester West and Castle Cary, and the Yeovil-Durston branch to a point on the Taunton side of Langport West - although for operational reasons the motive power depots at Weymouth and Yeovil Pen Mill remained under the control of the Western Region.

The only alterations to the infrastructure in the opening years of nationalisation were the removal, owing to its poor condition, of the Brunel overall roof of Weymouth station in March 1951, and the rebuilding of Culliford Road bridge, Dorchester. This opened to traffic on 21st May, 1951, the previous bridge having been closed to road traffic since August 1948.

The Festival of Britain was held in London between 3rd May and 30th September, 1951. To celebrate the event the 7.38 am Weymouth-Waterloo and the 4.35 pm return trains were named the 'Royal Wessex'. There were also a number of excursion fares available from various stations to Waterloo, the day return from Weymouth being 29s. 1d., and for those who could not visit the capital the Festival ship *Campania* visited Southampton between 4th and 14th May. However, the railways faced serious competition from coach operators which were also offering competitive day returns to London. Royal Blue, which already operated a substantial number of services between Bournemouth-Southampton and London, commenced several night services to allow more time in the capital. Fuel rationing had also ended on 27th May the previous year and for the first time since the beginning of the war the motorist was not restricted; it was the beginning of a new era in transport history.

A further attraction that year was the Bath & West show which visited Dorchester between 30th May and 2nd June. Again the railway was responsible for the cartage of a large number of the exhibits and livestock, although the growing competition of road transport was beginning to be experienced.

Although few in number compared with the later carnage of the Beeching era, a number of branch lines closed in the early 1950s - including the former joint GWR & LSWR branch from Weymouth to Portland, from which passenger services were withdrawn on 3rd March, 1952. The former GWR branch from

Upwey Junction to Abbotsbury followed on 1st December that year, this closure being complete except for the short section to Upwey (renamed Upwey Goods), which was retained to cater for wagonload traffic. This closure resulted in Upwey Junction being renamed 'Upwey & Broadwey' from 29th November, 1952. These two branches were very different in character, that to Portland being urban and serving a large population but suffering from keen bus competition, whilst that to Abbotsbury was distinctly rural and had never been a viable proposition.

Other minor economies made during this period included the closing of the small engine shed at Hamworthy Junction on 3rd March, 1954 (although the siding was not taken out of use until December 1956) and, the same year, the turntable at Branksome shed was removed, the pit being filled in and a length of track inserted to bridge the gap. As larger engines had gradually come into service over the years it became the custom to turn them on the Branksome triangle.

In October 1954 Walter Channon took over as station master at Dorchester upon the retirement of Stanley Arthur Smith after 50 years' service, having commenced his career at Ringwood as a junior clerk in August 1904 with an annual salary of £30. His retirement was marked by a dinner held in his honour by the local tradesmen and others at the Antelope Hotel.

Despite closures and economies, traffic levels were still high in 1954, the Lymington branch having a service of 14 trains each way on weekdays and nine on Sundays with three through trains in each direction between Lymington Pier and Waterloo on summer Saturdays. The Swanage branch had 16 trains each way daily; three of these conveyed through coaches to and from Waterloo, which became whole trains on summer Saturdays!

Both of these branches were straightforward operations, but services over the Old Road were more complex. On weekdays there were eight push-pull trains between Bournemouth and Brockenhurst and nine return workings. There were also several short workings: the 6.25 am Wimborne-Brockenhurst, a 6.45 am Wimborne-Bournemouth West, the 9.32 am Brockenhurst-Wimborne and the 11.10 pm Bournemouth West-Wimborne. There was also a 6.40 am from Weymouth to Brockenhurst via the Old Road and a 5.17 am Wimborne-Eastleigh service via Poole and Bournemouth Central, returning from Southampton Terminus at 5.05 pm, the stock being stabled overnight at Wimborne for the next morning working.

At that time Bournemouth was the popular place to visit in the evenings, with the last train departing from Bournemouth West at 11.10 pm and terminating at Wimborne 29 minutes later. Unfortunately, Bournemouth West was well out of the town centre from where a Hants & Dorset bus had for many years departed at 10.50 pm calling at Wimborne, West Moors and terminating in Ringwood just after midnight proving popular with picture goers and others.

Services over the Salisbury-West Moors line added a further five trains each way daily on the West Moors-Bournemouth section and there were Somerset & Dorset trains serving Broadstone, Creekmoor Halt and Poole. Summer Saturdays saw a few through trains routed over the Salisbury & Dorset line, and the Old Road was used by Waterloo-Weymouth (or Swanage) holiday relief trains to ease congestion at Bournemouth.

Cross-country traffic on summer Saturdays was also heavy. There were six down and eight up through trains from the Midlands and the North via the Somerset & Dorset most weekends, and four through trains in each direction from the North to Bournemouth via Oxford and Basingstoke; these, like those over the Somerset & Dorset would often have relief trains. With the Somerset & Dorset workings there was also the problems of late running on down trains as these movements had to be slotted into busy section between Holes Bay Junction and Branksome. Their late running could also cause problems at Bournemouth West, the commencing point and terminus of almost all Waterloo services where smart platform working was essential.

Added to this a considerable amount of freight traffic travelled via the Old Road, plus several freights over the Salisbury & Dorset line, these often remarshalling at Wimborne for Poole, Bournemouth and Dorchester line traffic. During this period Brockenhurst was also a focal point for the remarshalling of goods trains during the night. During the evening up goods from both the Old Road and the Direct Line arrived, and were sorted into trains for both the Southampton area and Nine Elms. Likewise down trains were also rearranged to be forwarded by both routes. A further interesting point was that, as well as traffic for Hamworthy Goods, traffic for Wareham and the Swanage branch was detached at Hamworthy Junction to be forwarded by the Swanage branch goods.

As a precursor for the future, early in 1954 two of the GWR diesel cars Nos. 36 and 38 with corridor third No. 1096 sandwiched between them underwent clearance trials between Basingstoke and Bournemouth before working a special from Southall to the resort on 23rd May.

The year also saw a marked decline in both passenger figures and goods tonnage, and there is little doubt that the Associated Society of Locomotive Engineers & Firemen (ASLEF) strike in the summer of 1955 acted as an escalating factor. Because of the strike many holidaymakers had to reach their destinations by coach for the first time and, having once sampled it and realising that they had guaranteed seats, cheap refreshments at the booked stops and generally a much lower fare, vowed to tolerate the somewhat longer journey times and desert the railway. Later, improvements to the road network allied to the growing popularity of the family car brought a further decline in rail traffic and the financial position of the industry was becoming serious. Until the end of petrol rationing in May 1950 road transport facilities had been limited, but thereafter the surplus on British Railways' operating account declined. In 1954 it became so small that it was unable to meet capital charges and the following year it disappeared altogether, with subsequent years bringing increasing losses.

In an attempt to combat the worsening position the British Transport Commission announced a 15 year plan for the modernisation and re-equipment of British Railways in January 1955. The steam locomotive was to be replaced by a mixture of diesel and electric traction. However, this plan was superseded two years later by the *Report on Diesel & Electric Traction and the Passenger services of the Future*, the publication of which made the earlier scheme seem rather half-hearted.

The outbreak of war in 1939 had caused many of the Southern's electrification plans to be postponed, although a report in May 1944 suggests that the matter was still under active consideration. It stated that:

Facilities for changing electric for steam locomotives, and vice versa, will be required at Basingstoke and Southampton Central. There would appear to be no doubt that, by the

Diesel-electric No. 10202 departs Dorchester with the 11.30 Weymouth-Waterloo service. It is a light winter load to be joined by the Bournemouth West section at Bournemouth Central. The steam heating boiler is working well by the amount of steam appearing from under the coaches. In the right background is the goods shed, the engine shed to the centre with the elevated signal box protruding from behind. To the left on the bank are railway cottages, the section at the far end being an engine crew dormitory.

Author's Collection

LMS-type main line diesel-electric No. 10001 pulls away from Bournemouth Central with an up train on 24th April, 1953; the different approach to the outline of the machine compared with the Southern version is noticeable. To the right is the former GPO sorting office, in the distance can be seen Bournemouth engine shed, and in the station yard a Pickfords removal van.

G.O.P. Pearce/C.L. Caddy Collection

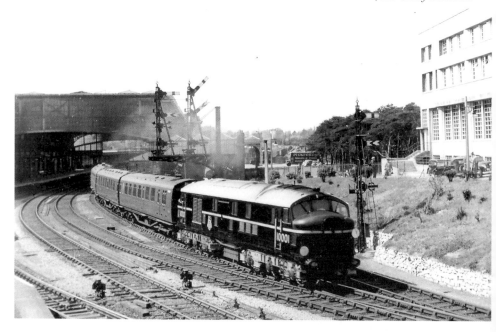

time they were required, adequate arrangements will have already been made at Basingstoke. On the other hand certain re-arrangements and the provision of additional accommodation will be necessary at Southampton Central and a covering figure of £50,000 has been included in the estimates in respect of these requirements.

It would suggest from the wording of the report that electric locomotives would be employed as opposed to multiple units. Also, around the same time, a senior management figure of the Southern Railway gave an after-dinner speech to Bournemouth businessmen suggesting they would proceed as soon as hostilities ended.

In the event it was 10 years before any serious plans were proceeded with, one report, published in 1951 and prepared by a committee appointed by the Railway Executive and London Transport Executive on the electrification of railways, came to the conclusion that the majority of existing systems were too widespread to render them easy to change - and that there were actually 'horses for courses'. Although 'overhead' AC was the preferred system, it was accepted that the former Southern Railway third-rail DC network was doing a good job and would be very difficult to alter. Part of paragraph 124 of the report makes interesting reading:

On the Bournemouth route it is also the practice today for trains to be divided at Bournemouth Central, one portion going forward to Bournemouth West and the other to Weymouth. No undue operating difficulty would be experienced if electrification on the third rail system terminated at Bournemouth. If, however, electrification is contemplated beyond this point - a somewhat remote contingency - it would seem logical to extend the third rail beyond Bournemouth for the 30 miles or so to Dorchester, and over the short section of the former GWR line into Weymouth. [Further on, in their summary of conclusions, it stated:] On operational and technical grounds, it is desirable that further extensions of electric workings in the south and south-east of England should be fully integrated with the existing installation. The Committee accordingly considers that for the time being an area should be earmarked for third rail electrification; this would consist of the Southern Region as far west as a line drawn to include Salisbury, Fordingbridge, Wimborne, Dorchester and Weymouth.

Whilst all these plans were being considered a number of trials were conducted of main line diesel locomotives. In 1951 the first of the Southern Region's three diesels - Nos. 10201-10203 - commenced running between Waterloo and Weymouth, followed in 1953 by the two ex-LMS machines, Nos. 10000 & 10001. The latter were precursors of the present main line diesel, but at the time they were considered revolutionary.

One of the more spectacular accidents in the history of the local railways occurred on the evening of Saturday 22nd January, 1955 at Bournemouth Central station. Shortly before 7.45 pm 'N15' class No. 30783 *Sir Gillemere* arrived 'light' from Bournemouth West and stood on the up through line awaiting its next duty, which involved crossing to the down platform line to work a portion of a train from Waterloo around to Bournemouth West.

When this engine came to a stand, the signalmen set the road for the up local line and cleared the signals for the 6.30 pm Weymouth to Waterloo service which consisted of six coaches hauled by 'H15' class No. 30485. As it approached the station at about 25 mph the driver was confronted with the 'N15' as it started to creep back along the up line! Both drivers were quick to realise the situation and

Southampton Central station viewed from the east end during 1953. The damage of the war years has been made good and would remain until the major alterations of the 1960s.

R.B. Gosling Collection

The results of the Bournemouth Central collision photographed the morning after on 23rd January, 1955. The Eastleigh crane. on the right, and the Bournemouth crane, on the left, commence to lift 'H15' class 4-6-0 No. 30485. 'N15' class 4-6-0 No. 30785 *Sir Mador de la Porte* can be seen to the right.

R.B. Gosling Collection

made the necessary emergency brake applications - but nothing could prevent a collision and the right-hand cylinders of both engines came together with considerable force. Both locomotives were derailed, the engine of the Weymouth train having its left-hand cylinder ripped off as it keeled over to an angle of about 45 degrees. The front bogie of the leading carriage was likewise derailed, but surprisingly only one of the 30 passengers on board was injured, although four members of railway staff required treatment.

It was indeed a lucky escape, for had the angle of impact been just slightly different or the speeds fractionally higher the outcome would have been very serious.

The incident blocked not only the up lines through Bournemouth Central but also access to the engine shed! Services were considerably disrupted, the impact of single line working all the way from Gas Works Junction to Boscombe being compounded by the fact that 15 engines were trapped in the shed and that others already on the main line were deprived of coaling and watering facilities.

Owing to the demands of traffic it was not possible to commence re-railing until 2.45 am on Sunday morning, despite the fact that the Eastleigh crane - which had been on its way to Dorchester for pre-arranged engineering work – had arrived on site at 8.15 pm on Saturday. The Bournemouth crane was of course useless as it was trapped in the shed, but was of limited lifting capacity, so the assistance of the Salisbury crane was summoned - although it had first to attend the work at Dorchester originally intended for the Eastleigh crane. The carriage was back on the rails at 5.50 am and the light engine (the 'N15') at 8.25 am, thus creating enough clearance to allow the Bournemouth crane onto the site, and at about 11.45 am it assisted the Salisbury crane to right the 'H15'. Unfortunately this proved rather too demanding, and after half an hour the chain between the Bournemouth crane and the front buffer of the engine parted. Consequently it was 2 pm before the tender was re-railed - and 3.15 pm by the time the locomotive itself was back on the track.

From 6.30 pm on the Sunday it became possible to confine single line working to the Gas Works Junction to Bournemouth Central section, greatly easing the congestion problem, with up trains returning to the right line via the crossover between the up and down through lines, near the signal box, then reversing into the up platform from the Holdenhurst Road end. Normal working through the station was resumed on Monday morning.

Although No. 30485 suffered nothing but superficial damage, she never ran again and was officially withdrawn in April 1955, the first 'H15' to be scrapped.

At the subsequent inquiry the driver of the light engine stated that he had stopped on the up through line - clear of shunting signal No. 27, and had in fact walked across the footplate to check that he was inside the signal and that it was at 'Danger'. He then returned to his own side of the cab and then seemed to become somewhat confused, as his subsequent testimony was vague and unreliable. Apparently he either saw the down through starting signal (No. 3) already 'off' or watched it come 'off' (he was unclear on this point) and, although he knew by his own admission that his authority to move was the shunting signal (27) he took this signal as applying to him and began to move his engine. His only excuse was that two earlier shunt movements of a like kind had been made very quickly and that he therefore assumed, without thinking, that any visible signal moving to 'clear' was for him! He admitted full responsibility for the mistake, but was unable to account for it.

Colonel McMullen, the investigating Board of Trade Inspecting Officer, in his report of 3rd March, expressed the view that the driver had been hindered somewhat by his fireman, an inexperienced youth aged 16 years! It must be remembered that part of a fireman's duties involved the observation of signals, and the Colonel's view was that the accident would have been averted - despite the driver's lapse - had his fireman been properly alert. During the 1950s he was not shielded from his share of the blame, and was expected to shoulder a man's responsibilities when doing a man's job.

In 1956 the Transport Commission finally decided to standardise on high voltage overhead main line electrification at 25kV 50Hz, and the following year a scheme was drawn up to electrify Waterloo to Weymouth and Worting Junction to Salisbury and associated lines on this system at an estimated cost of £20 million. A start was to have been made in 1962 with five years allowed for completion, but with estimated costs rising by £20 million in just two years this ambitious project was shelved until 1962, when it was reappraised.

In the meantime it was realised that there would be insuperable difficulties in the London area if the two systems were mixed, and the following May an alternative scheme envisaged the existing third rail extended to Basingstoke, whence 25kV would be installed to Bournemouth. The route from Pirbright Junction, through Aldershot, Alton, and over the Mid-Hants Line was going to be similarly equipped to provide a useful diversionary option! Yet another scheme suggested a 1.5kV side-contact third rail protected with wooden boards, as on the Bury-Manchester line.

How these different systems would have worked in conjunction with the existing suburban third rail system was not fully explained: certainly the variety of power supplies would have been a problem - for Channel Tunnel technology was in the future!

Despite its limitations, the existing 750v DC third rail system emerged as the only realistic way forward. In fact, the Southern had already invested heavily in it including the two recent Kent Coast schemes.

At this point we must leave prospective schemes and return to the changes taking place in the operational railway. Against all this talk of modern traction and faster services, closures were once again in the air - and this time the axe was not poised only over humble branches but lines of a semi-main character! The *Bournemouth Echo* for 3rd April, 1956 had this to say:

> British Railways, it was reported yesterday, are considering closing the branch line from Broadstone to Brockenhurst and the line from West Moors to Salisbury - two rural Puffing Billy runs. The news came as a surprise to railway officials affected. They had no details of the proposed closing, and at most stations plans have already been made for meeting the demands of the summer traffic. The proposed closing forms part of a plan British Railways have for shutting down twenty six branch lines to save up to £1 million a year. They follow the suggested closing of the stations and halts at Spettisbury, Charlton Marshall and Stourpaine - all part of the economy drive.

In fact, these three halts, together with Corfe Mullen - all situated on the lower part of the Somerset & Dorset - closed as from the 17th September, 1956, but for the time being no further action was taken towards the closure of either the Salisbury & Dorset line or the Old Road.

During the winter of 1956-1957 a number of cheap day returns were available after 9.30 am from various stations, including from Bournemouth West over the

Old Road to: Wimborne 1s. 11d., Ringwood 2s. 7d., and Brockenhurst 3s. 9d. Ironically, this was during the short period of petrol rationing created by the Suez crisis which caused bus and coach operators to reduce services as did road hauliers. However, this stay of execution was short-lived, reductions in the armed forces also caused a change in traffic patterns. Following the amalgamation of the Dorset Regiment with the Devon Regiment in 1958 Dorchester ceased to be a garrison town. Also it became customary to hire coaches with more flexible timings for weekend leave to London and other destinations for servicemen from Portland, Bovington, Lulworth and other camps. Later there were less servicemen travelling at weekends following the end of National Service, causing a further downturn in traffic for both the railway and coach operators alike.

The location of Bournemouth West station at the foot of a 1 in 90 gradient had always made it susceptible to mishaps; between 1946 and 1956 there had been six buffer stop incidents at the station! The most serious of these took place on the morning of Friday 17th August, 1956 at 10.15 am, when 13 coaches forming the stock for the 11.16 am Bournemouth West-York service ran down the gradient from the carriage sidings to collide with three coaches and a 10-ton covered van in the parcel bay. The impact of the collision forced the van and one of the coaches upwards, wrecking part of the station roof and severely damaging the parcel office. Part of the roof landed in the station forecourt, crushing one parked car and damaging another. The two occupants of the latter escaped without injury, as did passengers and staff on the platforms. Despite this services continued, the York train departing with alternative stock just 30 minutes late. Breakdown gangs and a crane were soon on the scene and by 3 pm most of the shattered roofing had been cleared away. By 10 pm workmen had completed the task of clearance and tidying up, as there was no time to waste with the busy summer Saturday timetable requiring all available space the next day.

A poor quality image of the scene of destruction at Bournemouth West station on 17th August, 1956 after 13 runaway coaches collided with other stock resulting in collapse of part of the station roof and severe damage to the parcel office. Twelve hours later all had been cleared away, the next day was a summer Saturday and the railway had a service to run, questions could be asked later! *Bournemouth Echo*

Contrasts in design, *above*, 'Q' class 0-6-0 No. 30549 arrives at Brockenhurst on 11th June, 1954 with an up goods that has travelled via the Old Road. No. 30549 was the last of the class of 20 solid traditional goods engines entering service in September 1939 and was withdrawn in July 1963. The closure of goods yards and reduced freight working assisted the early demise of the class. *H.F. Wheeler/R.S. Carpenter Collection*

Below, ugly duckling 'Q1' class 0-6-0 No. 33021 runs into Brockenhurst with a train of empty coaching stock on 17th August, 1957. Although of austere appearance their performance was not wanting, the most powerful 0-6-0 produced for a British railway. No. 33021 was completed in June 1942 and withdrawn in August 1963. The mixed LMS/GWR stock berthed in the down sidings would be stabled at Brockenhurst and used only for Saturday cross-country services. *H.F. Wheeler/R.S. Carpenter Collection*

The long-awaited reconstruction of Weymouth station commenced in 1956, two new platforms on the arrival side being opened for traffic in April 1957. At the same time the two former GWR signal boxes dating back to the 19th century were replaced by a new Southern Region structure containing a 116-lever Westinghouse 'A3' frame, this being the last large mechanical box to be installed by that region. Although the box was new a number of the old GWR signals remained, resulting in a mixture of Western lower quadrant and Southern upper quadrant signals that survived for several years. The track layout was largely unaltered, but greater flexibility of working was achieved by signalling all six platforms for both arrivals and departures. Unfortunately, at that point work ceased - and the original Brunel structure of 1857 (which had lost its overall roof during 1951) continued to be of service.

The 7th December, 1957 saw the closure of both Monkton & Came and Upwey Wishing Well Halts, both situated between Dorchester and Weymouth and only served by Western Region local services between Weymouth and Yeovil. Their demise was a loss to the few members of the local communities who used the facilities.

For some years Dorchester engine shed had suffered a slow decline. The wooden two-road extension of 1883 was demolished during 1955 and since March that year there had been no allocation of engines, the depot being run as a sub-shed of Bournemouth with responsibility for 10 turns each weekday. The end came at midnight on 16th June, 1957 when the shed closed, the 15 drivers, 13 firemen, and five shed staff being transferred to Weymouth. By late September the 1847 structure had been reduced to a pile of rubble, although the sidings serving the shed were not officially taken out of use until 26th January, 1958. The new arrangements at Weymouth engine shed were followed in February 1958 with the shed being transferred to the Southern Region, the previous Western Region shed code of '82F' being replaced by '71G', but a number of Western engines remained in the allocation.

Photographed on 21st July, 1957 'West Country' class 4-6-2 No. 34012 *Launceston* is seen passing over Lytchett crossing with the Saturdays-only 1.20 pm Weymouth-Waterloo which travelled via the Old Road avoiding Bournemouth. Note the line up of British manufactured cars waiting on the then A35 main road between Dorchester and Poole. *W. Newman*

Dorchester shed photographed in the early 1950s with 'West Country' class 4-6-2 No. 34044 *Woolacombe* in British Railways green livery, the tender of 'T9' class 4-4-0 No 30119 in a special green livery, 'U' class 2-6-0 No. 31632 in early British Railways plain black livery and 'O2' class 0-4-4T No. 30177 in British Railways lined black.　　　　　　　*G. Beale Collection*

Dorchester shed viewed after the removal of the 1883 wooden extension during 1955 leaving the vintage lifting gantry exposed, clearly showing the extent of the original shed. Standing outside the shed is 'West Country' class 4-6-2 No. 34020 *Seaton* and an unidentified 'West Country' stands alongside the shed with 'Q' class 0-6-0 No. 30543.　　　　　　　*G. Beale Collection*

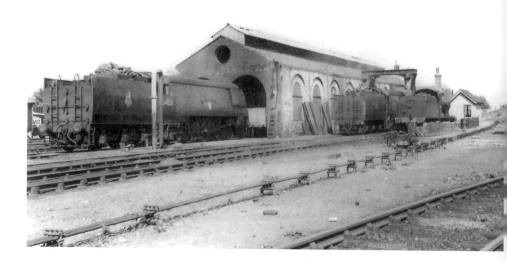

Propelling push-pull set No. 1 along the Old Road between Wimborne and West Moors, 'M7' class 0-4-4T No. 30111 has a Southern utility van in tow when photographed in 1957. Push-pull set No. 1 was converted from LSWR bogie stock in June 1937 forming first/third class 56 ft control trailer No. 6488 and 58 ft, 68 seat third No. 2620. *J.W.T. House/C.L. Caddy Collection*

Former Somerset & Dorset Railway Armstrong 0-6-0 No. 44558 pulls away from Christchurch with a pigeon special during 1957. Pigeon traffic was once heavy on the railways, the birds being released from various station yards, this often explaining the reason corks were threaded on telephone wires in the vicinity. *J.W.T. House/C.L. Caddy Collection*

Drummond 'T9' class 4-4-0 No. 30287 pulls away from Christchurch with the afternoon Brockenhurst-Bournemouth school train in June 1957. The 'T9' class were once known as the Greyhounds of the LSWR; No. 30287 was constructed in January 1900 and travelled a recorded 1,927,593 miles before being withdrawn in August 1961.   *J.W.T. House/C.L. Caddy Collection*

Drummond 'T9' class 4-4-0 No. 30101 makes light work of a three-coach Bulleid set near Wimborne on a Bournemouth West-Salisbury service in June 1959. When this photograph was taken No. 30101 only had weeks left in service, being withdrawn in the August after travelling a recorded 1,819,562 miles since construction in December 1900.

J.W.T. House/C.L. Caddy Collection

A special organized by the Railway Enthusiasts Club of Farnborough visited the Hamworthy branch on 7th June, 1958. Worked by 'M7' class 0-4-4 No. 30107 with push-pull set No. 738, the train started at Poole and after travelling over the branch continued to Weymouth, visiting the Portland branch before running to Maiden Newton to travel over the Bridport branch before returning to Dorchester Junction and then Poole.

On the 22nd February, 1959 the unusual signal box at Dorchester South was closed and replaced by a modern structure fitted with a 36-lever Westinghouse 'A3' frame, situated east of the former engine shed site on the down side. This repositioning brought all the points within the range of mechanical working and allowed the ground frame to be abolished.

The summer of 1959 saw the introduction of diesel multiple units on services between Weymouth and Bristol, thus reducing Weymouth's steam allocation. A further move towards Southern control was the diversion of the Paddington-Weymouth Channel Islands Boat Express to Waterloo after 26th September, 1959. This was the first part of a move in which all Southampton-Channel Islands' services were transferred to Weymouth. This caused great resentment in Southampton - one of Britain's premier ports and one having a railway-connected shipping service to the Channel Islands for a number of years prior to Weymouth's involvement. The new scheme involved the disposal of a number of the Southampton-based vessels and the two former GWR Weymouth-based passenger ships. With two new ships, *Caesarea* and *Sarnia* - and a refitted *St Patrick* - the new service commenced in May 1961.

The additional Channel Islands' traffic not only increased the use of the line west of Southampton but also brought a fresh prosperity to Weymouth. To handle it some extra sidings were laid at Weymouth and an extensive rebuilding programme embarked upon at the hopelessly inadequate Weymouth Quay station. Alterations and additions were made to the Weymouth Harbour Tramway, the details of which are outside the scope of this publication.

Whilst the Weymouth Harbour Tramway was being upgraded, the Poole Harbour Tramway was closed. Unlike Weymouth, there was no regular railway-connected shipping service, and it relied solely on a small amount of sea-borne freight, much of which had either ceased or been transferred across the harbour to Hamworthy. The line officially closed on the 5th May, 1960, the last train - hauled by 'B4' 0-4-0 tank No. 30102 – having run on Saturday 30th April.

Another closure that year - on 12th June - was 'Mansfield Siding', which was situated on the up side east of Dorchester station. It served the works of the Eddison Plant Hire Company, but by that date the company had disposed of the last of its once-extensive fleet of steam rollers and a siding to supply the yard with coal was no longer required. At the time of closure it had not been used for some time. Although officially named and referred to as 'Mansfield Siding' both the spelling was wrong and the Manfield connection long lost. William Hardy Manfield, the squire of Portesham, had taken the land on lease from the Duchy of Cornwall in 1866 for storing coal and other items, a siding being provided for the purpose. Manfield - the leading promoter and Secretary of the Abbotsbury

Drummond 'M7' class 0-4-4 tank complete with a Maunsell push-pull set crosses the newly re-decked bridge over the River Avon west of Ringwood station with a Brockenhurst-Bournemouth West service during the great freeze of 1963. The extended brick abutments in the foreground clearly show where the bridge deck that carried the third line serving the Hurn-Christchurch line was positioned. No. 30107 was constructed at Nine Elms in May 1905, converted to air-operated push-pull operation in July 1930 she served at Bournemouth for many years and was amongst the last members of the class to be withdrawn in 1964.   *J. Read*

'Lord Nelson' class 4-6-0 No. 30862 *Lord Collingwood* approaches Ringwood on a diverted down train during 1961, after the reconstruction of one of the bridges west of Ringwood that year allowed acceptance of the class. The lower quadrant signal with the concrete post in the foreground is not without interest. Today the site is an industrial and housing complex, although Crow Arch bridge in the background still survives.

S.C. Nash/Courtesy of Stephenson Locomotive Society

Railway - gave up the site in 1877, when it was taken over by Frank Eddison who had formed a steam ploughing company seven years earlier.

The autumn of 1961 saw the reconstruction of the viaduct over the River Avon west of Ringwood station. A new deck consisting of pre-cast concrete sections was installed utilising the existing iron piers and, despite the line's status as a 'secondary route' and the rumours of closure, the structure was rebuilt with double track.

Work commenced in September, with single line working over the down line from 9th September until 21st October, after which the reconstructed up side became the single line. Normal double line working over the viaduct was restored in December. During this work a temporary facing crossover, down main to up main, was installed opposite Ringwood signal box, together with an up main to down main connection and a trailing crossover west of the works. As the whole of this layout was deemed to be within 'Station Limits' with both ends of the single line worked from Ringwood signal box, no pilotman working or electric token instruments were necessary.

A legacy of cheap construction and short-sighted planning was the large number of level crossing which existed between Southampton and Dorchester, and these items - costly in staff and maintenance - were constantly under review and some of the minor ones were closed. On 18th August, 1951 Hyford (otherwise known as 'Heath crossing'), between Burton Common and Moreton, was reduced to the status of an accommodation crossing, and the same year Keysworth (No. 26) ceased to be a public right of way, being retained for the sole purpose of giving access to Keysworth House. No. 7 crossing, east of Brockenhurst, was replaced by a footbridge in June 1957 and Lewell (No. 39), between Moreton and Dorchester, was reduced to occupation status - as was Wool West (No. 34) in July 1958 followed by Taylor's crossing (No. 5), west of Lyndhurst, that December. On the Old Road Dolmans crossing (No. 20), between West Moors and Uddens, was reduced to occupation status on 16th June, 1959. During 1961 Syward crossing (No. 41), situated just to the east of Dorchester, was reduced to a foot crossing and the final such economy before the 'Beeching Era' had its effect was at No. 10 crossing - immediately west of Lymington Junction on the Old Road - where attendance was withdrawn on 7th January, 1964 and 'field gates' were substituted for the originals. At all those crossings downgraded to 'accommodation' or 'occupation' status it was possible to withdraw the staff, thus making a considerable saving on the wage bill.

It was not only crossings that were under review. November 1961 saw the modification of a working that dated back to the earliest days of the Southampton & Dorchester: the up and down night mail trains (later known as the Travelling Post Office had always terminated at Dorchester. From 27th November this train was extended through to Weymouth, and the familiar sight of three TPO vans standing in the up bay siding at Dorchester South throughout each day was no more.

Despite these various alterations the passenger service continued much as before. During 1961, along the Old Road cheap day returns were available on all trains to Bournemouth from Ringwood 3s. 4d., Ashley Heath 3s., West Moors

Drummond '700' class 0-6-0 No. 30692 enters Wimborne station with a goods train off the Salisbury & Dorset line. The train would be re-marshalled at Wimborne before sections proceeded to further destinations including Poole, Bournemouth, Hamworthy Junction, Swanage and Dorchester. One of a class of 30 engines, No. 30692 was constructed at Nine Elms works in March 1897 and withdrawn from service in February 1962. *Author's Collection*

A few British made cars wait as 'West Country' class 4-6-2 No. 34105 *Swanage* approaches Wool with a Weymouth-Bournemouth local service during August 1958. Although the signal box still survives, the scene at the crossing, 50 years later, is different as long queues of traffic quickly build up when the barriers are down. No. 34105 was constructed in March 1950 and withdrawn in October 1964. After spending 13 years in Barry scrapyard she has been restored and at the time of writing runs on the Mid-Hants Railway. *J.W.T. House/ C.L.Caddy Collection*

In characteristic pose complete with shunting pole a shunter watches Maunsell 'U' class 2-6-0 No. 31803 in the small goods yard at Parkstone during 1960. The line crossing the other trackwork at an angle was the end of the private siding leading from George Jennings' Parkstone pottery. *Lens of Sutton Association*

Maunsell 'Q' class 0-6-0 No. 30539 stands at Parkstone station with a Brockenhurst-Bournemouth West train that had travelled via the Old Road. To the left can be seen the small goods yard and part of the goods shed. *G.A. Pryer Collection*

Maunsell 'King Arthur' 4-6-0 No. 30788 *Sir Urre of the Mount* arrives at Holton Heath with a Weymouth stopping train after a snowstorm on 14th January, 1960. The blast proof shelters and two footbridges are of interest at this station built to serve the adjacent cordite factory. In the background Holton Heath signal box served the entrance to the factory complex.

R.A. Panting

Maunsell 'King Arthur' 4-6-0 No. 30777 *Sir Lamiel* heading away from Millbrook with the 11.50 am Bournemouth-Birmingham service on 16th July, 1960 forms the perfect Southern picture, a Maunsell engine with a mixture of Maunsell and Bulleid stock. No. 30777 was constructed in June 1925 and withdrawn in October 1961 after travelling a recorded 1,257,638 miles. Fortunately this excellent example of a Southern engine was saved and today forms part of the National Collection.

R.A. Panting

With Redbridge sleeper works in the background Urie 'S15' class 4-6-0 No. 30511 curves away from the old Redbridge viaduct with the 'Workmen's train', the 5.05 pm Southampton Terminus all stations except Beaulieu Road to Wimborne via Bournemouth. No. 30511 was constructed in January 1921 and withdrawn in July 1963 having travelled a recorded 1,287,933 miles.

Courtney Haydon Courtesy RCTS Collection

BR Standard class '5' 4-6-0 No. 73118 *King Leodegrance* climbs Parkstone bank with the 12.40 pm Eastleigh-Bournemouth West service, diverted via the Old Road owing to engineering work at New Milton on 27th March, 1960. The Old Road was a useful diversionary route that came to the rescue on many occasions, unfortunately its closure in 1964 and the lifting of the Lymington Junction-Ringwood section denied its use during electrification works to Bournemouth two years later.

Courtney Haydon Courtesy RCTS Collection

Bournemouth-allocated BR Standard class '5' 4-6-0 No. 75068 approaches Broadstone with the 11.20 am Brockenhurst-Poole freight on 4th June, 1960 with a number of Presflo cement wagons for Poole yard. No. 75068 was constructed in September 1955 at an official cost of £18,452 and was equipped with the BR1B tender for Southern Region use, not being fitted with water pick-up equipment; it had a water capacity of 4,725 gallons and 7 tons of coal. After less than 12 years work No. 75068 was withdrawn in June 1967.   *Courtney Haydon Courtesy RCTS Collection*

A Dorchester-Millbrook freight passes Lyndhurst Road on 27th September, 1960 headed by BR Standard class '5' 4-6-0 No. 75056. Being hauled dead behind is long serving Bournemouth Drummond class '700' 0-6-0 No. 30695 being transferred to Eastleigh from where she was withdrawn in December 1962 after 65 years' service. Forthcoming electrification ensured No. 75056 only completed 10 years' service when withdrawn in August 1966.

Courtney Haydon Courtesy RCTS Collection

Urie 'S15' class 4-6-0 No. 30509 heads a rake of ballast wagons past Redbridge signal box and the entrance to Redbridge works on 22nd December, 1960. Constructed in December 1920, No. 30509 was withdrawn in July 1963.   *P. Tatlow*

2s. 7d., Wimborne 2s. 6d., Broadstone 2s., Creekmoor Halt 1s. 8d. For some strange reason Holmsley only offered a cheap day return to Southampton Central at 4s. 3d. All other stations on the Old Road also offered cheap day facilities to Southampton Central, the Swanage branch, Wool, Dorchester and Weymouth.

The year 1962 was to see the beginning of the rundown of the Somerset & Dorset line. For the past 12 years the Western Region had had commercial control of the line north of Cole, with the peculiar arrangement of the motive power depots being under the control of the Southern Region. The Western's dislike of the Somerset & Dorset - which dated back to the territorial feuds of the 19th century - did not bode well for the future of the line. In February 1958 commercial control by the Western Region was extended south to a point between Templecombe (the main line station excepted) and Henstridge, and the motive power depots except Branksome transferred to the Western Region.

Documents that have now entered the public domain reveal that the fate of the line was already sealed. In May 1957 a memorandum from the office of the Operating Officer at Paddington set out proposals for diverting through passenger trains that ran over the Somerset & Dorset to Bournemouth West. Several alternative routes had been examined: from Salisbury, either via Fordingbridge or via Romsey and Eastleigh; or from Oxford via the Didcot, Newbury & Southampton line to Winchester or via Reading and Basingstoke. It is interesting to note that the MSWJ was not included in these proposals. However, as this was another cross-country route under the control of the Western Region clearly its long term future was already decided.

At that point the matter rested until June 1959 when a further note from Paddington, this time to the Operating Officer's Office of the London Midland Region stated:

Maunsell 'N' class 2-6-0 No. 31407 looks unkempt and slightly out of place shunting the private siding at the Eldridge Pope brewery, Dorchester. Interestingly, No. 31407 was until 1950 an Exmouth Junction-based engine and after that Ashford until the Kent electrification scheme resulted in transfer to Weymouth in 1961, from where she was withdrawn in July 1963.

Author's Collection

Maunsell 'N' class 2-6-0 No. 31816 stands at Parkstone with a down train in July 1962 whilst Maunsell 'U' class 2-6-0 No. 31617 climbs the 1 in 60 bank with an up train consisting of 10 former LMS coaches with rear end assistance. Today the factory on the right has been replaced by a block of flats, and the goods yard on the left has also been consigned to the history books. *Colour-Rail*

Ivatt LMS class '2MT' 2-6-2T No. 41305 pulls away from Southampton Central with a mixed train of empty oil tanks for the Fawley branch in June 1962; note the two obligatory barrier wagons between the locomotive and the tanks. The construction of additional oil pipe lines to distribution depots was later to drastically reduce oil tank traffic off the branch.

G.A. Pryer Collection

Eastleigh-allocated BR Standard class '4' 2-6-0 No. 76013 stands at Wimborne with an up freight during 1962. To the left are the goods shed and the various sheds used for the storage of cattle feed and other agricultural products with a Bedford delivery lorry loading from the building in the foreground. No. 76013 was constructed at Horwich in April 1953 and withdrawn in September 1966 and broken up in the yard of J. Buttigieg of Newport, Mon. in March the following year.

C.L. Caddy Collection

... as you are aware the diversion of all through freight traffic from the S&D line has already been agreed in principle and a first examination of the economies involved in closing the whole or the major part of the Western Region section of the line between Bath (Green Park) and Templecombe Junction shows that a financial saving of some magnitude would accrue.

From the above it is clear that the Western Region's policy was to divert all through traffic away from Somerset & Dorset line, a move that would ensure its later closure.

Saturday through train traffic over the Somerset & Dorset from the Midlands and North was still heavy. On 8th August, 1959 eleven through trains arrived at Bournemouth West, four were hauled by BR standard class '5' '4-6-0s, four by 'West Country' class 4-6-2s and three by S&D class '7F' 2-8-0s. Between 8.00 am and 12.20 pm 12 up through trains including two reliefs departed hauled by five BR class '5' 4-6-0s, three 'West Country' 4-6-2s, three S&D class '7F' 2-8-0s and one LMS class '4F' 0-6-0. Forgetting the logistics of working these trains over the Somerset & Dorset they also had to be fitted in with the other traffic between Branksome and Holes Bay Junction, and other traffic on the Old Road at Broadstone after which they often 'went off the timetable onto the calendar'.

A number of through trains used the Old Road on summer Saturdays to avoid Bournemouth, the 7.30 am Waterloo-Weymouth, the 9.15 am and 10.54 am Waterloo-Swanage services, and in the up direction the 11.34 am and 1.23 pm Swanage-Waterloo services and the 1.20 pm Weymouth-Waterloo. Several Saturday-only trains each way between South Wales and both Bournemouth and New Milton travelled from Salisbury over the Salisbury & Dorset line to West Moors before proceeding via Broadstone and Poole to reach their destinations. It is also of note that on 8th August, 1959 the three down Saturday-only trains between Waterloo and Lymington Pier were worked as far as Brockenhurst by 'Schools' class locomotives and two of the five return workings were in charge of BR class '4' 2-6-0s. The reported highlight of the day was 'T9' class 4-4-0 No. 30120 working the six-coach 12.50 pm Eastleigh-Wimborne train, departing seven minutes late from Southampton. Brockenhurst to Christchurch was covered in under 24 minutes and Bournemouth Central reached in a further 10 minutes, to depart on time towards Poole.

The early 1960s were to be the swansong for both the Somerset & Dorset and the Old Road, during 1962 summer Saturday extras were still using the latter to avoid Bournemouth. The 7.57 am boat train from Waterloo to Weymouth Quay travelled via Ringwood as did the 9.15 am and 10.54 am Waterloo-Swanage services, although in the up direction only the 6.10 am boat train from Weymouth Quay to Waterloo and the 11.34 Swanage-Waterloo service used the route.

Inter-Regional differences had stalled the Western desire to eliminate through services over the Somerset & Dorset. In the event the Fordingbridge line or the Didcot, Newbury & Southampton routes were not used, they too were to be victims of the Beeching cuts. All services were to be diverted via Basingstoke, Oxford and Banbury a route that allowed the Sheffield-Bournemouth train to take only 5½ hours against the previous 7½ via the Somerset & Dorset.

The summer of 1962 was the last in which through trains would run over the Somerset & Dorset. On Saturday 11th August, 1962 six down through trains reached Bournemouth West off the Somerset & Dorset, the motive power being two S&D class '7F' 2-8-0s, one BR class '9F' 2-10-0, two 'West Country' 4-6-2s and one BR class '5' 4-6-0. And the 10 up through trains that departed between 8.40 am and 12.20 pm were hauled by four BR class '9F' 2-10-0s, one S&D class '7F' 2-8-0, three 'West Country' class 4-6-2s, one BR class '4' 2-6-0 and one BR class '5' 4-6-0.

The withdrawal of through services included the much celebrated 'Pines Express'. Thus on Saturday 8th September '9F' class 2-10-0 No. 92220 *Evening Star* (the last steam engine built by British Railways) departed from Bournemouth West at 9.45 am with the last up 'Pines' driven by Peter Smith and fired by Aubrey Punter. The load consisted of 12 coaches weighing 426 tons - the heaviest authenticated load ever taken single-handed over the Mendips. The kudos of this historic event should have belonged to senior Branksome driver Donald Beale, but he allowed the honour to go to his regular fireman. To many it was inconceivable that a top driver should pass up the opportunity of working such a prestigious train, but that was the measure of Donald Beale. Peter Smith was a passed fireman capable of performing the job at the young age of 25 and - with an even younger fireman - the last 'Pines' passed into history. *Evening Star* later worked the southbound train with Branksome driver Peter Guy and fireman Ron Hyde. At 6.08 pm the last down 'Pines' stood at the buffer stops at Bournemouth West, thus bringing to a close a chapter in the history of the Somerset & Dorset and the beginning of the end for Bournemouth West station. With its demise the railways of south Dorset were never quite the same!

The last up 'Pines Express' to travel over the Somerset & Dorset departs from Bournemouth West on 8th September, 1962. Hauled by '9F' class 2-10-0 No. 92220 *Evening Star* driven by Peter Smith and fired by Aubrey Punter, it saw the closure of an important chapter in Somerset & Dorset Railway history.   *Dr J. Boudreau Collection*

A general view of Ringwood station looking east in later years. At the time the station was still situated towards the edge of the town giving it a rather rural appearance. It was not to be many years before the line closed and development swallowed up the site where a once important station had stood.   *Author's Collection*

Ringwood station viewed from underneath the down side canopy with an 'Ironclad' push-pull set No. 383 departing on a Bournemouth-bound train.   *Author's Collection*

Chapter Six

Beeching and the End of Steam

There is little doubt that British Railways (BR) were playing down the role of the Old Road by subtle means. Leaflets advertising cheap fares to Southampton Central for the 1962-1963 season of football at the Dell listed many stations from the surrounding area including the Old Road. However, the summer of 1963 saw leaflets for combined rail/road trips to Lyndhurst and the New Forest: passengers alighted at Brockenhurst from where they took a Hants & Dorset bus to Southampton, a break of journey being allowed at Lyndhurst, the return journey being undertaken by any train from Southampton. Although all stations from Weymouth to Hinton Admiral including the Swanage branch offered this facility, stations along the Old Road were conspicuous by their omission, whether this was purely for commercial reasons or other forces were at work we will probably never know. Still available were the ever popular Holiday Runabout Tickets, area No. 11 covering the main line from Pokesdown to Weymouth, the Swanage branch, the Old Road between Poole and West Moors, and the line to Salisbury. Available between the 28th April and 26th October, allowing seven days' unlimited travel, it was a bargain at 22s. 6d.

At the same time important changes were taking place that were to change the future of railways. The passing of the 1962 Transport Act allowed for the abolition of the British Transport Commission and a drastic reorganization of the industry. From 1st January, 1963 the British Railways Board became directly responsible to the Minister of Transport. A further change of Regional boundaries on the same date saw the Southern main line and all branches west of Salisbury, and the Somerset & Dorset as far south as Blandford, transferred to the Western Region as was the former Wilts, Somerset & Weymouth line between Dorchester West and Castle Cary. Indeed, a cynic might have said the stage was set for the publication of the Beeching report in March 1963, which was to change the face of the entire railway network. Locally the Old Road between Lymington Junction and Hamworthy Junction, the entire Somerset & Dorset line and the Salisbury-West Moors lines were to close, although the latter was under consideration before the report. The closure notice was issued at the end of June with closure due to take place on 9th September, with the Somerset & Dorset and the Old Road following on the 30th September.

However, the due process of the inquiry held by the Transport Users' Consultative Committee (TUCC) did not take place at Bournemouth until 17th September when the fate of the Salisbury line and the Old Road were considered. It was stated that both lines were losing £150,000 a year on passenger services alone.

Putting the case for British Railways, the inquiry was informed the losses incurred by the railways were more than the country could afford and they had to review the little-used lines. It was difficult to set a case for retaining the Ringwood and Fordingbridge lines at the losses they incurred. The movement expenses and terminal costs for passenger services on the Fordingbridge line were nearly 10 times the earnings and there was a shortfall of £45,000 a year between costs and earnings.

In the case of the Ringwood line costs were seven times the earnings and the shortfall was £103,000 a year. They could not bridge this gap by increasing fares, by increasing the number of passengers, by cutting fares or modernisation. So the disagreeable conclusion was reached that they must close the line for passengers, they also had in mind quite extensive rationalisation of freight services.

In general BR thought that bus services were a reasonable alternative. Unfortunately for the railway this was true, services in the area operated by Hants & Dorset Motor Services had been built up over the years following the war and were an attraction to the occupants of the many new houses in the area which were situated a distance from the railway on the more flexible routes offered by the buses. Wimborne, West Moors and Ferndown had all grown significantly. Ringwood was also fast developing, the bus company having a depot there from which it served Salisbury and Bournemouth and other surrounding places and it was quite prepared to offer additional services if required. Indeed the growth along the route of the Poole-Wimborne-Brockenhurst line was to be phenomenal; between 1961 and 1981 a reported 305 per cent population increase had taken place and by the 1990s it had become one of the fastest growing urban areas in Europe.

However, this was to be in the future, thus, despite the objections of various Councils, and objections from other organizations and people along the routes including 26 written objections, one with 900 signatures from Wimborne, three objections one with 180 signatures against the closure of Creekmoor Halt, the Minister of Transport gave consent to both closures on 3rd March, 1964. The closure of both lines would be effective from Monday 4th May, 1964.

This decision resulted in 1963 being the last time summer Saturday through trains would use either route. Over the Salisbury & Dorset line the up and down Bournemouth-Cardiff and New Milton-Swansea services ran. Over the Old Road in the down direction there was the 7.57 am Waterloo-Weymouth Quay boat train and both the 9.15 am and 10.54 am Waterloo-Swanage services, whilst up services consisted of the 11.34 am Swanage-Waterloo which joined onto the 11.00 am Weymouth-Waterloo service at Wareham, and the 2.45 am Weymouth Quay-Waterloo boat train. A further sign of the changing times was the introduction occasionally of Birmingham Railway Carriage & Wagon Co. Crompton type '3' Bo-Bo diesel-electric locomotives of the 'D65XX' class (later known as class '33') on the Waterloo-Swanage services. Also their extensive use on the Waterloo-Lymington Pier boat trains removed the necessity to change locomotives at Brockenhurst. A number of Waterloo-Bournemouth workings were also employing diesel power.

Services over both the Salisbury & Dorset line and the Old Road during the final eight months consisted of six trains between Bournemouth West and Salisbury and five return workings, plus the 1.10 am Waterloo paper train which divided at Salisbury, arriving at Wimborne at 4.17 am and terminating at Weymouth at 5.35 am.

On the Old Road there were seven trains each way between Bournemouth, Poole and Brockenhurst, with one short working from Brockenhurst to

Wimborne and two from Bournemouth to Wimborne the last up train terminating there at 9.24 pm. In addition there was the 6.35 am from Weymouth to Eastleigh via the Old Road, and the 5.17 am Wimborne to Eastleigh via Bournemouth, with a return working at 5.05 pm from Southampton Terminus. Additionally there was a 5.15 pm Southampton Terminus to Bournemouth West via the Old Road.

The Old Road was also dogged with motive power problems. The faithful 'M7' class 0-4-4 tanks that, with push-pull sets, had provided the main service for many years were becoming run down, although Bournemouth shed usually managed to supply enough for both the Swanage and Lymington branches. Their use on the Old Road was reduced, and by November 1963 Ivatt class '2' 2-6-2 tanks were covering some duties, although one of their number, No. 41261 fell from grace on the 25th November and required assistance. Within a short time Standard class '3' 2-6-2 tanks were allocated to Bournemouth to operate the service; again on 17th January, 1964 No. 82027 had difficulties raising steam. The introduction of the 2-6-2 tanks resulted in the demise of push-pull working except when an 'M7' was available as the 2-6-2 tanks were not auto-fitted. Also at times other engines including Standard 2-6-0s and light Pacifics were to be seen hauling push-pull sets.

For many years pupils attending Brockenhurst Grammar School from the Ringwood and Holmsley area had travelled on the school train. The last homeward journey on Friday 1st May, 1964 was hauled by Standard class '3' 2-6-2 tank No. 82028 complete with a special headboard. Departing from Brockenhurst at 4.07 pm with a six-coach train it was given a send off by about 500 other pupils, many in period dress. At Ringwood senior pupils made presentations to the driver, fireman and guard; for the driver Ernest Rabbetts it was his last day of railway service before retirement. The train then departed for Bournemouth West; from the following Monday four 39-seat buses would provide school transport!

On the final day Saturday 2nd May, 1964 many turned out to see the trains at stations along the line. At Wimborne the platform ticket machine refused to function, the station master selling tickets by hand to the many who required a souvenir of the occasion. 'M7' class 0-4-4 tanks Nos. 30053 and 30480 put in appearances during the morning as did Standard class '4' 2-6-0 No. 76027. The honour of hauling the final trains went to Standard class '3' 2-6-2 tank No. 82028 with push-pull sets Nos. 608 and 814 and a Southern utility van operating the 4.07 pm Brockenhurst-Bournemouth West, the 7.08 pm Bournemouth West-Brockenhurst and the final train, the 8.56 pm Brockenhurst-Bournemouth West, which carried the name board 'Last Day of Passenger Working'.

On the Salisbury & Dorset line Standard class '4' 2-6-0 No. 76066 worked the 4.50 pm Bournemouth West to Salisbury, with the last up train the 7.50 pm departing from Bournemouth West behind 'West Country' 4-6-2 No. 34091 *Weymouth* hauling eight coaches. The last down train departed Salisbury at 8.30 pm consisting of eight coaches behind Standard class '4' 2-6-0 No. 76066 with a wreath and locomotive headboard provided by the Bournemouth Railway Club.

In one fell swoop both the Salisbury & Dorset and the Old Road had lost their passenger services, the former closed completely, the latter reduced to a goods

Maunsell 'U' class 2-6-0 No. 31798 runs off the Salisbury & Dorset line into West Moors station with the 9.23 am Salisbury-Bournemouth West service on 4th April, 1964. Clearly shown are the up Salisbury line starting signal to the left, the Old Road up starting signal to the right and the ringed signal in the centre for access to the Army petroleum sidings.   *C.L. Caddy*

Shortly before the closure of the Old Road British Railways class '3' 2-6-2 tank No. 82029 runs into Ringwood with a Bournemouth West-Brockenhurst service. Constructed in December 1954 and allocated to the North Eastern Region until transferred to Guildford in 1963 and Bournemouth in January 1964 to replace the ailing 'M7' tanks, she was withdrawn seven months later and broken up at Birds Commercial Motors, Risca in January 1968.   *G.A. Pryer Collection*

A fine view taken from Crow Arch bridge looking west of the layout at Ringwood taken in the summer of 1963, a good number of wagons including oil tanks fill the scene as British Railways class '4' 2-6-4 tank No. 80083 with Maunsell push-pull set No. 615 departs with a Brockenhurst train. To the extreme right on the site of the old ballast hole is the crane of Thos J. Ward's scrapyard, in front of which the remnants of steam locomotives sent in pieces from Eastleigh works can be seen. No. 80083 built in May 1954 was a London Midland Region engine until transferred to Eastleigh in June 1962, withdrawn in August 1966 and scrapped in the following January. *J. Read*

With steam issuing from many places, LMS Ivatt class '2MT' 2-6-2 tank No. 41261 hauling Maunsell push-pull set No. 612 and a utility van departs from Holmsley with a Bournemouth West-Brockenhurst train shortly before the closure of the Old Road. *J. Read*

The shortage of serviceable tank locomotives at times resulted in the use of Bulleid 'West Country' class 4-6-2 engines for the Old Road service. During late 1963-early 1964 No. 34048 *Crediton* heads away from Ringwood with an afternoon train from Bournemouth West to Brockenhurst. No. 34048 was constructed in November 1946 and ran a recorded 539,988 miles before being rebuilt in March 1959, to obtain a final mileage of 847,615 when withdrawn in March 1966.   *J. Read*

Salisbury-allocated British Railways class '4' 2-6-0 No. 76005 approaches West Moors with a strengthened 10.04 am Bournemouth West-Salisbury train on 2nd May, 1964 the last day of passenger service over both the Old Road and the Salisbury & Dorset line. Standing under the ticket office sign is John Smith on his last day as station master before transfer to Kent.
Courtney Haydon/Courtesy RCTS Collection

The last day of service along the Old Road saw two of the faithful Drummond 'M7' 0-4-4 tanks brought back into service for the morning trains. No. 30053 pulls away from Ringwood with a train for Bournemouth West.   *J. Read*

The afternoon of the last day of service over the Old Road saw British Railways class '3MT' 2-6-2 tank No. 80028 operating the service photographed departing Ringwood with a strengthened afternoon train from Brockenhurst to Bournemouth West, a board fixed to the smokebox declares 'Last Day of Passenger Working'. No. 80028, built in December 1954, was allocated to the North Eastern Region until moving south in September 1963 and to Bournemouth in January 1964. Following a move to Nine Elms, the locomotive was withdrawn in April 1966.   *J. Read*

The single line between Hamworthy Junction and Broadstone was taken out of use on 5th June, 1966, the remaining spur at the Hamworthy Junction end being reduced to a siding, a fate that had befallen the former down line pre-war: shown on the right with stored wagons in 1968.

Author

The last of the cast-iron screw pile viaducts on the main line was the 30-span structure over the River Test at Redbridge. Opened in June 1883 it remained in use until May 1964. Photographed on 6th June, 1964 the disused 1883 viaduct is to the left with the new viaduct on the right.

G.A. Pryer Collection

branch worked from the Poole end. Station master at Wimborne since 1959, Edward Henbest moved to Poole as assistant station master until he retired during 1970. John Smith, station master at West Moors, was a third generation station master, both his father and grandfather had been station masters at Dorchester and he had been station master at Upwey & Broadwey between 1958 and 1960 before moving to West Moors. The closure saw him transferred as station master to Aylesford, in Kent, whilst Anthony Brooks, the Ringwood station master, transferred to the Central Section.

Thus a large nail had been put in the Old Road's coffin. Eighteen years later what everybody had suspected was quoted by Harold Ward, the Bournemouth area manager in an interview with the *Dorset Evening Echo* on 28th July, 1982:

> Cash was tight and the gamble of putting the third rail right through to Weymouth was just too great. We had virtually to close the Wimborne and Ringwood line to pay for the electrification to Southampton and Bournemouth.

Towards the end of April 1965 the line between Hamworthy Junction and Broadstone was severed at each end and stop blocks erected, the same procedure-taking place at the Lymington Junction end, with the Salisbury and Dorset line severed the following month at West Moors. The Old Road as far as Ringwood remained open for goods traffic being served via Holes Bay Junction, the remaining section was soon lifted commencing at the Lymington Junction end. Lifting had proceeded as far as Holmsley when in June 1965 eight wagons being loaded with sleepers made an uncontrolled journey to Ringwood. The first four started to move, followed by the next three and then the remaining wagon. Gathering speed they ran through four level crossings smashing the gates at Crowe; upon reaching New Street crossing at Ringwood station they collided with a diesel locomotive and two parcel vans, the latter being lifted off their bogies. Fortunately nobody was injured in this five-mile trail of destruction.

A little known side effect of the Beeching plan was the withdrawal of the circus train. Following the war Bertram Mills had again used the railways as a means of transporting its circus, visiting the south coast at various times: Southampton in 1948, Poole and Dorchester in 1957, Weymouth and Poole during both 1960 and 1963; the latter was to be the final visit to the Hampshire-Dorset area of the circus train. That year the circus made a financial loss of £37,555. The Beeching cut backs would also reduce the number of stations and routes available, also the contract with British Railways was shortly due for renewal and an increase of 150 per cent was proposed. As the circus vehicles were designed to clear the loading gauge and were equipped with small wheels and hauled by tractors the short distance from the station to the showground, all would have to be replaced at even greater cost. For the 1964 season one train was cut out, but that season saw the end of the touring circus and the circus train.

Following the closure of both the Old Road and the West Moors-Salisbury lines, Bournemouth West and Boscombe stations were then considered, although not in the Beeching plans - their closure was linked with the forthcoming electrification scheme. Boscombe's closure, it being situated only

The first up train crosses the new Redbridge viaduct hauled by 'West Country' class 4-6-2 No. 34031 *Torrington* on Sunday 31st May, 1964.   *Southern Evening Echo*

The through working of Western Region engines was not uncommon, here 'Modified Hall' class 4-6-0 No. 7912 *Little Linford Hall* eases the 8.30 am Newcastle-Bournemouth cross-country service off Redbridge viaduct on 25th August, 1964. Above the first coach demolition of the old Redbridge viaduct closed earlier in the year can be seen, and to the right, the expanse of the Redbridge sleeper and track works which closed in March 1989.   *Colour-Rail*

Bournemouth West, once a vital part of the Bournemouth railway scene, firstly saw the demise of through traffic over the former Somerset & Dorset Railway, then closure as part of the Bournemouth electrification plans. Photographed in July 1961 four years before removal from the railway map and the later construction of Wessex Way. *C.L. Caddy*

Boscombe changed very little over the years, instantly recognisable as the station that had opened in June 1897 when photographed in August 1963. Southern Railway style concrete fencing and electric lamp posts appear to be the obvious alterations. Two years later, on 4th October, 1965, Boscombe station closed. *C.L. Caddy*

43 chains west of Pokesdown with its advantage of through roads, was an operational expediency, whilst Bournemouth West's approach was on land required for the servicing sheds for the electric stock, there being very little other land suitable in the area.

The first public announcement of the closure appeared in the *Bournemouth Evening Echo* on 15th July, 1964, although the closure process was not hurried. Bournemouth West was a busy station and well suited to residents from the west of the town, Sandbanks, Canford Cliffs, and Branksome Park many who were not on a direct bus route to Bournemouth Central. There were also the older residents who preferred to join the principal trains at the West station where they were guaranteed a seat and did not have to hurry aboard as they would joining the train at Central. This also applied to many patrons of the 'Bournemouth Belle' who lived at that end of the town, and there were the many holiday makers who stayed in nearby hotels.

All these points were discussed when objections to the closures were discussed at the TUCC hearing held at Bournemouth Town Hall on 27th April, 1965. The alternative use of Branksome station, which the railway admitted was a disgrace, was criticised, but now that BR was satisfied with its economics they would do something to make it a little more attractive.

The No. 25 trolleybus route also came in for criticism. Although its route from Boscombe to County Gates passed Boscombe, Bournemouth Central and Bournemouth West stations its recent reduction to a 12 minute headway at both ends of its route past Boscombe and the West stations was considered by many as unsatisfactory. Although closure of Boscombe station was discussed at the same inquiry, its plight was lost under the weight of opposition to the fate of Bournemouth West.

During 1964 British Railways had been seeking to develop the site of the former station master's house at Dorchester South, which was unoccupied, and adjacent land by the building of a petrol station, workshop and showroom, office block and six shops. Following an inquiry, permission was refused in the December, the Council stating 'it would be an undesirable extension away from the town centre'.

In the same period the amount of goods traffic handled also declined, one example being coal, there being less demand from both industry and the domestic customer as other fuels became popular. Household coal once a staple traffic for the railways was in far less demand, the cost in 1964 being £13 6s. a ton having risen from £1 5s. a ton in the past 53 years.

The number of stations handling goods traffic was reduced, this varied from complete closure to only handling traffic collected by the customer, this applying mainly to coal and other bulk items. Stations including Beaulieu Road and Holton Heath were reduced to unstaffed halts from 1st June, 1964, freight facilities were withdrawn from Lyndhurst Road on 7th July, Moreton became an unstaffed halt from 1st March, 1965. And the withdrawal of goods facilities from Lymington Town on 9th August changed branch-working patterns.

These closures compared with passenger services attracted little publicity, after all the origin of the lorry delivering to the door was of little interest or concern to the public providing the service was still provided. The Achilles heel was the freight concentration scheme where a few selected larger goods depots would deliver to the surrounding area, in reality an extension of the earlier zonal delivery service!

Two depots were to serve the majority of Dorset, Yeovil (also serving south Somerset) covered north Dorset down to Shillingstone commenced on 1st March, 1965, whilst on 5th April Weymouth covered an area including Portland, Bridport, Maiden Newton, Dorchester, Moreton and Wool. In the east of the county Hamworthy Junction, Parkstone, Broadstone and West Moors lost all their freight facilities from 20th September, 1965, and smalls traffic ceased from Wimborne on 28th February, 1966 and Poole on 18th July, traffic being transferred to the Bournemouth concentration depot. On 13th February, 1967 most of Blandford's freight was transferred to Bournemouth, as was Ringwood's freight from 7th August.

After the closure of the Old Road, the Swanage and Lymington branches became the last bastions of branch line steam. Swanage was the first to go over to diesel traction, following the demise of the 'M7' tanks the previous year, the branch in the interim was worked by Ivatt class '2' 2-6-2 tanks and Standard class '4' 2-6-4 tanks. However, on 4th September, 1965 the 8.14 pm from Swanage hauled by Standard class '4' 2-6-0 No. 76010, was the last regular steam passenger working. The following day Hampshire diesel units took over, steam only appearing on freight workings.

The 1960s saw an increasing number of steam-hauled rail tours over the line between Southampton and Weymouth. Of the more interesting of these, 'Battle of Britain' class 4-6-2 No. 34050 *Royal Observer Corps* hauled an Ian Allan special from Paddington to Weymouth on 22nd September, 1962. A Southern Pacific working the entire former GWR route to Weymouth was unusual, to be followed by S&D '7F' 2-8-0 No. 53808 performing the return journey from Weymouth to Bath Green Park via Hamworthy Junction to Broadstone, and over the Somerset & Dorset. There was then a pause until 25th August, 1963 when the Southern Counties Touring Society ran a special from Waterloo to Hamworthy Junction behind LNER 'A3' class 4-6-2 No. 60112 *St Simon*, 'M7' class 0-4-4 tank No. 30052 working the stock over the Hamworthy Goods branch after which the train proceeded to Weymouth. A further demonstration of LNER motive power appeared on 12th September, 1965 when 'A3' class 4-6-2 No. 4472 *Flying Scotsman* visited Weymouth with a special organized by the Gainsborough Model Railway Society.

Few steam-hauled rail tours travelled over the Old Road east of Broadstone. On 18th September, 1960 the 'South Western Limited' was organized by the Locomotive Club of Great Britain (LCGB). Running from Waterloo various locomotives were involved, 'H16' class 4-6-2 tank No. 30516 hauling the train from Eastleigh to Totton and over the Fawley branch, after which 'N15' class 4-6-0 No. 30782 *Sir Brian* worked the train forward over the Old Road to Broadstone. Here S&D class '7F' 2-8-0 No. 53804 came on the rear and took the train over the Somerset & Dorset to regain the main line at Templecombe for its return journey.

The lifting of the Lymington Junction-Ringwood section of the Old Road resulted in the final two steam-hauled tours being worked from the Broadstone

The only ever known visit of a Somerset & Dorset class '7F' 2-8-0 to the lower section of the Southampton & Dorchester line took place on 22nd September, 1962. Photographed heading towards Wool station No. 53808 is working the Weymouth-Bath Green Park via Hamworthy Junction section of a railtour organized by Ian Allan. No. 53808 was constructed at Derby in July 1925 and withdrawn in March 1964, after rusting away in Barry scrapyard it was purchased by the Somerset & Dorset Circle. Today fully restored it is operated by the Somerset & Dorset Railway Trust on the West Somerset Railway.   *C. L. Caddy*

Drummond 'M7' class 0-4-4 tank No. 30052 stands at Hamworthy Goods on 25th August, 1963 waiting to return the Southern Counties Touring Society railtour to Hamworthy Junction where LNER 'A3' class 4-6-2 No. 60112 *St Simon* continued with the tour to Weymouth.   *R.A. Panting*

The LCGB 'South Western Limited' railtour was worked between Totton and Broadstone on 18th September, 1960 by Maunsell 'King Arthur' class 4-6-0 No. 30782 *Sir Brian*. Photographed at Wimborne the use of the class over the Old Road with its bridge restrictions was rare. No. 30782 was constructed in July 1925 and withdrawn from service in September 1962 having travelled a recorded 1,197,719 miles. During her later years, was a Bournemouth-allocated locomotive.   *R.K. Blencoe Collection*

The 'Hampshire Venturer' railtour on 18th April, 1964 headed by Maunsell 'Q' class 0-6-0 No. 30548 climbs towards Broadstone on the single line section from Hamworthy Junction on the return working via the Old Road to Southampton Central. The carriages in the background are stored on the remaining stub of the original Southampton & Dorchester up line, the Poole and Bournemouth line running to the left of the photograph. No. 30548 built in August 1939 was the first of the three surviving members of the class in 1965 to be withdrawn that March.   *Author's Collection*

Almost certainly the last visit of a Southern Railway locomotive and stock to the Old Road. Bulleid light pacific 'West Country' class 4-6-2 No. 34006 *Bude,* complete with a rake of four Bulleid coaches, stands at Ringwood station before returning to Broadstone with the British Young Travellers Society 'Hampshire Explorer' special on 21st May, 1966.   *R.A. Panting*

The LCGB 'Hants & Dorset Railtour' with British Railways Standard class '3' 2-6-0 No. 77014 leading and Standard class '4' 2-6-0 No. 76026 behind pass the army petroleum depot just east of West Moors station on their way to Ringwood on 16th October, 1966.   *D.E. Canning*

end. On 21st May, 1966 the British Young Travellers Society organized the 'Hampshire Explorer' tour with 'USA' class 0-6-0 tank No. 30073 hauling the special from Southampton to Fawley and back to Totton. BR Standard class '3' 2-6-0 No. 77014 then took the train forward to Bournemouth and Blandford, returning to Broadstone, from where 'West Country' class 4-6-2 No 34006 *Bude* hauled it to Ringwood before returning to Bournemouth and Southampton.

The same year saw the final steam-hauled passenger train over the remaining section of the Old Road when the LCGB ran a 'Dorset & Hants' railtour on 16th October. 'West Country' class 4-6-2 No. 34023 *Blackmore Vale* brought the train to Broadstone, from which point BR Standard class '3' 2-6-0 No. 77014 and BR Standard class '4' 2-6-0 No. 76026 took over to work the special to Ringwood and back, then up the Somerset & Dorset to Blandford and finally over the Hamworthy Goods branch before Nos. 34023 and 34019 *Bideford* double-headed it back to Waterloo.

Passenger services over the Fawley branch ceased after 11th February, 1966 when diesel-electric multiple unit (demu) No. 1128 departed from Southampton at 4 pm on the final journey. However, its closure was under different circumstances: the service had mainly been timetabled to suit the requirements of the oil refinery employees rather than the general public, but as the number of employees using the train decreased, the need for increased branch availability for oil trains sealed the passenger services fate.

The closure of the Somerset & Dorset was to be a far more protracted affair. It only provided a local service and by the nature of the line progress was pedestrian; the loss of through services had not helped its case.

A closure process that had commenced covertly in 1957 was eventually announced on 9th September, 1965 with the closure taking place from 1st January, 1966. At the last minute unexpected complications with the replacement bus services caused this to be postponed, until the Traffic Commissioners approved the necessary licences on 16th February with the closure eventually taking place on 7th March. Certain parts of the line were retained for goods traffic, including the southern section between Broadstone Junction and Blandford, virtually the original Dorset Central!

The Old Road, now only accessible from the Poole end was further rationalised with the singling of the section between Broadstone and Wimborne when the down line was taken out of use on 24th July, 1966. Further reductions took place on 8th January, 1967 with the down line between Wimborne and Ringwood being taken out of use, together with the ground frames at Wimborne, Canford Crossing, Uddens, Ashley Heath, and Ringwood.

A number of goods trains were steam-hauled over the remaining line to Ringwood almost to the end; unfortunately for some locomotives Ringwood was the end. Two BR class '4' 2-6-4 tanks Nos. 80096 and 80102 were broken up in March 1966 by Messrs T.W. Ward in their yard adjacent to Ringwood station, to be followed by BR class '4' 4-6-0s Nos. 75072 and 75073 the following month. Following the withdrawal of freight facilities from Ringwood on 7th August, 1967 the West Moors-Ringwood section was closed and the track recovered as far as West Moors War Department depot.

The long awaited announcement of the £15m scheme to electrify the main line as far as Bournemouth was made on 29th September, 1964, with plans to extend

The last ever steam-hauled passenger train has arrived at Ringwood on 16th October, 1966. British Railways Standard class '4' 2-6-0 No. 76026 stands at the head of the LCGB 'Hants & Dorset Rail Tour', the piloting engine Standard class '3' 2-6-0 No. 77014 having already moved to position itself at the other end for the return journey. *Author's Collection*

British Railways Standard class '3' 2-6-0 No. 77014 waits to depart from Hamworthy Goods with the LCGB 'Dorset & Hants Rail Tour' on 16th October, 1966; at the rear of the nine-coach train is British Railways Standard class '4' 2-6-0 No. 76026. Since this photograph was taken the waterline in the foreground has been reclaimed and forms part of the ferry terminal complex. *R.A. Panting*

An unidentified British Railways Standard class '4' 2-6-0 stands on the down line at the west end of Ringwood station during early 1967. Removal of the down line had already commenced and a close examination of the track in front of the engine reveals that a number of fishplates have been slackened off and keys have already been removed. *R. Smith Collection*

Ringwood viewed from Crow Arch bridge during early 1967. An unidentified British Railways Standard class '4' 2-6-0 shunts the yard, at the time the down line between Ringwood and West Moors was being lifted. *R. Smith Collection*

Complete with home-made numberplate British Railways Standard class '4' 4-6-0 No. 75077 arrives at Ringwood with a lightweight goods on 11th February, 1967. Standing in the down track is a tractor belonging to the track removal gang and a bogie bolster loaded with rail from the down line of the West Moors-Ringwood section. No. 75077 was to follow the fate of the track, withdrawn at the end of steam in the July and broken up the following year having only given 12 years' service.   *SOUTHERN-IMAGES*

Ashley Heath crossing on 11th February, 1967. British Railways Standard class '4', 4-6-0 No. 75077 passes with a bogie bolster of rail recovered from the down line between Ashley Heath Halt and Ringwood.   *SOUTHERN-IMAGES*

The Ringwood scrapyard of Messrs T.W. Ward was responsible for the breaking-up of four complete British Railway Standards that arrived on site complete, they also handled a vast amount of scrap from Eastleigh that arrived by the wagon load. The remains of 'M7' class 0-4-4 tanks Nos. 30034, 30112, 30107 and 'E4' class tank 0-6-2 No. 32479 along with other unidentified locomotives are piled high in this engine graveyard. *J. Read*

Crompton type '3' No. D 6527 (33110) waits to depart from Ringwood with a short freight shortly before the complete closure of the West Moors-Ringwood section. Already the down line through the station has been removed leaving only the run-round facilities at the goods yard end of the layout. *J. Read*

The prestigious 'Bournemouth Belle' ran to and from Bournemouth West. 'Merchant Navy' class 4-6-2 No. 35024 *East Asiatic Company* runs into the station with the down train on 29th February, 1964.   *C.L. Caddy*

Millbrook signal box and goods yard viewed from the station footbridge. 'Merchant Navy' class 4-6-2 No. 35016 *Elder Fyffes* has shut off steam in preparation for the stop at Southampton Central on 1st May, 1965. Today the signal box has gone and the goods yard is now a container terminal.   *C.L. Caddy*

the existing Southern Region 750 volt DC third rail for 80 miles from Sturt Lane Junction, Brookwood to Bournemouth Central. The third rail would be extended to Bournemouth West where the existing carriage sheds would be expanded into full maintenance facilities. Three National Grid supply points at Basingstoke, Southampton and Bournemouth and 25 sub-stations would supply the line with power.

The hub of the system consisted of 11 high-powered multiple units classified as '4REP' which consisted of two driving motor seconds, a buffet car and a brake third. Twenty-eight four-car trailer units classified as '4TC' consisting of two driving trailer seconds, a trailer brake second and a first class corridor, and three, 3-car sets classified '3TC', these units not having the first class trailer. The associated diesel locomotives consisted of 19 'D65XX' Bo-Bo diesel-electrics (later classified '33/1'), these, the 'REP' units and the 'TC' units all having control wiring to allow working in various formations. The usual practice for through Weymouth trains was the '4REP' unit propelling two '4TC' units from Waterloo to Bournemouth where a class '33/1' would back onto the front of the formation which was then split, the diesel and one or two '4TC' units proceeding to Weymouth, the 'REP' unit moving over to the carriage sidings.

Later the unit would proceed to the top end of the up platform where the '4TC' units propelled by a class '33/1' which had arrived from Weymouth would be joined to the rear, the train then proceeding to London hauled by the 'REP'. The class '33/1', having been uncoupled, then proceeded to the down side to await the next down working.

The new timetable planned for a two-hourly Waterloo-Weymouth fast service, covering Waterloo to Southampton in 70 minutes and Bournemouth in 100 minutes, an hourly Waterloo-Bournemouth semi-fast with alternate trains extended to Weymouth, and an hourly Waterloo-Bournemouth slow train. The fasts and semi-fasts would be worked by the 'REP'/'TC' combinations and the slows by '4VEP' sets.

To put the plan into operation was a major undertaking. It required the electrification of 90 route miles involving 236 miles of trackwork, the laying of power cables and the construction of sub-stations and associated works, the complete relaying of the main line west of Woking replacing 60 ft lengths of rail on wooden sleepers with continuous welded rail on concrete sleepers and the reballasting of the track bed. Signalling had to be modernised, and other works included the lengthening of platforms at nine stations to accommodate the 12-coach trains, and refencing much of the line owing to the presence of the third rail.

Much of this work required occupation of various parts of the line. East of St Denys this could be arranged by diverting trains via Guildford and Portsmouth, or 'over the Alps' via Alton rejoining the main line at Winchester Junction. However, further west the earlier closures of both the Old Road and the Salisbury-West Moors lines gave no alternative to prolonged single line working and replacement bus services.

To enable the laying of continuous welded rail single line working was commenced between Beaulieu Road station and Brockenhurst over the down line between 3rd October and 6th December, 1965. A temporary signal box was brought into use at Beaulieu Road for the purpose, and Woodfidley signal box

Deep in the New Forest at Sway station the tranquil scene is disturbed by the arrival and departure of British Railways Standard class '4' 2-6-0 No. 76010 on an up train. In the background through the trees one of the two Pullman camping coaches can be seen; once a familiar sight at a number of stations they provided an interesting holiday environment. *P. Tatlow*

'Merchant Navy' class 4-6-2 No. 35024 *East Asiatic Company* climbs the 1 in 150 gradient between Holdenhurst Road tunnel and Bournemouth Central Goods signal box with a Waterloo train on 27th September, 1964. To the left can be seen the track work and buildings of Bournemouth Central goods depot, the locomotive is passing over the site of the original Bournemouth East engine shed and the first East station occupied the right side of the goods yard. A comparison with diagrams and photographs on pages 174 and 175 of Volume One will clarify the situation. *A. Trickett*

was taken out of use during the single line working. On 2nd January, 1966 single line working was instituted over the up line between Hinton Admiral and New Milton. Work was suspended during the 1966 summer service; however, other events in connection with the improved service were taking place. Early in the summer it was announced that the contract had been let for the construction of the new repair facilities to be built on the site of the Bournemouth West approach tracks. In Southampton, there having been few objections to the closure of Southampton Terminus and Northam stations, the Minister of Transport announced that their closure would take place from 5th September, 1966. All services were transferred to Southampton Central, where reconstruction work did little to assist with the increased station usage. The main buildings on the up side including the landmark clock tower were demolished in the September. Temporary huts situated at the London end of the up platform were provided whilst reconstruction took place. Ironically, platforms 1-4 at Southampton Terminus reopened over the Christmas period to handle mail and parcels traffic.

Work recommenced with the new rail works at the end of the summer service, single line working operating between Sway and New Milton from 18th September until 3rd November.

The signalling between Woking and Bournemouth was of the conventional semaphore type controlled from 48 signal boxes. This was all to be changed to an automatic and semi-automatic colour light system. In July 1966 Woking box took control as far west as Pirbright Junction and during November Basingstoke and Eastleigh power boxes opened, the latter covering to St Denys in the west. It had originally been planned to extend the Eastleigh control area to Bournemouth and beyond, however, in the event the scheme was reduced in scale.

The laying of the feeder cables was not without interest. On one Sunday in September 1966, what at the time was considered to be the longest continuous length, 2,016 yds of three-core oil filled cable was laid between Bournemouth and Branksome, a specially converted wagon carrying the 11 ft diameter cable drum.

The previous closure of goods facilities had allowed the removal of sidings, thus the section between Totton and Brockenhurst A was converted to semi-automatic colour light operation using track circuit block from 23rd October, 1966 with the closure of signal boxes at Ashurst, Lyndhurst and Woodfidley. Lymington Junction to Christchurch was converted on 26th February, 1967 with the closure of Sway, New Milton and Hinton Admiral signal boxes. This left two sections of mechanical signalling, one between Brockenhurst A and Lymington Junction, and the line west of Christchurch.

In the meantime work had proceeded well east of Swaythling, and on 5th December, 1966 pick-up shoe clearance tests commenced between Swaythling and Brockenhurst. The switching on of current between Swaythling and Lymington Junction on 18th January, 1967 introduced electric power to the east end of the Southampton & Dorchester line, with a test train consisting of two '2EPB' units, an electro-diesel locomotive and a three-car 'EPB' unit running from Wimbledon to Brockenhurst on the same day.

With steam having less than a year to run, an unidentified 'Merchant Navy' class 4-6-2 heads across Rockley viaduct with a Weymouth-bound train on 24th September, 1966. The first and third coach are of Bulleid construction, the second is a British Railways Mk I already in the then-new blue and white livery.   *P. Tatlow*

Electro-diesel No. E6043 hauling a brake van and former Southern Railway '6PAN' motor coach No. 3031 carrying out conductor rail positioning checks at Lyndhurst Road on 2nd January, 1967. This was prior to the switching on of current as far as Lymington Junction on 18th January.
                                                                SOUTHERN-IMAGES

Type '3' Crompton (later class '33') No. D 6504 passes through Southampton Central on 12th March, 1967 with a train of recovered track panels during electrification works. In the background the up side buildings including the clock tower have been demolished and reconstruction has commenced. The remaining building is the District Offices built in 1913 and demolished in 1971.   *C.L. Caddy*

On 26th February shoe clearance test were conducted between Brockenhurst and Bournemouth, the train consisting of electro-diesel No. E6043, a goods brake van and withdrawn motor coach No. 3031 from a '6PAN' unit. The section from Lymington Junction to Bournemouth Central was energised on 6th March, and on the 28th the final section from Bournemouth Central (Merrick Park TP hut) to Branksome, with selected tracks in Bournemouth West carriage sidings was energised. Thus electric power was now available from Waterloo to Bournemouth, the longest electrified main line on the Southern Region, although much work and testing had to be carried out before regular services could commence.

The alterations in the Bournemouth area had been of a more complex nature. The carriage shed and sidings at Bournemouth West were extended to include a depot for the maintenance of the new stock. As Bournemouth West station had lost much of its traffic following the closure of the Old Road and the Salisbury-West Moors line and the diversion of the remaining Somerset & Dorset trains to Bournemouth Central its sole remaining traffic was the portions of Waterloo trains that commenced or terminated at the station. It was decided to close the station ahead of its official closure date which had been set for 1st November, 1965 to allow work to commence with the new depot. The station closed on 5th September, 1965, from which date buses transferred passengers to and from Bournemouth Central until the official closure date.

The connection between Branksome and Bournemouth West Junction signal box had already been taken out of use on 1st August. Branksome shed closed the following day and was quickly demolished. Bournemouth West Junction box and the curve over the viaduct to Gas Works Junction signal box was taken out of use on the night of 30th/31st October, as were the associated signals. The line between Branksome and Bournemouth West Junction was reinstated on the same date to allow stock to and from Bournemouth Central to gain access to the carriage sidings. At the same time Bournemouth West Junction box reopened as a ground frame, with work proceeding on the construction of the new depot which covered the approach to Bournemouth West.

The first revenue-earning electric train to depart from Bournemouth Central on Monday 3rd April, 1967 was 'REP' unit No. 3001 in all-blue livery departing with the 8.33 am service to Waterloo. Note the 'Brute' trolleys on the down platform loaded with parcels and mail traffic now no longer carried by rail. Forty-one years later the background has completely changed, St Paul's church and other assorted buildings being replaced by a bus interchange and a supermarket.   *Bournemouth Evening Echo*

Ahead of the full change-over to electric traction 'REP' set No. 3009 with two 'TC' units in all-blue livery heads an up train past Sway on 3rd June, 1967.   *C.L. Caddy*

The introduction of automatic signals between Branksome and Bournemouth Central saw in the closure of Gas Works Junction signal box on 15th January, 1967. The layout at Bournemouth Central was remodelled to provide for the new service. There had been plans to completely demolish the station and construct one consisting of a central island platform, however, this scheme was dropped and the new arrangements carried out within the constraints of the Victorian train shed and surrounding area.

The up and down through lines and associated pointwork were taken out of use on 9th November, 1966, and with a concerted effort the new layout was introduced complete with the two middle sidings at the west end, all signalling converted to colour light and all points power-operated, although the box retained its Westinghouse 'A2' 60-lever frame. The work was completed and became fully operative from 11th December, at the same time Bournemouth Central Goods signal box was reduced to a ground frame released from Bournemouth Central box. An unusual feature arose from the fact that Bournemouth engine shed had to remain open until the end of steam operation, the points controlling its entrance being hand-operated as a temporary measure.

Further east the continued operation of the Lymington branch was assured by its inclusion in the Bournemouth electrification scheme. Not only did it serve Lymington and was a convenient railhead for several small resorts along the coast, more importantly it connected with the British Railways ferry to Yarmouth which served the west part of the Isle of Wight.

Owing to the need to make layout alterations at Lymington in connection with the electrification, from April 1967 'Hampshire' diesel units replaced steam. Like both the Swanage branch and the Old Road, Lymington had for many years been supplied with 'M7' tank engines from Bournemouth shed, and then for the final few years with Ivatt class '2' 2-6-2 tanks and Standard class '4' 2-6-4 tanks. Historically Lymington was the oldest branch (1858) off the original Southampton & Dorchester Railway and also had the distinction of becoming the last steam-operated branch line in the country. On Sunday 2nd April Ivatt class '2' No. 41312 worked the final services, bringing to an end to yet another chapter in railway history. 'Hampshire' unit No. 1103 took over services the following day, when the entire branch was also reduced to 'one train only' working.

Electric power was switched on along the branch on 1st June when several trial trips were made with an electric unit; gradually electric units took over and from the 26th of the month completely replaced diesel units. Both diesel and electric traction had gradually been introduced into various workings along the main line in the period leading up to full electrification. The first passenger-carrying electric train departed from Bournemouth on Monday 3rd April, 1967 headed by '4REP' unit No. 3001 with the 8.33 am service to Waterloo, although leaving 12 minutes late due to the late arrival of the Weymouth section. However, time was more than made up with a three minute early arrival at Brockenhurst; passengers were impressed by the quick acceleration and smooth running and the buffet car in the leading unit. Slight delays there might have been whilst crews who had spent their life on a steam locomotive came to terms with something entirely different.

Looking back to the pre-war days when the Southern Railway was forging ahead with massive electrification schemes, it was almost inconceivable that the Waterloo-

The various railtours that ran in the final years of steam involved a number of interesting locomotives. Amongst these was former LNER 'A4' class 4-6-2 No. 4498 *Sir Nigel Gresley* in LNER blue livery photographed passing through Christchurch on 3rd June, 1967 with a special from Waterloo to Bournemouth and return. *J. Read*

Weymouth line would be the last in the country to operate steam-hauled express trains. This was to cause a proliferation of steam specials to be arranged over the final two years, inclusion of too many of which would make boring reading.

However, those run during the final months are not without interest as enthusiasts attempted to cram in every route available. Of these, 25th March, 1967 saw the 'Hants & Dorset Branch Flyer' cover the Fawley and Lymington branches, a run over the truncated Somerset & Dorset to Blandford and a run over the Swanage branch before returning to Southampton. Whilst the LCGB-organized 'Dorset Coast Express' from Waterloo via Guildford concentrated on a double run over the Swanage branch before continuing to Weymouth and returning to Waterloo.

A return of LNER steam saw 'A4' class 4-6-2 *Sir Nigel Gresley* in LNER blue livery make a run between Waterloo and Bournemouth on 3rd June and the following day repeat the performance but extended to Weymouth. The Warwickshire Railway Society ran a special from Birmingham on 11th June via Clapham Junction which took in the Swanage branch *en route* to Weymouth.

The final steam tour was operated by the Railway Correspondence & Travel Society (RCTS) on 18th June when a selection of motive power worked the special from Waterloo to Weymouth via Guildford and Fareham; a visit to the Swanage branch was included before reaching Weymouth. The return ran to Waterloo via Eastleigh and Salisbury.

During the final months the remaining locomotives appeared in a very run-down condition, lack of cleaning and removal of nameplates to deter souvenir hunters made them a sad sight as, in reduced numbers, they maintained the gradually diminishing number of steam-hauled services On 1st January, 1967 the four motive power depots involved, Nine Elms, Eastleigh, Bournemouth and Weymouth, were allocated respectively 27, 33, 21, and 14 locomotives. From the April Weymouth had no official allocation and by the end of steam Nine Elms had 25, Eastleigh 21, and Bournemouth 15, numbers having been still further reduced.

By the final week there were few steam workings; on most days only about 18 steam-hauled passenger trains passed along the line between Southampton and Weymouth. On Sunday 2nd July the official 'Farewell to Steam' specials were run from Waterloo. 'West Country' class No. 34025 *Whimple* departed at 9.33 am with a special to Bournemouth, returning at 4.30 pm. 'Merchant Navy' class No. 35008 *Orient Line* departed at 9.55 am with the second special to Weymouth; an added bonus for those travelling was the piloting of the return working between Weymouth and Bournemouth by sister engine No. 35007 *Aberdeen Commonwealth*. This averted the necessity of a banker from Weymouth to Bincombe tunnel and between Poole and Branksome.

The celebrated 'Bournemouth Belle', which had already succumbed to diesel haulage, was steam-hauled twice during the final week. The penultimate steam working was hauled by 'West Country' class No. 34025 *Whimple* in both directions on Monday 3rd whilst on Wednesday 5th July 'West Country' class No. 34024 *Tamar Valley* hauled the down train and sister engine No. 34036 *Westward Ho* the up working, the last steam-hauled 'Bournemouth Belle' and the final steam-hauled Pullman on the Southern Region. The 'Channel Islands Boat Express' between Waterloo and Weymouth was for the majority of the final week steam-hauled; on the last day 'Merchant Navy class' No. 35023 *Holland-Afrika Line* took the up train to bring the last steam-hauled titled train into Waterloo.

Other trains of note steam-hauled during that period included the 2.45 am Waterloo-Bournemouth paper train, 'West Country' class No. 34095 *Brentor* taking the last such working out of Waterloo in the early hours of Saturday 8th July. This engine had also worked the final 9.00 pm Bournemouth-Weymouth (6.30 pm ex-Waterloo) that evening, this service having been steam-hauled all the final week.

Saturday 8th saw few steam trains on passenger services. The final down steam express, the 8.30 am Waterloo-Weymouth, was hauled by 'Merchant Navy' class No. 35023 *Holland-Afrika Line*. BR Standard class '3' 2-6-0 No. 77014 hauled the 10.43 am Southampton-Bournemouth service.

On the very last day Sunday 9th July there were even less steam movements. Enthusiasts who had hoped that the final 'Bournemouth Belle' would be steam, hauled were disappointed, officialdom had decreed this not to be, thus a rather grimy Brush type '4' No. D1924 hauled the well-known Pullman train in both directions. In the early hours 'Merchant Navy' class No. 35030 *Elder Dempster Lines* departed Waterloo with the Sundays-only 2.30 am service to Poole, and BR Standard class '5' 4-6-0 No. 73018 worked the 10.02 am Bournemouth-Weymouth service.

However, at Weymouth an historic event was unfolding. In place of a diesel that had reportedly failed, 'Merchant Navy' class No. 35030 *Elder Dempster Lines* in charge of driver Allen and fireman Groves took the 2.07 pm Waterloo express out of Weymouth, the last steam-hauled passenger train to depart Weymouth and indeed to run on the Southern Region.

Crowds stand on the down platform of Bournemouth Central on 9th July, 1967 as Brush type '4' (later class '47') No. D1924 pulls into the station with the last down 'Bournemouth Belle'. The clientele associated with this prestige service were in decline, and it failed to fit in with the new electric service. Unfortunately other standards were also falling, a look at the time worn and damaged end screen of the station roof was a sign of the times.   *SOUTHERN-IMAGES*

The final steam train from Weymouth, the 2.07 pm Weymouth-Waterloo hauled by 'Merchant Navy' class 4-6-2 No. 35030 *Elder Dempster Lines*, takes water at Southampton Central on 9th July, 1967.   *SOUTHERN-IMAGES*

LMS-designed Ivatt class '2MT' 2-6-2 tank No. 41320, taking water at Bournemouth West on 9th July, 1967 whilst on shunting duty at the nearby carriage sidings, can lay claim to being the last steam locomotive to use the then disused Bournemouth West station.

A. Trickett

Although the last steam-hauled passenger train had departed for Waterloo, there was a final working of steam up the Western line to Westbury in the form of three Channel Islands' fruit specials. The first had departed at 10.20 am behind 'West Country' class No. 34095 *Brentor*, the second at 2.20 pm behind 'Battle of Britain' class No. 34052 *Lord Dowding*, the final departing at 2.45 pm behind BR Standard class '5' 4-6-0 No. 73092. Thus the final revenue-earning steam train had departed from Weymouth; later in the day the trio returned light engine to Weymouth shed to join the other assembled engines awaiting their fate.

Two Ivatt 2-6-2 tanks remained in the Bournemouth-Poole area: No. 41224 ran light to Weymouth during the afternoon, No. 41320 at Poole carried out the last steam banking duty up Parkstone bank. At approximately 6.45 pm bunker first she assisted an electro-diesel with an up empty stock working; her work done No. 41320 also headed for Weymouth.

There was one final steam working for the day to bring down the curtain on Southern Region steam operation. BR Standard class '3' 2-6-0 No. 77014 left Bournemouth at 8.50 pm with a van train; after shunting at Poole to add two more vans, at 9.25 pm the last revenue-earning steam train departed for Weymouth. One hundred and twenty years after the first steam trains had entered the county over the Southampton & Dorchester Railway, it was the end of an era. There was regret amongst enthusiasts and mixed feelings from enginemen at the replacement of a faithful servant.

Quickly all remaining steam engines were hauled to Salisbury and Weymouth sheds to await their fate; 26 had gathered at Weymouth by 23rd July. Gradually they were hauled away to the breaker's yard, the last three departing from Weymouth on 20th January, 1968, exactly 111 years since the first steam train had departed from the town.

Photographed leaving Poole, British Railways Standard class '3' 2-6-0 No. 77014 hauling the very last revenue earning steam train to run on the Southern Region, the 8.50 pm Bournemouth-Weymouth vans on 9th July, 1967, thus ending 120 years of steam locomotive working. *C. Stone*

The scene at Weymouth engine shed on 15th July, 1967 as withdrawn engines gather before their last journey to the scrapyard. *Author*

Chapter Seven

Electric Trains to Bournemouth

Monday 10th July, 1967 was an important date in Southern Region history; it saw the virtual completion of a 50 year programme of main line electrification. However, in the early stages the new service suffered teething troubles. Although a number of electric units had already entered service and push-pull operation performed for a short period, delays and cancellations took place until the new system had been well practised and experience gained. There was also the problem of late delivery of both '4REP' and '4VEP' units and class '74' electro-diesels, resulting in various combinations of diesels, 'TC' units and other stock to make up trains during the first few weeks of the service.

Although when all the stock had been delivered there was little in reserve, the timetable required the maximum utilization of stock and the '4REP' sets were used to the limit. Timekeeping problems were mainly caused by reduced turn-round times plus the increased number of trains, which intensified problems at already busy main line stations. This situation was resolved by adjustments to the timetable, and a revision of platform arrangements at Waterloo to reduce the number of crossing movements in and out of the station at busy times.

On 10th October, 1968 the Southern Region press office released the following statement entitled 'Electrification a Success:

An increase in passenger travel by 20% was Southern Region's forecast when the Bournemouth Electrification scheme was first announced. In fact, this target has been reached in the first full year, with the number of passenger journeys on the line between Waterloo and Bournemouth going up by over 1¼ million.

This has meant a corresponding jump of 21.9% in actual receipts, over a period in which there was no increase in fares. But the story doesn't end there. The figures are still rising. In the four weeks of this year corresponding to the first month of electrification, there has been a further increase of over 11% in the number of passenger journeys, with receipts up by almost 9% on the same period of 1967. And again, this had happened at a time when fares had remained static.

By 1970 there had been a remarkable growth in traffic on the Bournemouth line, although to be fair it was not all brought about by electrification itself. Residential development and the expansion of other activities encouraged commuters, in particular from the Southampton area.

In the five years between 1965 and 1970 the annual season ticket sales from Brockenhurst had risen from 590 to 900 and Southampton from 4,500 to 6,800. During the same period ordinary ticket sales from Bournemouth had risen from 305.5 to 415.5 thousand, Brockenhurst 68.4 to 94.4 thousand and Southampton 586.2 to 818.8 thousand.

At the same time the shape of future freight services appeared with the opening of Millbrook Freightliner Terminal on 29th January, 1968 with direct services and connections serving many places in the Midlands, North East and North West and Scotland. Exactly a year later there were further major changes as the Transport

Bournemouth engine shed stands empty with the rails removed shortly after the end of steam, the site was quickly cleared to enlarge the station car park. With the station's shunting movements reduced to the splitting and joining of units, one of the new 'REP' sets waits its next journey in the new carriage sidings. *Author*

Bournemouth carriage shed in June 1976 with its extended sidings and the new maintenance depot, the latter sitting astride the former route into Bournemouth West. Amongst the stock in view are a class '07' shunter, a former Southern Railway '2HAL' electric unit converted into a de-icing unit and a class '74' electric locomotive. To the extreme right stands Bournemouth Carriage Sidings ground frame, formerly Bournemouth West Junction signal box that originally controlled the curve over the viaduct to Gas Works Junction. *Author*

Despite the closure of a number of small goods yards the late 1960s still saw a considerable amount of freight traffic over the main line between Southampton and Weymouth. On 7th August, 1969 non push-pull fitted Crompton type '3' No. D6518 departs from Wareham with the 2.10 pm Wareham-Dorchester goods. Although steam had disappeared the water tower of LSWR vintage remained a station feature for a number of years. *G.A. Pryer Collection*

Act of 1968 came into force on 1st January, 1969 to cause further complications within the industry. The formation of the National Freight Corporation, resulted in British Rail's recently established Sundries and Freightliner Divisions being passed to National Carriers Ltd and Freightliners Ltd, both subsidiaries of the National Freight Corporation, a move that was to see the further decline of freight traffic by rail. The Act also saw a distinction made between 'commercial' and 'social' passenger services, the latter being eligible for grant aid. A situation where again politicians have hesitantly handed out subsidies when politically expedient, but then cutting them back at the first opportunity.

Although looking forward to a modern railway, arrangements from the past could often make an unwelcome appearance. Following the closure of the Old Road to passenger traffic and the lifting of the line east of West Moors, attendance at the remaining level crossings was withdrawn, the gates being opened by the train crew on each goods train. All went well until 25th March, 1968 when the driver of the Poole-West Moors freight misjudged his brake application resulting in No. D6538 running into the gates at Oakley crossing. This was followed by correspondence between British Railways and the Ministry of Transport in which the latter could trace no previous papers relating to the crossing and ask for confirmation of its name. Although the railway had altered the method of operating the crossings along the line it appeared they still needed authority to be released from their former obligations to provide attendance.

There was a Royal visit to Dorset during July 1969, the Royal Train being stabled on the Hamworthy Goods branch on the night of the 9th before proceeding to Dorchester the following morning. Having arrived at the down platform the train was shunted over to the up line then drawn into the up platform to allow the Royal party to alight without having to proceed through the subway. The Duke of Edinburgh, no doubt taking note of the station's unusual layout, enquired of the station master Mr Desmond Rawlings as to the reason for all the shunting. Following a visit to Duchy of Cornwall properties the Royal party travelled by road to the Atomic Energy establishment at Winfrith and then to Poole where the Queen opened the new general hospital. Rejoining the Royal Train at Poole station

Wimborne station viewed during the summer of 1971 the top photograph looking west and the lower to the east. Although the signalling has been reduced and a general air of decay has fallen over what was once the busiest station in Dorset, a considerable amount of goods traffic still occupies the yard.

(Both) Author

An unidentified push-pull fitted Crompton type '3' enters Wimborne off the viaduct over the River Stour during the summer of 1971 with a freight for Wimborne and West Moors petroleum depot. *Author*

it proceeded to Wimborne for a further engagement. After staying at Wimborne overnight, at 6.50 am on the morning of 12th July class '47' No. 47811 departed with the last Royal Train to visit the Old Road.

A press release on 2nd December, 1969 stated that electrification of the Weymouth-Bournemouth line to give an all-electric service to Waterloo was contained in the £217 million 10 year investment programme. Pressed on the subject the Southern Region General Manager was unable to be precise, whereas the divisional manager stated Weymouth could expect a new station in about two years. A further statement was made that it was planned to operate the entire Southern Region by 15 power signal boxes within 15 years and the Weymouth line would be controlled from Eastleigh.

Throughout the region the rationalisation of freight terminals would continue and the 80 public terminals in use would be reduced to about 40, and the 120 parcel depots would be reduced to about 30 for greater efficiency. However, the railway's political masters had other ideas, and with the exception of the freight and parcels business in which they excelled in the quest for efficiency almost to the point of destruction, some of the other matters had not been fully implanted 30 years later.

The remaining section of the former Somerset & Dorset line between Broadstone Junction and Blandford had closed to goods traffic on 6th June, 1969. Following track removal the connection to the Old Road at Broadstone was removed in October 1970 and the signal box closed on 18th October. On the same date the down line between Broadstone and Holes Bay Junction was taken out of use, and the previous arrangement where the points at Holes Bay were controlled from Poole B signal box was altered as the connection was reduced to a single point on the up Hamworthy Junction-Poole line worked by a ground frame released from Poole B box. These works had effectively reduced the line to West Moors into a long siding.

Further attempts to close the Swanage branch in January and May 1970 came and went. However, progress was being made with the construction of the new station buildings at Poole erected on the west end of the up platform and accessed by a new entrance that was formerly part of the goods yard. They were

Dorchester South viewed from Maumbury Rings in June 1970 just before construction was completed on the new up platform. A Crompton class '33' departs from the down platform for Weymouth with a '4TC' unit, in the background two '2TC' units are backing into the old up platform with a Weymouth-Waterloo train.   *Author*

Dorchester South photographed from Maumbury Rings on 19th February, 1977 showing the new up platform in the centre with the old up platform with the offices still in use behind, and the back of the down platform shelter visible to the right.   *Author*

Poole's second station, photographed in 1978, the two curved platforms survive whilst station buildings of 'Clasp' construction serve the public. In the background wagonload traffic including bulk cement is still handled in the goods yard.   *M.J. Tattershall*

brought into use on Sunday 15th February, 1970, allowing the demolition of the old buildings, parts of which dated back to the opening of the line, the old station footbridge being removed at the same time. During the first weekend in March the line was closed for 30 hours whilst excavations took place and a pre-cast pedestrian subway was installed at the east end of the station in readiness for the later removal of Towngate Street level crossing.

Further down the line between Dorchester and Weymouth the signal boxes at Bincombe tunnel and Upwey & Broadwey were closed from 1st March, when colour light signalling was introduced between Dorchester Junction and Weymouth, although semaphore signalling remained at Weymouth itself.

The archaic arrangements at Dorchester South where up trains had to reverse into the up platform finally came to an end on the 28th June, 1970. A new concrete platform had been constructed alongside the up line from Dorchester Junction on the curve opposite the down platform. The existing station buildings remained in use with a short walkway across the line of the original up platform and up sidings trackbed to give access to the new platform.

At the same time Dorchester South signal box was reduced to a ground frame to control points and shunting signals. Dorchester Junction box took over the control of running signals, with colour lights coming into use between Dorchester Junction and Moreton. Moreton signal box was reduced to a gate box controlling the signals protecting the crossing in both directions.

Weymouth engine shed ceased to be used as a signing-on point in October 1970, the staff being housed in wooden huts erected in the down side station forecourt at Weymouth. On 29th November the track work at Weymouth shed was officially taken out of use.

The following year was reasonably uneventful; the road bridge to carry traffic over the railway at Towngate Street, Poole was completed, resulting in Towngate Street crossing being taken out of use from 6th November.

The fate of the Swanage branch was also sealed during the year. Never a candidate for closure under the Beeching plans, it had fallen victim to later railway policy. It was announced that the branch would close after 1st January, 1972, thus at 10.15 pm demus Nos. 1110 and 1124 departed from Swanage with the final train. Shortly afterwards the track was lifted between Swanage and a point south of Norden Siding, from which clay traffic would continue.

Economies were also made at Dorchester West (former GWR station) from 2nd January when the station became unstaffed. Although not directly connected with the Southampton-Weymouth line, it remained the responsibility of the Dorchester South station master. The 16th February, 1972 saw the level crossing gates at Moreton replaced by automatic half barriers and the gate box closed, the structure being demolished in May.

The Maritime Freightliner Terminal, which had been under construction at Southampton, was connected to the main line at both Millbrook and Redbridge on 28th February, 1972. At Weymouth the complete withdrawal from 1st March of freight services between the port and the Channel Islands in favour of Portsmouth (which was not rail connected) reduced the freight traffic in the area to very low ebb, with further reductions from the August when goods facilities were withdrawn from Weymouth.

Controversy was raised in November when on the 8th the *Dorset Evening Echo* reported that,

... 'Dorsetway', launched yesterday by the Southern Region of British Rail to attract more passengers on the Weymouth to Bournemouth line, is not a last-ditch campaign to save the line from closure. 'We have no plans to close the line' said Mr Llew Edwards the region's South Western Regional Manager told a press conference.

Although he had to admit the line was receiving something in excess of £500,000 a year in Government subsidy. The Dorsetway campaign resulted in 100,000 envelopes being delivered to local homes giving details of services and six 5p travel vouchers!

The introduction of colour light signalling and track circuit block on 3rd December, 1972 between Christchurch and Pokesdown resulted in the closure of both signal boxes. In the same month there was a reduction in siding capacity at Weymouth, to be followed in May 1973 by the removal of track from Weymouth goods yard, the resulting space opening as a 300-space car park in the August. At Poole the disused Gas Works Sidings were taken out of use in September.

By the summer of 1973 the Maritime Freightliner Terminal at Southampton was fully operational with Freightliners operating to and from Birmingham, Glasgow, Leeds, Liverpool and Manchester. At the east end of Southampton the curve between Southampton Terminus and Tunnel Junction, part of the original Southampton & Dorchester Railway, was taken out of use from 5th February, 1973 and lifted over the weekend of 9th-10th December.

The year had also seen the commencement of a service between Hamworthy and Cherbourg by Truckline Ferries thus putting Poole back on the cross-channel ferry map after 105 years. Albeit not directly rail-connected, it enhanced Poole's status as a port and was to later introduce additional traffic to the Hamworthy Goods branch.

With a train of vans an unidentified Crompton type '3' takes the curve between Tunnel Junction and Southampton Junction on 15th March, 1967. This curve was the original link between the London & Southampton Railway and the Southampton & Dorchester Railway, and although the third rail was laid with the electrification scheme the curve was closed in 1973.   *SOUTHERN-IMAGES*

On 2nd April, 1974 the 11.42 am Waterloo-Bournemouth stopping train upon leaving Totton took the Fawley branch in error; having run clear of the third rail the train was propelled back onto the main line by the 1.16 pm Fawley-Eastleigh freight. The signalman having accepted the down passenger then set the road for the branch, the driver compounding the error by passing the down main starting signal at danger and accepting the branch starter.

During this period Weymouth was enjoying the service of 19 trains daily to Bournemouth, the majority continuing through to Waterloo, all worked between Weymouth and Bournemouth by the unique Crompton-'TC' push-pull sets.

Following the closure of so many sidings and other facilities the opening of a Motorail terminal at Brockenhurst in May 1974 was a welcome event providing a weekend service to and from Stirling in Scotland, the loading ramp facility being established on the down side adjacent to the Lymington bay platform. A further development was the provision of a siding into the Atomic Energy Authority's establishment at Winfrith in October 1974. However, as it was for the handling of nuclear flask trains its opening was of a special nature. Situated 3,500 yards from Wool on the down line, all traffic had to run forward to Dorchester South before returning eastwards. Although the Winfrith establishment had opened during the late 1950s and was situated alongside the main line no halt had ever been constructed to cater for the many workers at this isolated site, who were conveyed in fleets of buses from Weymouth, Dorchester, Swanage, Poole, Bournemouth and the surrounding area.

A non push-pull fitted Crompton type '3' heads the Brockenhurst-Stirling overnight car sleeper train through the New Forest. The service united with the Dover-Stirling service in West London to form a combined train travelling via the West Coast main line. *J. Dedman*

A Crompton type '3' stands at the head of the Brockenhurst-Stirling Motorail train at Brockenhurst on 8th June, 1980, consisting of two sleeping cars, a corridor first, a corridor brake first and carflats. Owing to improved motorways and a sharp fall in bookings the Brockenhurst section was withdrawn after the 1980 season. *J. Dedman*

At Bournemouth the site of Bournemouth West station and the remaining part of its approaches had been cleared and in January 1973 construction commenced on the Westbourne spur road. This opened in May 1974, by which time construction on stage two of the Wessex Way urban trunk road had commenced including the bridge over Bournemouth Central, this section opening on 13th July, 1975.

During the summer of 1974 two temporary level crossings were brought into use on the freight-only section between Holes Bay Junction and Broadstone at Fleetsbridge and Hamosford for use in conjunction with adjacent road construction work. As with other crossings on this section of line the gates for these two short-lived crossings were controlled by train crews.

The remaining section of the Old Road attracted a number of enthusiasts' railtours at this period. On 18th September, 1971 the Poole Grammar School Railway Society ran the 'Dorset Venturer' railtour commencing at Bournemouth Central with No. D6528 propelling '4TC' unit No. 414 to Weymouth. From here a run was made to Yeovil Pen Mill and back to Dorchester Junction. This was followed by a run over both the Swanage branch and the Hamworthy Goods branch returning to Bournemouth West, and finally a visit to Wimborne before returning to Bournemouth Central.

The 3rd March, 1973 saw the Locomotive Club of Great Britain organize the 'Hampshire Ferret' tour from Waterloo embracing the Hamworthy Goods branch and the Old Road to West Moors, the train consisting of Crompton No. 33101 and two '4TC' units with a buffet car wired for multiple working sandwiched between. One further enthusiasts' special penetrated the line as far as West Moors on 1st June, 1974 when the Swanage Railway Society ran the 'Wessex Wanderer' a three-car demu No. 1130, this was to be the last passenger-carrying train to proceed beyond Wimborne. Earlier in the day the 'Wessex Wanderer' was also the last enthusiasts' special to visit the former GWR Bridport branch.

The sands of time were running out for a further section of the Old Road. With only military traffic proceeding beyond Wimborne to West Moors, this was due to end at the beginning of June 1974 when the freight service from Poole was reduced to three trains a week terminating at Wimborne. However, it continued to run to West Moors for a further six weeks to clear the military stores depot. The Wimborne-West Moors section was officially placed out of use on 14th October, after which date only track recovery trains entered the section, the track having been removed by the end of December. At Wimborne traffic was confined to coal and full wagonloads and the exhibition trains that were refurbished by a local company in the yard.

A further event of historic interest during 1974 was the granting of Grade Two Listed Building status to Bournemouth Central station, a matter that 25 years later was to lead to its restoration.

The first proposals for the redevelopment of Bournemouth Central station were mooted during 1975 when a local plan for the station area was agreed by Bournemouth Borough Council and the Dorset County Council (Bournemouth having become part of Dorset the previous year). This plan, published in July 1976, involved a much larger area than just the station making provision for a new road network, and consisted of three alternative schemes.

On 3rd March, 1973 the LCGB organized a railtour from Waterloo that included a visit to the Hamworthy Goods branch and the Old Road which by then terminated at West Moors. Passing the hand-operated gates Crompton type '3' No. D6511 (shortly to become No. 33101) enters West Moors station. *G.F. Gillham*

Another view of the LCGB railtour of 3rd March, 1973. No. 6511 stands at the remains of West Moors station with two '4TC' units with a buffet car wired for multiple working sandwiched between. *G.F. Gillham*

The last passenger train to West Moors, the 'Wessex Wanderer', arrived at a flag-bedecked station, the parish council greeted the train and music was played by the Verwood Band with many local residents turning out to witness the historic occasion. Twenty minutes later at 7.20 pm on 1st June, 1974 the last passenger train to travel between West Moors and Wimborne departed into the sunset.   *C.R. Jones*

Hampshire diesel-electric unit No. 1130 stands at Wimborne with the 'Wessex Wanderer' railtour organized by the Swanage Railway Society on 1st June, 1974. Having returned from West Moors this was the last ever passenger train to proceed east of Wimborne; the two young boys running down the old up line with exhibition coaches in the background are no doubt unaware of the historic significance of the occasion.   *R.A. Panting*

Scheme One - Which would have cost an estimated £24m at current land values and construction costs at that time was the boldest, it proposed a major redevelopment of the whole area at a high density and included the remodelling of the railway station and the provision of a new road network. The existing tracks and platforms would be retained, but it was probable that at least 80 per cent of the existing buildings (including the listed building) would be removed. A bus-rail interchange would be provided by constructing a deck above the railway track to include a circulation system for all vehicles bus and coach parking bays, with a waiting area for taxis and cars with access to adjoining multistorey car parks. New railway booking offices and other public facilities would be constructed on the upper deck, centrally placed over the tracks to provide direct access by escalators to each platform.

Scheme Two - Proposed partial redevelopment of the area at a moderate density and improvement in the circulation facilities with most of the listed buildings and existing roads retained. The existing station platforms would be retained as would the main hall of the railway station and various other buildings, with the existing single storey buildings each side of the main hall replaced creating improved facilities for British Rail, and a new public footbridge over the railway provided west of the station buildings. There would also be limited bus and coach parking facilities on the down side of the station.

Scheme Three - Was a variation of scheme two, only including a redevelopment of the site of St Paul's Church in addition to the requirements of the previous scheme.

In conclusion it was considered that a scheme based on either scheme two or three would best achieve the objectives identified in the consultative document, and there the matter rested for a number of years.

The Associated Portland Cement Marketing Company, who had previously handled bagged cement at Hamworthy New Quay, moved to a former clay siding at Hamworthy Junction. Here a purpose-built powdered cement receiving facility was constructed, served by Prestflo wagons, during 1975.

The next year was embroiled in controversy. Firstly, there was disagreement between local councils and other interested parties concerning the siting of the controversial Wytch Farm oil terminal, with Holton Heath being proposed as an alternative to Furzebrook on the Swanage branch. The Swanage Railway Society, which had been formed during 1972 with the aim of reopening the Swanage branch, was in favour of that proposal as the Furzebrook scheme would deny them future control if they ever restored a passenger train service between Swanage and Wareham. However, despite Holton Heath's previous status as an industrial site it was denied the opportunity and Furzebrook later became the terminal.

Secondly, British Rail announced that it intended to replace Poole A signal box and the gates in Poole High Street with barriers controlled from Poole B box. The second proposal that the footbridge be removed caused dismay and objections from both townspeople and High Street traders. British Rail claimed that the 1872 bridge was coming to the end of its useful life and would cost more than £30,000 to replace.

At Hamworthy the original station buildings, which had stood empty since 1946, were due to be demolished, the site having been acquired by Messrs James Bros, an adjacent engineering company. The Poole Industrial Archaeological Group and other organizations had been fighting to save the building as a specimen of Southampton & Dorchester Railway architecture. The group's first aim was to restore the house and use it for their long-awaited industrial

Runaways had always been a problem on the approach to Bournemouth West, a situation that has not chnaged since the closure of the station, as both stock and locomotives have continued to escape from Bournemouth depot. 'TC' unit No. 303 attempted an escape on 27th March, 1972. Photographed on 5th March, 1976 'REP' unit No. 3004 also ran through the stop blocks at the end of the head shunt to cause interest to motorists on the adjacent Wessex Way. *M. Thresh*

museum. However, despite the fact the petitioners stated it should be listed as a building of local historic interest because it played an inestimable part in the development of the town, unfortunately, it could not be saved and was demolished on 29th July, 1976.

Other reductions included the closure of Worgret Junction signal box on 23rd May, the remaining section of the Swanage branch being controlled by a ground frame connection from the down main line released by Wareham signal box. Further west East Burton crossing ground frame was closed on 28th November when control of the previously-fitted barriers was taken over by Wool signal box.

May 1977 saw the final closure to freight traffic of the remaining section of the Old Road between Holes Bay Junction and Wimborne. To mark the passing of this historic section of the line on 1st May the Lea Valley Railway Club ran the 'Corkscrew Shuttle' consisting of class '33' No. 33107 and two '4TC' units on three trips between Bournemouth and Poole to Wimborne. Two days later on 3rd May, the final freight train ran over the line hauled by class '33' No. 33012 fitted with a handwritten headboard inscribed 'The Last Train from Wimborne 3 May 1977'.

Shortly after closure, the East Dorset Railway Society had plans for its partial reopening as a tourist attraction. Also a consortium calling themselves the Railway Antiques Company had plans for the station at Wimborne. The *Bournemouth Evening Echo* for 12th December, 1977 reported that 'the idea is to open between six and twelve antique shoplets in the station buildings with craft stalls along the platforms and tourist attractions in other parts of the station area. Also proposed were a skateboard park, a crazy golf course, a scent garden for the blind, café and restaurant facilities and possibly a miniature steam railway', needless to say neither scheme was proceeded with.

On Saturday 1st May, 1977 the final revenue earning trains ever to travel over the remains of the Old Road were when the Lea Valley Railway Club ran three special trains entitled the 'Corkscrew Shuttle' between Bournemouth, Poole and Wimborne operated by Crompton type '3' No. 33107 and two '4TC' sets. Passengers view the scene at Wimborne before returning to the main line. *D.M. Habgood*

Demolition work is well advanced on the viaduct that carried the Old Road over the River Stour south of Wimborne station on the 11th February, 1978, bringing to an end 147 years of railway history. *Author*

A Southern Region '2HAP' electric unit turns onto the Lymington branch at Lymington Junction in the late summer of 1978 when construction work was almost completed on laying an independent third track from Brockenhurst thus eliminating the junction. On 17th October Lymington Junction was abolished, the other junction curving right onto the Old Road having been removed in March 1965. *Author*

The weekend of 13th-15th November the demolition of Poole A signal box with Poole High Street level crossing replaced by full barriers with CCTV, controlled from Poole B signal box which had the suffix 'B' removed.

On 5th February, 1978 the trailing connection into the up main line at Holes Bay Junction was removed, thus severing the last physical connection with the Old Road. By the following month the girder bridge over the River Stour, south of Wimborne was being demolished. At Wimborne, once the most important station in Dorset, the downside station buildings were demolished. Rail removal was completed by July 1978, and after 90 years, the Old Road had finally succumbed to the later Direct Line.

Later in the year major alterations were to take place between Brockenhurst and Lymington Junction, to enable the Lymington branch to operate as a separate entity without impinging upon the main line between Brockenhurst and Lymington Junction. This was achieved by laying a new third track parallel to the down main line, being brought into use on 17th October, 1978 when the connection between the main line and the branch at Lymington Junction was removed. Colour light signalling replaced the remaining semaphores and both Lymington Junction and Brockenhurst B signal boxes were closed; following the removal of the pointwork at Lymington Junction the main line speed limit at that point was raised from 60 to 70 mph. From 19th October the Westinghouse 'A3' type lever frame in Brockenhurst A signal box was replaced by an NX panel.

By 1978 the majority of freight traffic was concentrated on Poole yard and the Hamworthy branch where Freightliner traffic had been introduced. A trial service had been carried out between January and March 1977, this was followed by the construction of a loading gantry and from late 1978 a daily service commenced linking with the main terminal at Millbrook, Southampton. Although the service commenced well, the level of use rapidly declined resulting in its withdrawal as early as May 1980.

West of Hamworthy Junction there was a small amount of clay traffic off the truncated Swanage branch, army traffic from Wool and wagonload traffic at Dorchester, mainly fertilizer, which by its nature was a fluctuating trade. The only freight traffic to Weymouth consisted of oil tanks between Hamble and Weymouth Quay to fuel the cross-Channel steamers.

However, the situation was about to change: for a number of years past the small output of the Kimmeridge oilfield had been brought to Wareham by road tanker and transferred to rail wagons for forward shipment. The opening of the Wytch Farm oilfield resulted in the construction of an oil terminal at Furzebrook on the Swanage branch. Following a trial run by class '47' No. 47369 on 19th June, 1978 for testing the new sidings, the first loaded train consisting of fifteen 45-tonne tanks hauled by class '33' No. 33032 departed for Llandarcy at 5.00 pm on 12th December, 1978, thus setting in motion a valuable source of traffic from rural East Dorset. However, at Bournemouth the Central goods depot closed as from 2nd July, 1979.

Wareham level crossing, signal box and goods yard looking east on 24th June, 1976. Standing in the up sidings are oil tank wagons, at this stage the small output from the Kimmeridge oil field was transported to Wareham by road tanker and pumped into rail tank wagons. Just over two years later this practice ceased when the new oil terminal opened on the Swanage branch at Furzebrook. In the down sidings a push-pull fitted Crompton type '3' shunts wagons for the clay siding at Furzebrook.   *Author*

Chapter Eight

Electrification through to Weymouth

On 3rd April, 1980 the notorious level crossing at Wareham was taken out of use, a new road bridge spanning the line east of the goods shed. Further improvements were carried out in the Southampton area during the year; a new booking office was opened on the down side to replace accommodation provided following wartime bomb damage. A number of semaphore signals were also replaced by colour light ones in preparation for the later expansion of Eastleigh panel, and the Northam curve was realigned resulting in the previous speed restriction of 15 mph being raised to 25 mph.

By August 1980 the negotiations between British Rail and the Dorset County Council for the purchase of the trackbed of the former Old Road from Leigh Road, Wimborne to Fleetsbridge, Poole were formally concluded, thus allowing the Council to carry out a number of road improvements. This brought down the final curtain on part of the original Southampton & Dorchester line.

The status of Dorchester was further reduced in December 1980 with the withdrawal of the remaining goods facilities. On 5th December one week after the final freight had called, class '33' No. 33109 cleared the remaining wagons from Dorchester South yard. On 7th December Dorchester Junction was relaid to ease the speed restriction from 15 mph to 35 mph for trains using the curve to Dorchester South. However, trains taking the line to Dorchester West had their speed reduced from 40 mph to 25 mph. The junction was simplified to a trailing connection between the up and down main lines, followed by a facing point off the up main towards Dorchester West, before the line again became double track through to Dorchester West station. At the same time the Southern route was designated as the main line and the former Wilts, Somerset & Weymouth line as the branch.

The fortunes of the Hamworthy Goods branch continued to fluctuate; following the failure of the Freightliner traffic a brief venture was undertaken in the import and export of cars with double deck car transporter trains visiting the branch. However, with the transfer of the vessel to a rival port the traffic was lost.

For a short period during 1982 the transportation of an intermodal type container by a company called Novatrains was tried using the Freightliner gantry. By this time the future of the branch lay in the traffic that could be generated by ships at the quayside, handling facilities having been withdrawn from Hamworthy Goods yard on 2nd March, 1981, although the branch remained open to serve the private sidings at Hamworthy Quay.

Although not directly connected with the Southampton area the reopening on 28th August, 1981 of the Laverstock Curve east of Salisbury, a spur that had closed 122 years previously, saved the reversal of diverted London-bound trains at Salisbury. The area controlled by Eastleigh panel box was extended on 8th November, 1981 with the closure of both Southampton and Millbrook signal boxes, with Redbridge and Totton following on 23rd and 28th January, 1982.

Further west Bournemouth Central Goods box, which for many years had been reduced to ground frame status, closed in the April. In the previous January, outline planning permission had been granted for the use of the former Bournemouth Central goods yard for light industrial use and a warehouse complex. On the traffic side it was announced that the twice-weekly Stirling-Brockenhurst Motorail service would not run that summer as a sharp fall in bookings the previous year had made it unprofitable.

During the early 1980s rumours of closure of the line west of Bournemouth were sufficiently rife for the South Western divisional manager, Mr Whitehall, to publicly refute them on 23rd September, 1983 with a statement that the future of the line was secure. He further promised that new rolling stock would be introduced within six years.

The station buildings at Moreton were demolished towards the end of the year and were replaced by platform shelters. This was followed by the surprise closure on 31st December, 1983 of Radipole Halt, near Weymouth. This was brought about by the allegedly unsafe condition of the platforms, which British Rail estimated would cost £51,000 to repair.

Southampton tunnel was to cause disruption to traffic between 1983 and 1985, the mortar of the brick lining being in such poor condition it was decided to reline the tunnel. As the centre of the tunnel had previously been renovated and was still in good condition, the new work commenced for about 67 metres each side, to be followed by a further 85 metres to the London end of the tunnel, with the second phase being the 160 metres at the station end of the tunnel.

Owing to the density of traffic at Southampton it was impossible to close the tunnel for anything other than short periods, causing the contractors Messrs Edmund Nuttall having to work whilst trains still passed through. This was achieved by single line working, and following the laying of additional crossovers either end of the tunnel single line working commenced in May 1983.

The first two phases involved removing the original brick base to the tunnel and replacing it with a much deeper concrete base. To enable this work to proceed and keep the tunnel open with a minimum of delay to traffic through this busy bottleneck, special signalling was installed to enable single line working over either line as required with a safety fence between the tracks to protect workmen.

The method employed was interesting, in any one week about 20 metres of track was removed from one of the lines, then five strips of the brick floor well separated were dug out and replaced by concrete. Following completion, the track was replaced to allow trains to revert to that track, then the opposite track was lifted to allow the other half of the base to be installed, after which five more strips were replaced with work continuing in this manner until completed.

The second part of the operation was to replace the arch; this was achieved by laying a single line down the centre of the tunnel again employing single line working. A 10 metre-long movable safety shield spanning the track to protect the trains was employed. Hoists fitted to the shield lifted the new cast-iron tunnel lining segments into position, the materials for this work being transported into the tunnel on a narrow gauge railway laid from the station end,

Work in progress in Southampton tunnel in December 1984. During single line working '4TC' unit No. 432 squeezes under the special support bridge used during the relining of the tunnel, the new concrete segments can be clearly seen in the surrounding view.
Southern Evening Echo

again fenced off from the running line. Using these techniques it was possible to keep services running with only minor delays, the only closures being whilst the tracks were realigned or relayed. The work was completed and the tunnel returned to normal working on 8th July, 1985.

In what has since proved to be a retrograde step in the protection of revenue and station security, the 'open station' concept was introduced between Millbrook and Weymouth from 19th March, 1984 with on-train ticket checks replacing barrier examination. The same year saw Weymouth without a station master for the first time in its 127 year history, the station being brought under the area management scheme. The last station master was John Smith, who after moving from West Moors to Kent, later became assistant station manager at Maidstone West for the area, then assistant station manager at Salisbury before taking his appointment at Weymouth in 1979 which also covered Dorchester.

The dilapidated station at Weymouth was causing concern and its replacement was again discussed. In June 1982 it was stated that negotiations to develop a combined office development and new station were being discussed, and as the existing station had reached the end of its life a temporary station would be erected until the plans were finalised. This resulted in the arrival side buildings being demolished in September 1983, followed by the departure side buildings and platforms in August 1984 after temporary buildings had been erected. The office block scheme failed to materialize; a short third platform was constructed to the west of the two 1957 platforms which formed the basis for the new station with the stone block booking office and other facilities being constructed across the platform ends. The new station was officially opened on 3rd July, 1986.

Further signalling alterations had taken place at Dorchester in June 1985 with the reopening of Dorchester South signal box (reduced to a ground frame in 1970) on 2nd June as a panel box to control the section from there to a point just west of Moreton which was reduced to single track from the same date. A week later Dorchester Junction signal box closed, Dorchester South taking over control of the junction and the single line section to Maiden Newton.

Although having served well, the stock used on the Weymouth-Waterloo service, most of which was modified former steam stock, was below the standard of that employed on other routes of comparable distance and journey times. It was also nearing the end of its economic life.

For a number of years the future of the non-electrified section west of Bournemouth had been open to speculation with rumours circulating, even closure west of Poole had been talked about! The question had to be asked, was electrification beyond Bournemouth or Poole viable? Several options were considered including that of electrifying to Poole and providing 'Sprinter' diesel multiple units (dmus) onwards to Weymouth. Another alternative was to replace the 'REP'/'TC' fleet with 168 new 20 metre Mk III vehicles and continue using the '33/1' Cromptons over the Weymouth section, or rebuild the 'REP' units and construct new trailer units. This option remained open to the last minute when it was eventually decided to electrify the remaining 32 miles to Weymouth and provide a fleet of 24 new five-coach units for the service, later designated class '442'.

Announcement of the new £34.5 million plan was made in the House of Commons on 28th January, 1986; of that sum of money £30m would be for the new rolling stock and £13.5m for the electrification of the route. The depot at Branksome would be extended; sections of the route from Waterloo would have their maximum train speed increased from 90 mph to 100mph and the journey time from Waterloo to Weymouth reduced by 17 minutes.

The Southern Region General Manager said at the time of the announcement that electrification would be completed by January 1988 and the first new trains would start running to Bournemouth in May 1987. However, there was a considerable amount of work to be done before this could happen, the new stations at Dorchester and Weymouth had to be completed, and other stations required platform lengthening to accommodate the new trains. The track had to be relaid, the third rail installed and supply cables laid, with two new sub-stations. To save costs, the power supply west of Wareham would only allow trains to consist of a single class '442' unit, class '432' units and class '73/1' electro-diesels having similar restrictions, although these arrangements can be modified in an emergency.

Following years of negotiations, at the end of March 1986 it was announced that Dorchester South station was to be rebuilt under a development partnership between British Rail and Dorchester brewers Eldridge Pope Ltd. The plan provided for a new station building alongside the 1970 up platform, a new access road from Weymouth Avenue, a spacious car park, and a footbridge to replace the existing subway with reconstruction of the existing down platform. The new station buildings were in brick under a slate roof in a style similar to the brewery and therefore be in keeping with adjacent buildings. This would be followed by the conversion of the former station master's residence into a public house.

Work on the construction of the new station proceeded through the summer with the footbridge replacing the subway from 7th July. Work was nearing completion when the station caught fire on 18th October, fortunately the situation was quickly brought under control by the fire brigade and only about a third of the roof was destroyed. However, the damage was rectified by 25th November, 1986 when David Mitchell MP, Minister of State for Transport, officially opened the new station.

On 16th December it was announced that British Rail was intending to replace Bournemouth station with a multi-million pound combined station and shopping centre which would be constructed mostly of stainless steel and tinted glass with the structure suspended from 36 double pylons. These plans were approved by Bournemouth Borough Council early in the following year.

However, the station having become a grade two listed building in 1974 resulted in the matter going to a public enquiry, which was held in June 1987 with the various interested parties representing their case. British Rail stated that the station building was too large for current business requirements and costly to maintain and the physical condition of the building was causing concern. A survey by consultant engineers indicated that the costs of renovating it to sound condition would be £1.84m. An important element of the approved development of the site to the south of the station was a transport interchange which could not be provided unless changes to the station buildings and access arrangements were carried out.

The Railways Board had considered four options,

1.   To put the existing station into good repair without any restoration and without any provision of land for the interchange.
2.   As above with a limited amount of restoration.
3.   To retain and restore the main features of the existing building, demolish the mainly single-storey projecting buildings, build new staff and public facilities and enable land sale for the interchange.
4.   To demolish the existing station and build a new one, provide a bridge link from the adjacent proposed development and enable the sale of land for a traffic interchange.

The costs at the time were quoted as: Option 1 - £1.848m, Option 2 - £3.66m, Option 3 - £6.120m (less £0.9m land sale value), Option 4 - £4.487m.

In conclusion British Rail stated that the County Council had sought to secure the provision of a rail, coach, bus and taxi interchange adjacent to the existing station since 1976. Both the County Council and Taylor Woodrow Property Co. Ltd had invested heavily in assembling the necessary land for the interchange, access road and commercial development. The council wanted a new station which reflected the architectural ambitions of the 20th century, a theme upheld by the Bournemouth Chamber of Trade, Bournemouth Hotel & Restaurant Association, the Bournemouth & District Committee for Tourism, and Transport 2000.

The case for the retention of the station was put by the Bournemouth Civic Society, the Historic Buildings and Monuments Commission for England

(English Heritage), and the Victorian Society. The latter in a letter pointed out that of only five other British stations had lateral ridge-and-furrow glazing, two had been demolished and only Glasgow Central retained its original roof which is in any case very different from Bournemouth. Furthermore ridge-and-furrow roofs are generally low and gloomy, whereas Bournemouth is high and capable of having a 'lofty airiness'. Bournemouth station was therefore unique and should not be demolished.

English Heritage, also stated that the roof structure was particularly impressive and there was no other example of that period to match it. The only other remaining through stations with roofs supported on cross-girders rather than carried on iron arches or braced with ties were Carlisle of 1847 by Sir William Tate, and Stoke-on-Trent of 1848 by H.A. Hunt.

However, English Heritage did make one interesting suggestion in that the Commission would support a proposal to incorporate the listed building in a new passenger exchange facility. This might be done within the repaired building with railway use being concentrated on the up side, with the down side track moved over and a new platform constructed beside it. Taxis could be introduced under the overall roof, probably at either end of the passenger concourse, the down side could be given over to bus and taxi offices, and the forecourt of the down side could be used for the larger and longer distance buses. In this way the whole of the main building could continue in busy and effective use.

The case for demolition and retention having been well argued by all interested parties, the Inspector later recommended that the station be retained, stating,

> Only part of the less attractive and less interesting single-storey projections on the down side needs to be demolished in order to enable development proposals for a station improvement scheme, new travel interchange and retail shopping complex to proceed. As for the importance of the building in the light of its unusual design and style and in relation to its surroundings, it is certainly worth its Grade II status on the statutory list and it may indeed be, as the Historic Buildings and Monuments Commission for England stated, that it is under graded, and as the Victorian Society pointed out, its high level, lateral ridge-and-furrow glazed roof is almost unique.
>
> The station has little or no importance in relation to its surroundings, but is of considerable architectural and historic importance because of its unusual design and style.

After describing varying aspects of the rundown station the Inspector continued,

> ... the surrounding area was very rundown and unattractive. It is not surprising therefore that many Bournemouth people hold their station in low regard. However, if the missing glazing were replaced, the remaining parts cleaned up, the end screens replaced and the decorative steelwork painted, the station's possibly unique roof would be restored to its former glory. If, in addition, masonry were repaired and cleaned, attractive new buildings added, the footbridge removed and the subway opened, Bournemouth could have a very handsome Victorian station once again. The Inspector recommending that, listed building consent to demolish the whole station be refused, but listed building consent to demolish the single-storey buildings on the down side be granted.

Needless to say British Rail were less than impressed by the inspector's findings, now having to take measures to restore a historical station which in their view was far from suitable for their requirements in the late 20th century.

Other general improvements carried out during the year included the provisional of additional car parking at both Brockenhurst and Poole stations. To mark the official commencement of electrification works west of Branksome a 'Golden Pot' ceremony attended by Bob Reid the British Rail Board Chairman and many Southern Region managers took place at Branksome on 6th October.

Changes had also taken place with the commercial side of railway operating; the decision to set up five British Rail business sectors resulted in further change on 10th June, 1986 when the Waterloo-Weymouth line became part of the newly-formed Network SouthEast. The new sector covered 2,500 route miles from Kings Lynn and Harwich in the east to a northern boundary around Banbury, Northampton, Bedford and Huntington, and embracing the entire South East of England to include Weymouth in the South West and the Salisbury-Exeter line in the West. During the same period slight changes to the Waterloo-Bournemouth service included the addition of a Clapham Junction stop for the semi-fasts with the 1986/7 timetable, and Southampton Airport added to the fasts in the same winter.

Work on the electrification scheme proceeded quickly and by April 1987 stacks of third rail insulators at Weymouth, Dorchester and other places were a sign that progress was being made. A start was also made on various station improvements along the line, Branksome, Parkstone, and Hamworthy Junction were renovated and painted, as were the listed buildings at Wareham. Other improvements included a £653,000 facelift to the 1960s up side buildings at Southampton Central, including an enlarged ticket hall with a travel centre.

South of Dorchester Junction the construction of the Dorchester bypass required the provision of a bridge in the embankment, this work resulting in the complete closure of the line between Dorchester and Weymouth from the 4th to 11th April. During the same period improvements were carried out to Upwey & Broadwey including new platform shelters, new station access and provision of a car park. Historically this section of line was the first part of the former Great Western Railway (London Transport lines around Paddington excepted) ever to be worked by electric trains!

Between 11th and 15th May single line working over the up line was in operation between Hamworthy Junction and Wareham to facilitate tamping, joint welding and other works on the down line. The long disused signal box at Holton Heath was demolished on 12th May, other improvements there including a new entrance and shelters on both platforms.

Poole station, a building that could be best described as basically a pre-fab, was replaced by what was described as a 'Grand Marquee' style building. Work on reconstruction began on 7th October when the ticket office was transferred to a Portacabin in the car park, to allow demolition of the old station building.

Work continued on the preparations for electrification, the layout at Weymouth was reduced with most sidings being removed and on 19th September Weymouth's 1957-built signal box closed and the simplified layout was controlled from a new panel in Dorchester South box. During November a temporary down

Photographed on 24th May, 1988 two class '73' electro-diesels wait in the sidings at Bournemouth Central with a 'TC' set before proceeding to the up platform to receive the Weymouth portion of an up fast to Waterloo. At this time the class was employed to haul either 'TC' units or unpowered 'REP' units when their electrical equipment had been removed for incorporation in the new '442' electric units. *Author*

No. 73129 leads a pair of class '73' electro-diesels waiting to depart from Bournemouth Central with an up fast for Waterloo on 24th May, 1988. *Author*

platform constructed of scaffolding was erected at Wool to the east of the station to allow for the reconstruction and lengthening of the down platform.

Unfortunately, the delivery of the new stock and technical difficulties were to cause problems. It became clear that one of the reasons for the delay was the rundown of staff at the carriage works and there had to be a temporary halt to the 1,420 redundancies so more staff could be put on class '442' construction.

To enable the traction motors and other equipment to be removed from a number of REPs for use in the new class '442' units it would be necessary to use class '73' electro-diesels with reformed sets consisting of two '4TC' units, the 'FK' coach from one being removed and replaced by a buffet car from a 'filleted' 'REP' unit to maintain the buffet facilities. Recoded '4TCB' this combination lacked the power of a conventional 'REP' and to allow for this the timetable had been extended by seven minutes for the semi-fast service from 26th September, 1986.

Meanwhile along the line the various improvements were proceeding, it being reported in January 1988 that the new Poole station was 'taking shape', and in February the platform alterations at Wool were completed and the temporary down platform dismantled. By the end of the month the redundant down line between Moreton and Dorchester South had been recovered.

To mark the switching on of current to the Branksome-Weymouth section, a ceremony was held at Wareham station on 11th January, 1988 attended by the Southern Region General Manager Mr Gordon Pettitt and members of the junior section of the St Johns Ambulance Brigade (called Badgers), the current being switched on by one of their number. The first trial run with an electric unit took place on 1st February when units Nos. 1611 and 1621 with class '33' No. 33106 as back up ran through to Weymouth the third run the following day was carried out without the class '33'.

The temporary down platform at Wool during December 1987; constructed to the east of the station it was used during the lengthening of the station platform.   *Author*

Sunday 28th February saw the first passenger-carrying electric multiple unit (emu) working through to Weymouth when '4VEP' unit No. 3008 arrived with a down Bournemouth working, returning with the 12.51 pm from Weymouth. Delays in delivery resulted in the first unit No. 2401 not arriving at Bournemouth and running under its own power until 18th February, 1988, making its first visit to Weymouth with a crew-training run on 8th March. By mid-March only sets 2402 and 2403 had arrived, although without seats in order to facilitate the crew-training programme.

Despite the delay in the delivery of new units which threatened the commencement of the new service, an open day was held at Branksome depot on 24th March when various locomotives were on display including one of the completed '442' units. In the circumstances it was a brave to attempt a highly publicised record breaking run between Waterloo and Weymouth on 14th April. Units 2401 and 2403 broke the record completing a non-stop run in 1 hour 59 minutes 24 seconds for the 142¾ miles, with 109 mph being recorded between Woking and Basingstoke and between Worting Junction and Winchester. It was also a speed record for third rail pick-up, the invited guests only being carried in unit 2401, as 2403 had still not had all the seats fitted!

Whilst the new railway was being introduced, the old order put in an appearance on 3rd April with a railtour organized by the Plymouth Railway Circle using a 3-car and a 2-car Western Region dmu visiting the Weymouth Harbour Tramway, the Swanage branch as far as the oil terminal at Furzebrook, and the Hamworthy Goods branch.

A completely recast timetable had been published for the new service which was due to commence on 16th May, 1988, by which time only four of the 24 units had been delivered and were available for service. This resulted in the trailer units with pairs of class '73/1' electro-diesels hauling/propelling between Bournemouth and Waterloo with a shuttle service of older emus between Weymouth and Bournemouth. Instead of shaving 17 minutes off the service passengers were now arriving up to 30 minutes late, and at times the connection was not held at Bournemouth in the up direction causing further extension of journey times. By the end of May only six units were available, increasing to eight six weeks later, gradually units arrived until the complete fleet was available by the following February.

Unfortunately as the new units entered service there were irritating problems mainly with the automatically controlled plug type doors. As public discontentment mounted over the service the class '442' units quickly gained a nickname amongst staff, 'Plastic Pigs', Pig standing for 'personal inconvenience guaranteed', and small lapel badges of pigs appeared on some staff uniforms. So embarrassed were management that it became a disciplinary offence to either refer to the units as 'Pigs' or display the badge. However, mud sticks and to this day many enthusiasts still refer to the '442' units as 'Pigs'!

However, their introduction saw a vast improvement over the previous arrangements: a 12-coach 'REP'/'TC' combination was 265 yds long and had 471 second class and 108 first class seats, whereas two '442' units in multiple was 251 yds long with 596 second class and 100 first class seats. Over the Bournemouth-Weymouth section a single '4TC' unit could only accommodate 160 second class and 42 first class passengers, whereas a five coach '442' unit had 248 second class and 50 first class seats. Not only had seating capacity risen but so had inflation; when the line was first electrified 21 years previously the first class return fare between Bournemouth and Waterloo was £4 8s., by 1988 it had risen to £43.10.

Although electrification of the line through to Weymouth was to provide an improved service, there were several disadvantages, firstly, the loss of the South Western TPO, a service dating back to July 1876, the last up postal train departing at 10.13 pm on 14th May 1988.

Secondly, the electrification of the section between Bournemouth and Weymouth had been carried out on a limited budget resulting in a limited power supply. Although 12-coach trains can work as far as Poole, the maximum load west thereof is eight coaches which effectively means only a five-coach '442' unit can form a single train. Between Wareham and Weymouth the number of electric units in the electrical power section at any one time must not exceed four, although this can be stretched to five in exceptional circumstances. There are also delay problems with the single line section between Moreton and Dorchester when trains do not adhere to the timetable.

The construction of the new station at Poole had not proceeded without problems, by September 1988 the new buildings were virtually complete but British Rail refused to accept them owing to structural defects. This had not been resolved in November when problems were still being experienced with leaking roofs and public access doors. At Bournemouth the subway that had been closed to the public when a footbridge was provided during the original electrification works was reopened in July 1988, mainly to ease the work of Post Office and Travellers Fare staff.

Although no work had yet taken place to restore Bournemouth Central station, 11 years after it was first conceived a new £1.25 million coach and bus interchange situated on the down side of Bournemouth station, on the site of a former laundry and St Paul's church, was officially opened on 23rd November, 1988. Included in the development was a supermarket, a multi-storey car park and associated road improvements, the completed works giving a fresh outlook to the previous rather cluttered approach road.

The opening of a siding to serve the expanding industrial estate that was developing on the site of the former Cordite factory at Holton Heath was looked upon as a move towards generating goods traffic on the lower part of the Weymouth line. Served by a trailing connection off the up line released by Wareham signal box, it came into use on 7th November, 1988. Sadly within months it was to be the scene of a tragic accident involving a goods train that had just called at the siding and a light engine travelling towards Bournemouth.

Just after midday on Thursday 20th April, 1989 electro-diesel No. 73002 had just completed shunting the siding and after the guard had closed the ground frame the train had just begun to move towards Hamworthy when the rear wagon, a 'VAA' van loaded with bagged and palletised clay, was struck by class '33' No. 33107 travelling at an estimated speed of 60 mph, killing its driver. An inspection of the severely-damaged cab revealed that the controller was in the off position and the driver's brake valve was in the emergency application position. It appears that the driver had attempted to escape from the cab and was thrown from either the cab doorway or off the steps, as his body was found lying in the cess.

Class '47' No. 47246 attempted to gain access to the non-existent Bournemouth West through the stop blocks on 12th December, 1985, an event witnessed by the driver and passengers of a passing bus. *M. Thresh*

A head-on view of No. 47246 later in the day, with the locomotive firmly planted over the stop blocks as the men in hi-vis jackets and white helmets decide on the next move. *M. Thresh*

Clearance began as soon as the Eastleigh breadown train arrived, the engine of which pulled No. 33107 away from the damaged wagons, which No. 73002 then slowly hauled to sidings at Hamworthy as an out of gauge load owing to the damage to the rear wagon. The damage to No. 33107 resulted in the locomotive subsequently being withdrawn from service. The accident occurred 'because of a series of failures in the application of operating procedures' by the guard and driver of the freight train and the Wareham signalman. The driver of the light engine, tragically killed, was blameless.

Whereas Bournemouth West had in past years been the scene of a number of runaways, there were still minor incidents at Bournemouth carriage sidings involving the headshunt that formerly led to the station. Two of the most serious were when class '47' No. 47246 ran through the stop blocks onto the ground beyond on 12th December, 1985, to be followed in September 1989 by a class '442' unit with spectacular results.

As the decade closed the changing policy of British Rail towards its workshops saw the closure of Redbridge Civil Engineers works as from 3rd March, 1989, after having supplied track and pointwork to the LSWR and its successors for over 100 years.

By the spring of 1990 the deteriorating state of Bournemouth station was causing concern. With permission recently refused for the station's demolition to protect passengers from the possibility of injury from falling glass in the overall roof, a temporary 'ceiling' suspended from the roof girders was erected which would remain in place until funds could be allocated for the restoration of the station.

The oil traffic from the Furzebrook terminal was drastically reduced with the opening of a pipeline to the refinery. This resulted in the final oil trains running at the end of June 1990, it being recorded that 4,500 oil trains had left the branch in the past 11 years. By the autumn liquid petroleum gas tanks had taken their place, running a service between Furzebrook and Hallen Marsh, near Bristol. However, this new working was not without public concern owing to the nature of the traffic.

The first visit of a High Speed Train (HST) west of Bournemouth took place on 17th November, 1990 with a demonstration run as the 8.15 am Birmingham-Weymouth and the 3.45 pm return working, the power cars being Nos. 43010 *TSW Today* and 43188 *City of Plymouth*. This was a forerunner to the gradual introduction of these trains on summer services from Poole and Bournemouth to the North of England and Scotland the following summer, when the 'Dorset Scot' the 8.40 am Poole-Edinburgh commenced on 8th July, 1991. The 10.40 am Edinburgh-Poole was the return working, after which the unit would proceed via Reading to Old Oak Common for servicing. The first working of the Saturday-only 6.55 am Aberdeen-Weymouth service, which was at the time the longest station-to-station run on the British Rail network, just failed to reach the south coast resort on Saturday 13th July, it having been terminated at Dorchester South owing to a failed power car. However, the following week on 22nd July the first timetabled HST left Weymouth for Edinburgh with power cars Nos. 43071 and 43155 *BBC Look North*. These services were short-lived, the Weymouth extensions not running the following summer, although from

During 1988 an unidentified class '47' passes through Wareham station with an up oil train of high capacity bogie tank wagons from Furzebrook oil terminal on the Swanage branch.

J.E.R. Jackson

Hamworthy Goods photographed in April 1990 showing the changes: the land to the left behind the fence has been reclaimed to form the new ferry terminal and the original 1847 station building has been demolished. Class '09' diesel shunter No. 09025 waits its next move as a pair of class '20s' arrive with the annual weed-killing train.   *L.N. Thomas*

Bournemouth the 11.19 am 'Wessex Scot' continued to serve both Edinburgh and Glasgow, as did the 12.19 pm 'Dorset Scot'. Eight Inter-City services continued to serve Bournemouth daily, although the overnight Scottish sleeper to and from Poole was discontinued after 8th May 1992.

Early in 1992, with British Rail being prepared for privatisation and loss-making sections coming under scrutiny, it was announced that the Hamworthy Goods branch would close from 31st March. However, the Poole Harbour Commissioners assisted by Poole shipping agents John Carter Ltd negotiated an arrangement with British Rail whereby the rail track to the new quay below the level crossing into the ferry terminal would be the responsibility of the Commissioners who would also load wagons and provide a diesel shunter. Thus on 8th May class '09' diesel shunter No. 09025 performed the last British Rail shunting duties on the branch, the Commissioners having hired a shunter until a suitable machine could be purchased. With a reduction of trains from five to two a week hauled by more powerful locomotives and a reduction of staff, Dorset's oldest branch line was saved!

Between 1990 and 1994 a repatriated Stanier '8F' steam locomotive underwent restoration in the former Blue Circle cement siding at Hamworthy Junction. Built as WD No. 348 in 1940 it ran as LMS No. 8274 until shipped to Turkey towards the end of 1941, later becoming Turkish State Railways No. 45160 until repatriated in 1989. In the summer of 1992 four former British Rail class '20' diesel locomotives purchased by the French Railway Company Chemin de fer Departementaux travelled to their new home via Hamworthy and the Poole-Cherbourg Ro-Ro ferry. Later body shells for London Underground and the Irish Railways were shipped into Hamworthy for transportation by road.

The running of steam specials over the third rail had been taboo, until history was made on 11th September, 1992 when Bullied Light Pacific No. 34027 *Taw Valley* departed from Waterloo at 8 pm, with stops at Basingstoke and Southampton. Upon arrival at Bournemouth, the special returned behind class '33' No. 33102, whilst No. 34027 proceeded light engine to Bournemouth depot for exhibition at the depot open day. Although the journey had been made in the evening, no doubt to deter line side photographers, it was the first time in 25 years that a steam engine had made the journey. This was to be followed on the 13th November by *Taw Valley* working a steam special out of Weymouth, the first since the end of steam traction in July 1967.

During the summer of 1993 the site of Redbridge works was advertised for sale as Redbridge Wharf, 44 acres for industrial/warehouse use. Further west at Totton, the removal in December of the points connecting Eling Wharf with the main line ended a rail connection that had existed for 142 years.

The 1993 Transport Act, which came into force on 1st April, 1994, involved huge changes in railway management, far too complex to fully explain in this work. Suffice it to say that the system was broken up. The track, signalling and infrastructure became 'Railtrack', whilst both passenger and freight train operations were sold off to train operating companies. Put simply, the train operating companies would pay access charges to run their trains over the Railtrack system.

Although the railways had always employed contractors for major civil engineering works and the building of stations and bridges, this was now to be taken much further with both track and signalling maintenance being put out to contract. Ironically, but unsuccessfully, John Major the Conservative Prime Minister had considered a return to the pre-1948 'Big Four' as a method of privatisation; unfortunately this idea was not pursued, resulting in fragmentation of the system.

In due course the various sectors were privatised, the Waterloo-Weymouth line was part of a seven-year franchise awarded to Stagecoach Holdings Ltd to operate as South West Trains from Sunday 4th February, 1996. The first private train since 31st December, 1947 was the 5.10 am Twickenham-Waterloo formed with unit No. 5871. On 7th February the first unit appearing in Stagecoach colours was No. 2402 forming the leading unit of the 5.15 pm Waterloo-Weymouth service. The remaining freight services along the Southampton-Weymouth line were worked by English, Welsh and Scottish Railways (EWS), a company owned by the American Wisconsin Railway Group.

At Redbridge the site of the former civil engineering works had been acquired by Associated British Ports during 1994 and was cleared and levelled by the summer of the following year. Additional traffic was brought to Hamworthy Junction from 2nd July, 1997 when regular stone traffic from Merehead for the Puddletown bypass began arriving at the former cement siding. This traffic, continued until December 1998, with, from July 1998, scrap steel loading outwards from the former cement siding bolstering freight revenue. Army traffic made a return to Wool on 8th May, 1998, this time using the remaining siding situated behind the up platform. February 1999 saw the timber footbridge at Ashurst replaced by a new structure, and renovation work undertaken on the station house.

The dilapidated state of Bournemouth Central station was not helped by the 'Great Hurricane' of 16th October, 1987, which caused extensive damage, smashing much of the remaining glass in the roof and damaging the sheeting forming the end screens, after which a scaffolding umbrella was erected over the platforms to protect passengers from the possibility of falling debris. So it was not before time when work commenced early in 1999 on the £6.7m restoration scheme for the station. The 18-month project carried out by Keir Rail covered a variety of work to restore much that had fallen into decay. The principal part was to restore the 12 massive riveted wrought-iron trusses supporting the overall roof, by removing the existing covering and shot-blasting the ironwork cleaning and replacing any if found necessary and then re-glazing the roof and replacing the glazed end screens. There were also 6,000 square metres of brickwork to restore. With a busy station that handled 1.7 million passengers a year any form of closure was not an option. To protect the running lines and the platforms during the work a series of short 'Possessions' allowed the erection of a 3,133 square metre crash-deck above the platforms supported by scaffolding, to enable the work to proceed to restore this Victorian masterpiece to its former glory.

Before bringing our story right up to date, we will look at some methods of train operation in the past and more recently, at signalling and at the architecture and infrastructure along the route.

Chapter Nine

Railmotors and Push-Pull Working

For almost 60 years push-pull trains were a feature of train working across the area. Although in official documentation for many years it was referred to as 'Pull-Push', with the passage of time the term 'Push-Pull' became generally used in both official railway circles and, it would appear, always by enthusiasts. Following the unsuccessful expedition into steam rail motors and the early lightweight push-pull locomotives, the 'M7' class 0-4-4 tanks were to become synonymous with the Lymington and Swanage branches, and the Ringwood-Christchurch branch until its early demise. They also operated around the Old Road and other local services radiating from Bournemouth shed, which was responsible for their operation, and that of the Lymington branch after January 1934 when its working was transferred from Eastleigh to Bournemouth.

Although the operation of a push-pull train travelling sedately through the countryside may appear simplistic, its operation was complex as was its history and development. It also required an experienced crew, in particular the fireman who had to be capable of being left in sole charge of the locomotive when propelling and able to respond very quickly to any unforeseen emergency. Therefore a brief outline of push-pull development and operation is not out of place in the history of an area they served well.

The first to appear were the steam railmotors originally introduced to counteract the threat of urban tram services. Apart from the two Joint company railmotors built for the Fratton-Southsea branch, the first railmotors built by the LSWR were Nos. 1 and 2 of the 'H12' class constructed during 1904. After running in and modifications they were sent for trials around the Bournemouth area during the middle of August, which were reported to have been successful, before taking up service on the Bishops Waltham branch in the October. No. 2 returned to Bournemouth in February 1907, usually employed on the New Milton service until its departure in December 1912.

Convinced that steam railmotors could successfully operate many branch services, a further order was placed for 13 cars. However, these 'H13' class railmotors were of a more pleasing outline having the boiler and engine unit enclosed within the coachwork, which followed the general design of LSWR stock of the period, whereas the two earlier cars had the business end enclosed in what could only be described as a steel box! Cars Nos. 3 and 4 commenced to operate the Poole-Bournemouth-Christchurch service on 5th November, 1905, and cars Nos. 9 and 10 took up the Bournemouth Central-New Milton service, which included the occasional trip to Ringwood via Hurn, from 1st March, 1906. However, there was a continual interchange of cars owing to mechanical failures and visits to works. For example car No. 4 spent the winter of 1906/7 in store at Bournemouth before transfer in March 1907. Car No. 7 served at Bournemouth between early 1907 and December 1912, and during the summer of 1913 Nos. 3, 8 and 13 were employed in the Bournemouth area and No. 10 operated on the Lymington branch in September 1914; by mid-1915 Nos. 9, 12 and 13 were at Bournemouth.

The prototype 'H13' class steam railmotor No. 3 runs into Boscombe station with a Poole-Bournemouth-Christchurch service *circa* 1906. The bodywork including that around the boiler section was in keeping with the carriage outline of the period and painted in the salmon pink and brown livery which was also extended around the ends of the vehicle.

C.L. Caddy Collection

Class 'H13' LSWR steam railmotor No. 3 in the cutting through Talbot Woods, Bournemouth on 30th June, 1908. In the foreground the Gas Works Junction distant signal is off for the Bournemouth West curve.

R. Smith Collection

A poor quality image of an unidentified 'H13' steam railmotor stands at Meyrick Park Halt. Although undated the fact that it appears to be a posed photograph would suggest that it was taken around the time of the halt's opening in March 1906.   *M. Thresh Collection*

Their temperamental nature and wartime traffic levels being far beyond their capacity led to their withdrawal, and with the power units removed the cars were all converted into push-pull trailer cars, thus ending the London & South Western's brief flirtation with steam railmotors. Ironically, the boilers from units 3, 4, and 10 ended their days heating the Bournemouth Corporation greenhouses!

The next development came in 1906 when the LSWR introduced its first push-pull trains with specially designed 'C14' class 2-2-0 tanks Nos. 736-745 to work with pairs of 48 ft trailers. Nos. 737, 738 and 739 were recorded as working both the Bournemouth Central-New Milton and the Poole-Bournemouth Central-Christchurch services and No. 744 the Lymington branch in May 1907, and in the autumn of 1911 Nos. 737, 743 and 745 were employed in the Bournemouth area. Although giving a better performance than the steam railcars they were still under normal conditions incapable of hauling two trailers. They were shortly afterwards withdrawn and placed on light shunting duties (one was recorded as working at Dorchester), whilst others were set aside.

However, in March 1915 Nos. 741 and 745 were returned to traffic for the conveyance of workmen between Bournemouth West and Holton Heath where a cordite factory was being built. Of the 10 members of the class seven were sold out of service whilst Nos. 741, 744 and 745, having been rebuilt as 0-4-0 tanks, were retained, the former two shunting Southampton Town Quay until 1957 and the latter as No. 77S was employed as Redbridge sleeper works shunter until 1959.

Drummond 'M7' class 0-4-4 No.110 heads away from Ringwood station with the 2.49 pm Ringwood-Brockenhurst service on Saturday 10th September, 1927 after having been shunted to allow the 1.50 pm Swanage-Waterloo express to pass. The wire and pulley control gear is just visible on the roof of the locomotive. The two coaches are half a former LSWR four-coach bogie block set, a number of which were split up and converted to push-pull operation.

R.J. Harvey Collection

Push-pull set No. 28, formerly half of an LSWR four-coach bogie block set, emerges from Crow Arch bridge, Ringwood with a Brockenhurst-Bournemouth West service on 10th September, 1927. Apart from converting the end of the guard's van into a driving control trailer and the fitting of conventional buffers to the other end of the set, very little other work was required to form these units. Set No. 28 ran in this form from December 1926 until withdrawn in August 1939.

R.J. Harvey Collection

Drummond 'S14' class 0-4-0 No. 147 stands with a two-car vestibule gate set on the Hurn branch at Christchurch with the original Christchurch station in the background No. 147 was constructed in October 1910 and together with sister engine No. 101 often worked the Bournemouth West-New Milton service, although the location and lack of people would suggest this was an official photograph. No. 147 was sold to the Ministry of Munitions in May 1917, and after later use by a contractor was shipped out to Basra in 1927 for use by the Anglo Iranian Oil Company. *South Western Magazine*

The failings of the 'C14' class resulted in the development of the slightly larger 'S14' class during 1910. Originally five locomotives were to be constructed, but by this time the use of such small locomotives had fallen from favour resulting in only two actually being built, Nos. 101 and 147.

Again, both were found incapable of hauling two trailers on either the Seaton or Portland branches, but could manage two fully-loaded trailers on the easier graded Lymington branch and on the Bournemouth West-New Milton service. The Lymington branch reverted to conventional operation in early 1911, leaving the New Milton service their sole duty until the locomotives were put into departmental use during mid-1914 and sold three years later.

By 1912 it was realised that neither the steam railmotors nor the small push-pull units were entirely satisfactory for the work intended. The former also had the drawback that the entire unit had to visit the engine shed, an environment not conducive for coaching stock, also attention to the power unit placed the entire vehicle out of service. Neither had sufficient power to haul additional vehicles at busy periods resulting in ordinary train working being resorted to. Therefore it was decided that conventional tank locomotives with their greater reserve of power and flexibility would perform future push-pull operations.

In June 1912 a series of tests were conducted with 'M7' class 0-4-4 tank No. 481 over various lines including the Lymington and Swanage branches and between Bournemouth Central and New Milton, also along the main line between Southampton and Weymouth. Various combinations, including propelling six coaches and having up to three coaches each side of the engine, were carried out. It was concluded that three coaches was the maximum that could be propelled safely, no doubt on account of the wire and pulley control arrangements, and the idea of propelling coaches in front of the locomotive was abandoned.

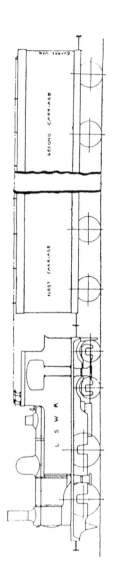

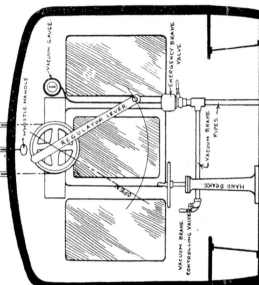

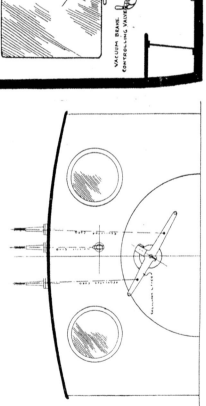

A diagram published in the March 1916 *South Western Magazine* of the LSWR three-wire push-pull control gear as used between 1906 and 1930, a very basic ineffective system that survived for 24 years.

END VIEW OF GUARDS VAN

END VIEW OF ENGINE CAB

The trials having been successful, a number of 'M7s', 'O2s', 'T1s' and '0415' class engines were equipped for push-pull working. 'M7s' Nos. 21, 109 and 667 were sent to Bournemouth to operate the Bournemouth Central-New Milton service, and push-pull working also appeared at times on the Lymington branch where 'T1' class 0-4-4 tanks Nos. 11 and 18 were noted during the spring of 1918.

The control of all the push-pull trains was by the wire and pulley system. This consisted of a regulator facing downwards mounted on the front bulkhead of the driving trailer to which was attached a drum around which the wire was wound, the wire entering and leaving the compartment through holes in the roof then via pulleys, guides, and connectors along the carriage roof to the roof of the locomotive cab, then via pulleys to a second drum attached to the regulator. Thus by the driver manipulating the regulator in the driving trailer the wire was both pulled in and paid out to operate the regulator on the locomotive. However, it required accurate adjustment of the various connectors and no doubt assistance of the fireman in its operation, and doubtless there were times when, like with the SECR rod system, it was unofficially disconnected with the fireman working the regulator at a given signal!

Other controls consisted of a third wire to work the locomotive whistle, a vacuum brake valve and an electric bell circuit to signal between the trailer and locomotive. The fireman had to notch up the reversing gear and work the locomotive stream brakes and also release the vacuum brake after the driver had made an application. In addition to his normal duties of looking after the fire and water level he also had to keep a good lookout and be prepared to take full control in the event of the push-pull equipment failing to operate. Indeed there were reports of a number of malfunctions, as there had been with the SECR rod-operated system. In March 1929 the Rolling Stock Committee recommended that this rudimentary method of control be abandoned and the compressed air control system, already employed on the former Brighton section, be fitted to all push-pull units.

These more complex arrangements required the locomotive to be equipped with a Westinghouse steam air pump, air reservoir, and an operating cylinder, which via linkage operated the locomotive regulator. Control of these arrangements was carried to the cab of the driving trailer via pipe work and three hose connections, back pressure, main storage, and regulator control, a miniature regulator in the driving trailer cab controlling the air operating cylinder on the locomotive either opening or closing the regulator. Other controls consisted of a vacuum brake valve, an electric bell circuit and a whistle operated by compressor air which was fitted to the outside of the driving trailer cab. On the locomotive the firemen carried out the duties as required for the previous system.

Conversion to the air system took place during 1930, the first air-equipped 'M7s' Nos. 21, 27, 45, 47, 49, 50, 51, 56 and 59 arriving at Bournemouth between July and October to operate the Old Road, Bournemouth-Christchurch-Ringwood, and the Swanage branches, whilst Nos. 57 and 60 allocated to Eastleigh served the Lymington branch.

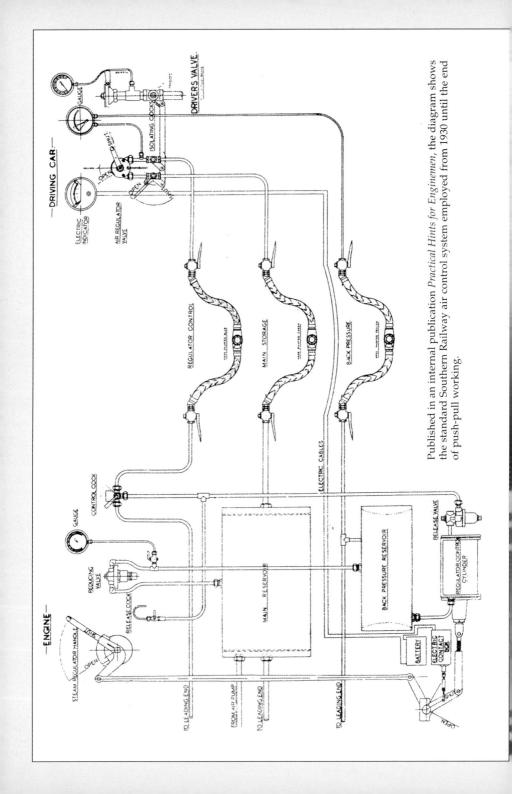

Published in an internal publication *Practical Hints for Enginemen*, the diagram shows the standard Southern Railway air control system employed from 1930 until the end of push-pull working.

Drummond push-pull fitted 'M7' class No. 30106 stands at Bournemouth West with a push-pull train during the early 1950s, the air pump and regulator control gear are clearly shown above and behind the front splasher. The coach next to the engine is a 58 ft rebuilt brake third with seven compartments and short brake van with a pressed-steel lookout fitted. *Author's Collection*

Rolling Stock

Only the stock to operate with the 'C14' and 'S14' locomotives was especially constructed as push-pull sets. Internally the large windows with curtains and the open saloon with the majority of the seats of moulded plywood were as those of the steam railmotors, both types in general, although roomier, giving the impression of the modern tramcars of the period! Also a feature of both types was the central transverse entrance vestibule equipped with Bostwick-type folding lattice gates. However, these fittings, a cut-down version of those once popular with lifts in hotels, department stores and other buildings, were prone to trapped fingers and clothing and were later replaced by an ornamental 'garden gate'. In general following the introduction of later push-pull stock the 'Gate Sets' mainly operated in the West Country and two sets on the Portland branch (until 1941). The final gate set No. 373 survived until October 1960, having made a brief appearance on the Swanage branch during its final summer.

Further expansion of push-pull working required additional vehicles, these being obtained by converting existing stock, a practice that continued until the end of push-pull operation. This was first accomplished in 1915 with the splitting of LSWR four-coach bogie block sets into two-coach units, the brake ends being converted into driving trailer cabs with conventional buffers and draw gear fitted at the other end; the first sets so converted were intended for service in the London area. In 1922 set No. 12B was split to form two push-pull sets for the Swanage branch. However, after a short while both the trailer brake thirds were reduced from seven to six compartments to allow extra luggage space. Further block trains were converted but whereas the earlier sets retained their guard's lookout duckets in the brake ends, those converted by the Southern Railway had theirs removed forming a more pleasing outline to the trailer end.

During the 1930s a number of the earlier conversions were withdrawn and further adapted stock added to the pool of push-pull sets, such units were sets 1, 3, 4, 6, 31, 35 and 36, all of which worked in the Bournemouth area. All six were produced from LSWR stock, the driving trailer being former 56 ft coaches whilst the non driving trailers were 48 ft seven-compartment lavatory brake thirds, lengthened and mounted on 58 ft standard Southern Railway underframes. However, wear and tear took its toll, resulting in the driving trailer of set No. 31 being replaced by a former SECR 60 ft brake third No. 3474 during 1951, and unfortunately the set was withdrawn in March 1959 following damage at Bournemouth Central. Other replacements included the non-driving trailer No. 4749 in set No. 36 being replaced by No. 4752, a 60 ft all-third of SECR origin in June 1957. This gave the set to give a further two years' service before withdrawal, and in May 1958 non-driving trailer No. 2612 of set No. 6 was replaced by No. 1103, also a 60 ft all-third of SECR origin.

Except for the replacements mentioned above, in general the push-pull stock of the pre-Grouping companies usually remained on their former territory. However, in September 1950 former SECR 60 ft coaches Nos. 3546 and 5503 were removed from 3-set No. 637 and converted into push-pull set No. 662, based at Eastleigh as a Western Section relief set often working Bournemouth area services in the red livery that many sets were painted at that period. In late 1961 set 662 was transferred to Tunbridge Wells, and when withdrawn the following May was the last push-pull set formed from ex-SECR stock in service.

For a number of years strengthening coaches had been used on both the Lymington and Swanage branches. Equipped with push-pull connections and pipework the extra coach was marshalled between the engine and the two-car push-pull set (three coaches being the maximum allowed to be propelled).

Between late 1913 and the end of 1915 a two-coach arc roof set was converted for push-pull operation on the Lee-on-Solent branch. No. 375, the only arc-roof set on the LSWR, eluded photographers until this one appeared of it standing at Broadstone Junction with a train from the Hamworthy direction in about 1924. *South Western Circle/Eyers Collection*

At various times the service was not run in push-pull mode. One such occasion was in August 1958 when non push-pull fitted Drummond class 'M7' No. 30127 was in charge of an Old Road train near Oakley Crossing. *J.W.T. House/C.L.Caddy Collection*

About 1944 the earlier coaches were replaced by two former SECR 10-compartment 60 ft thirds Nos. 1093 and 1098, their 100-seat capacity proving useful at busy periods. No. 1093 survived until November 1961 and No. 1098 to December 1962, the latter is today preserved on the Bluebell Railway. In later years three Maunsell open thirds Nos. 1331, 1342 and 1343 were converted as replacements.

A noted feature of the Bournemouth West-Wimborne-Ringwood-Brockenhurst push-pull trains was the luggage van inserted between the locomotive and the coaches, often referred to as a 'Pram Van'. Five former SECR utility vans Nos. 2001/2/4/5 were converted by the fitting of through Westinghouse pipes and other equipment in August 1939 for use on the Old Road and other Southern Railway branches. These five vans were the last pre-Grouping vans in ordinary traffic when they were withdrawn in 1962, to be replaced by plywood-bodied vans Nos. 1621-1625 built in 1950. However, by the time of conversion their use was virtually restricted to the Old Road, and following its closure the push-pull fittings were removed and the vans returned to normal traffic.

To replace older stock, during 1949 Ironclad two-car sets Nos. 381-384 were converted into push-pull sets. Both coaches had their corridor connections removed with the brake thirds having their luggage compartments reduced by the construction of an additional seating compartment. The toilet was also removed and this space at the end of the coach converted into a six seat coupé, with the brake end converted into a driving end fitted with four windows in groups of two. The composite brakes simply had both their toilet compartments converted into two-six seat coupés. Set No. 385 was converted to the same specification during 1962.

The reconstructed sets remained on the Western Section, although a certain amount of movement took place. Set 382 was noted on the Lymington branch during 1951 whilst set 385 was acting as a relief set at Bournemouth West in the summer of 1952. Following fire damage at Bournemouth West on 20th August, 1959, set No. 382 was the first to be withdrawn; the remaining sets were withdrawn in late 1962.

The family with the high pram gives a feeling of the period as Drummond 'M7' class No. 30058 propels a converted 'Ironclad' two-coach corridor set and utility van away from Wimborne with a Bournemouth West-Brockenhurst train in the early 1950s. Five 'Ironclad' two-coach sets were converted to push-pull operation during 1948 and 1949, pre-war they had been used as two-coach sets for through working of expresses on both the Lymington and Swanage branches.

Author's Collection

Looking every part the archetypal branch train Drummond 'M7' class No. 30052 has just passed under Ashley bridge west of Ringwood propelling a converted Maunsell push-pull set and utility van on a Brockenhurst-Bournemouth service during 1961. No. 30052 was constructed in December 1905 and converted to push-pull operation in July 1937 and withdrawn from service in May 1964.

J. Read

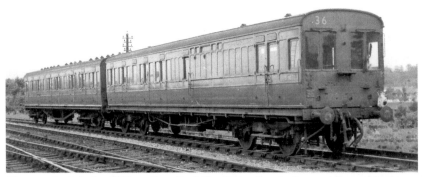

Photographed during 1958, push-pull set No. 36 standing in the up siding at Wimborne had been regularly employed in the Bournemouth area since conversion during 1939. In November 1956 the left-hand coach was rebuilt with an LSWR eight-compartment body fitted on a Southern Railway underframe and renumbered as No. 4752. The driving trailer No. 3070 was not rebuilt. it remained an LSWR five-compartment brake. The entire unit was withdrawn in June 1959.   *R. Smith Collection*

In June 1959 it was decided to replace the remaining wooden-panelled coaches, as these included a number of pre-Grouping vehicles employed on push-pull services. Twenty further push-pull sets were converted from 1935 Maunsell corridor stock taking set Nos. 600-619, each set consisting of a six-compartment brake composite and a seven-bay open third. These conversions were less complex than the previous 'Ironclads'. The toilet compartments were simply sealed; the gangways were retained between the coaches, only the end gangways being removed, with the brake compartment having two small windows emu-style fitted in the driving end. To complete the conversion large electric-stock pattern buffers were fitted to each end of the sets.

Originally the sets were distributed across the Southern Region where push-pull operation was in operation. However, there were a number of transfers of various sets, e.g. set 604, which was operating on the Hawkhurst branch in the summer of 1961, subsequently moved to Bournemouth. The introduction of diesel units, branch line closures, and the transfer of lines west of Salisbury to the Western Region caused many moves with the result that by the spring of 1964 the Old Road, and the Swanage and Lymington branches were the last push-pull services operated by the Southern Region. However, by that date a shortage of 'M7s' at Bournemouth often resulted in any locomotive available hauling push-pull sets on the Old Road.

Fortunately 'M7s' Nos. 30053 and 30480 were available to haul trains on the last day of operation of the Old Road on 2nd May, 1964, a fitting tribute to a class that had faithfully served the area for so many years, thus bringing an end to steam-operated push-pull working on the Southern Region. Ironically, several of the Maunsell push-pull sets remained working until the autumn on both the Swanage and Lymington branches hauled by Standard tanks, after which ordinary stock was employed until dieselisation.

'REP' unit No. 2003 waits to depart from Bournemouth Central with an up Waterloo stopping service on 24th May, 1988. Whilst working the 6.14 am Poole-Waterloo service on 12th December the same year No. 2003 was involved in the Clapham Junction disaster and subsequently withdrawn. *J.E.R. Jackson*

An undated photograph at Totton shows 'REP' unit No. 2004 with two 'TC' units in tow on an up stopping service easing past derailed tank wagons being attended to by the Eastleigh breakdown crane. *Peter (Hussey) Smith*

Chapter Ten

The Waterloo-Bournemouth-Weymouth Push-Pulls and the '442s'

The entire concept of the electric service between Waterloo and Bournemouth with the diesel haulage of trailer units onwards to Weymouth was a major step forward in railway operation, the first time that coaching stock had been propelled at high speed. Until that time push-pull working had been confined to steam operation with a limited number of coaches at low speeds mainly on branch and secondary routes. During the early 1960s the Southern Region had conducted experiments employing electric locomotives propelling electric units at speeds of up to 90 mph. The Ministry of Transport being fully satisfied with the results of the trials sanctioned its use in general service. It was also to break new ground for train operation by its flexibility of working with other electric units, electric and diesel-electric locomotives.

The hub of the system was 11 high-powered multiple units classed as '4REP' which consisted of two driving motor seconds, a buffet car and a brake first. There were 28 four-car trailer units classed as '4TC' consisting of two driving trailer seconds, a trailer brake second and a first class corridor, and three, three-car sets classified '3TC', these units not having the first class vehicle.

The diesel locomotives employed were a sub-class of 19 class '33/1' diesel-electrics, these, the 'REP' units and the 'TC' units all having control wiring to allow working in various formations.

The compatibility of the 'TC' sets, 'VEP' units and the class '33/1' diesel locomotives and the class '73' electro-diesels was demonstrated on many occasions, one being on 3rd April, 1993 when units 410 and 417 topped and tailed by electro-diesel No. 73019 and class '33/1' No. 33109 worked a special from Bournemouth to Weymouth, where after detaching the electro-diesel No. 33109 and the 'TC' sets made four trips over the Weymouth Harbour Tramway before rejoining the electro-diesel for the return to Bournemouth.

In everyday service the flexibility of class '33/1', 'TC stock' and '4VEP' units was demonstrated by the 5 pm Waterloo-Yeovil Junction service. Hauled by a class '33/1' with a '4TC' trailer unit, in rear of which was two '4VEP' units, the whole 3,550 hp being controlled from the '33/1', at Basingstoke the forward part would proceed to Yeovil, whilst the two '4VEP' units continued to Eastleigh.

A majority of the rolling stock for the scheme was a case of history repeating itself; the former Southern Railway had converted existing steam-hauled stock for both push-pull and for inclusion in electric multiple units. To this end the same principle was again applied, only the driving trailers for the '4REP' units being of new construction, the remaining 145 vehicles were converted from existing Mk I locomotive-hauled coaches which were already around 10 years old.

The 11 four-coach high-powered tractor units classed as 'REPs', Nos. 3001-3011, consisted of a power car each end designated driver motor second (DMS), a trailer restaurant buffet car (TRB) and a trailer brake first (TBF). The capacity of the DMS vehicles was 64 in 2+2 seating with a wide central gangway. The TRB had seating for 24 in a 2+1 arrangement whilst the TBF vehicle contained four first class

'TC' unit No. 8017 is propelled into Wareham station by push-pull fitted Crompton type '3' No. 33117 on 29th March, 1987. Although not yet energised the third rail is in position and the replacement of mechanical signals by colour lights had commenced. *C.L. Caddy*

Three car 'TC' unit No. 8104 is propelled out of Dorchester under Culliford Road bridge with an up fast. The train has just entered the single line section to Moreton, the line to the left is an engineer's siding and to the right are the disused loading docks that had proved invaluable in years past when the Bath & West show visited the town. *Author*

compartments seating three each side, other accommodation consisting of the guard's compartment and a security cage for parcels and luggage.

The driving trailers were of new construction to Mk I outline, however, that was where the similarity ended. Each Mk IV bogie carried two axle-suspended English Electric four-pole EE546/B traction motors of 385 amps, 675V and 320 hp. The resistance grids, air compressors and brake control gear was suspended from the underframes between the bogies. The heating of both the 'REP' sets and trailer stock consisted of two different systems, one for compartments the other for open saloons. The power for this on the 'TC' stock was supplied from the '4REP' set via jumper cables, and west of Bournemouth the power supply for both heating and lighting was provided by the class '33/1' locomotive.

The 'TRB' vehicles were existing restaurant/buffet cars refurbished with the kitchen equipment converted to electric operation, this being supplied by a motor-generator unit fitted to the underframes which were remounted on SR modified Mk V bogies. The finishing touch was the naming of each of these cars, the name being applied to a glass panel behind the serving counter.

The trailer brake first again were rebuilds from existing stock having previously been Mk I composite corridor vehicles, major rebuilding having taken place. The second class accommodation was completely removed and replaced by the guard's van area, whilst the first class compartments were refurbished, and the underframes mounted on SR Mk I bogies.

All the units had their vacuum brakes replaced by the Westinghouse air system, buckeye couplings, rubbing plates, retractable buffers, and the necessary wiring and control gear for multiple unit working fitted.

To operate in conjunction with the 'REP' tractor units, 28 '4TC' four-car trailer units Nos. 401-428 and three 3-car trailer units Nos. 301-303 were provided. All this stock was converted from existing BR Mk I vehicles; the four-car sets were formed with two driving trailer seconds (DTS), between which was a trailer brake second (TBS) and a trailer first corridor (TFK).

The driving trailer seconds were rebuilt from TSO vehicles and required the most alteration, the outer ends being fitted with a driving cab to the same design as the 'REP' units as was their interior layout. The trailer brake seconds were rebuilt from BSK vehicles and apart from refurbishment of the seating very little interior alteration was required; likewise apart from refurbishment there was very little alteration to the corridor first vehicles.

However, all the stock was fitted with SR 'B5' bogies and converted to air/EP braking, this along with other auxiliary equipment being mounted on the underframes. The air brake compressor which derived its power from either the 'REP' unit or diesel/electric locomotive was mounted under the trailer brake second. Again buckeye couplings, rubbing plates and retractable buffers were fitted, as were high-level air and electric connections. The three '3TC' units were identical except for the omission of the trailer first, and as with the 'REP' units the prototype of each was reconstructed at Eastleigh, the remainder of the rebuilds being carried out at York.

When introduced both the 'REP' units and the trailer sets were painted in all-over rail blue livery with early deliveries having just a small yellow warning panel on the end unit corridor connection door. This was quickly amended to

'REP' unit No. 3015 in the sidings at Bournemouth Central in August 1985. Having earlier arrived from Waterloo it will proceed to the top end of the up platform and wait for a 'TC' unit from Weymouth to be coupled on before returning to Waterloo.   *Author*

The operation of joining 'TC' unit No. 411 to the rear of a '4REP' set taking place at Bournemouth Central in April 1971. Having propelled the 'TC' unit from Weymouth the Crompton at the rear will next proceed to the down side of the station to wait the arrival of a down train and then haul its 'TC' unit to Weymouth.   *Author*

an all-over yellow end and within a few years all units received the standard blue/grey InterCity livery.

There was very little in the way of spare stock in the fleet to allow for failures. For the original service 10 'REP' units were required, this leaving one set to cover maintenance and failures, a very optimistic scheme where each unit was annually achieving 160,000 miles and the entire fleet was averaging 3.5 million miles per year. Each unit was covering 3½ daily round trips between Bournemouth and Waterloo averaging 700 miles at high speed, some duties saw a unit cover 756 miles in 17 hour 11 minutes of revenue earning service.

These punishing schedules, together with alterations to the service in 1974, gave a requirement for an additional four 'REP' units. Nos. 3012-3015 were constructed, the eight driving trailers being amongst the last Mk I coaches ever built, whilst the intermediate vehicles were again taken from existing stock, the four buffet cars being reconstructed from restaurant cars built originally by the Birmingham Carriage & Wagon Company. Again the three additional '4TC' units Nos. 432-434 were formed from reconstructed Mk I vehicles, as were the three trailer firsts which were added to the three existing '3TC' sets Nos. 301-303 to bring them up to '4TC'. The additional stock allowed the mileage of 'REP' units to be reduced to 141,000 annually.

Thus with additional stock the service was maintained with the distinctive whine of the 'REP' power units until the introduction of the Wessex Electrics (class '442') concluded an interesting chapter in Southern Region train working. However, it was not the end of the line for either the 'REP' or 'TC 'units, a number of 'REP' units were strengthened to '6REP' and for a few years covered various duties. As late as November and early December 1991 the remaining undiagrammed units were covering for a shortage of '442s' between Poole, Bournemouth and Waterloo. It was whilst working the 6.14 am Poole-Waterloo service on 12th December, 1988 that set No. 2003 hauling 'TC' sets Nos. 8015 and 8027 was involved in the Clapham Junction disaster and subsequently withdrawn, the final 'REP' unit being withdrawn in February 1992.

By virtue of their versatility a number of 'TC' trailer sets survived longer. One unit No. 417 was refurbished, fitted with fluorescent lighting and restored to all-blue livery to become part of the Network SouthEast tour train in company with unit No. 410. In later years with the withdrawal of a number of vehicles others were regrouped to form the remaining stock, and others were sold. Six vehicles including three driving trailers passed to the Dartmoor Railway at Okehampton. Eight were sold to London Underground early in 1992: consisting of four driving trailers, two BSK and two FK vehicles repainted in brown livery with red driving trailer ends they were employed in the 'Steam on the Met' events during 1992 and 1993.

Later four of the coaches, driving trailers Nos. 76298 and 76322, TK No. 70855 and TBSK No. 70824 which had been formed up as unit No. 413 were acquired by the 4TC Group with the ultimate plan to operate the unit with a class '33/1' on the Swanage Railway. However, at the time of writing the stock remains in storage. The remaining London Underground set, consisting of driving trailers 76297 and 76324, BSK 70823 and FK 71163, which had not seen operational service since 2001 was overhauled during 2007 and has since been used on

Non push-pull fitted Crompton type '3' No. D6551 in green livery heads a 'TC' unit in all-blue livery past Radipole on 1st July, 1967, days before the switch over to full push-pull operation on the Bournemouth-Weymouth section.   *C.L. Caddy*

Crompton class '33' No. 33103 propels a 'TC' unit out of Weymouth on 27th August, 1978. The unoccupied ballast in the right foreground was formerly the site of the up and down lines between Weymouth station and the GWR engine shed.   *D.M. Habgood*

special trains in conjunction with No. 12 *Sarah Siddons*, the preserved Metropolitan electric locomotive.

The locomotive selected to operate the push-pull section of the Waterloo-Weymouth service was already in service on the Southern Region; BRCW type '3s', later re-classed as the class '33' and had quickly gained the name 'Cromptons' from their Crompton Parkinson electrical equipment. The class of 98 were constructed by the Birmingham Railway Carriage & Wagon Co. of Smethwick. Originally numbered D6500-6585 and D6586-6597, the latter batch had bodies constructed to suit the narrower Hastings line loading gauge.

Powered by a Sulzer eight-cylinder 8LDA28 turbo-charged diesel engine with a continuous rating of 1,550 bhp at 750 rpm, driving a group of three Crompton Parkinson generators, the main generator gave a continuous rating of 1,012 kw and 1,760 amps at 750 rpm, a second generator producing 110 volts to supply locomotive equipment whilst the third generator produced 750 volts at 250 kw and 313 amps for train heating. Power from the main generator was supplied to the two four-wheeled bogies via four Crompton Parkinson C171C2 motors with a continuous rating of 305 hp at 580 volts and 440 amps; the two four-wheel bogies had a nose-suspended axle-hung motor for each axle. All were equipped with dual braking, both vacuum and Westinghouse, the engines themselves being air braked. All were with equipped electro-pneumatic multiple control equipment to enable one driver to control up to three locomotives coupled together.

The class made its first regular appearance in the area in July 1962 when 12 were allocated to Eastleigh to handle a number of general freight and oil train workings in the Southampton area, working both singly and in tandem, often working off the Southern Region. They were also employed on summer Saturday passenger workings between Waterloo and Bournemouth, and over both the Lymington and Swanage branches

With the planned Bournemouth electrification the feasibility of converting members of the class to push-pull working was considered, with No. D6580 modified during June 1965 to be followed by testing under various conditions before it was decided to convert a further 18 locomotives. The work was carried out at Eastleigh commencing with No. D6521 in November 1966 and concluding with No. D6528 a year later, all returning to service in the new Rail Blue livery except No. D6580 the prototype. This was the only push-pull Crompton to run in green livery until receiving further modifications in November 1967.

To enable the locomotives to carry out their new task a considerable number of modifications were involved: buckeye couplings and vestibule rubbing plates were fitted, as were retractable buffers, control jumpers and air pipe connections were fitted at high level. To control the locomotive from the driving trailer of a train it was propelling it was necessary to devise a control system, this consisted of a four position controller connected to a 'Westcode' transcoder which provided shunt, series, parallel and weak field, the commands translated via electro-pneumatic valves into different air pressures to run the engine at 430, 570, 720 and 750 rpm. Other refinements included a system whereby the engine could be both started and stopped from the trailer cab.

An unidentified push-pull fitted Crompton type '3' propels a '4TC' unit past the remains of the former Upwey Wishing Well halt into Bincombe South tunnel towards the end of the stiff climb out of Weymouth with an up train during April 1980. *Author's Collection*

Crompton class '33' No. 33108 approaches Weymouth with two '4TC' units, on a Waterloo-Weymouth service, on 29th May, 1982. The housing complex above the train (*far left*) was once the site of the GWR engine shed. *D.M. Habgood*

No. D6580 with 'TC' units undertook high-speed trials over the Bournemouth line during August 1966, by which time crew training had commenced with 'TC' units appearing at Weymouth. Training took until December when No. D6521 commenced the first push-pull operated service between Waterloo and Bournemouth, albeit to steam train timings, and with the arrival of more converted locomotives and stock the number of push-pull and other diesel workings increased.

From the commencement of the new service the '33/1s' (as they were later known) proved their worth. For the next 21 years they faithfully propelled and hauled 'TC' units between Bournemouth and Weymouth. Four members of the class were required daily to operate the service with eight intermediate stops in a 34¾ miles journey which took one hour. They never had any difficulty with either the climb out of Weymouth or Parkstone Bank with one or two 'TC' units (the latter giving a load of 264 tons), reliability was high and failures few.

Again their versatility often found them employed as in earlier days on Saturday extras over both the Lymington and Swanage branches but with 'TC' units in push-pull mode. Later the Clapham Junction-Kensington Olympia shuttle was added to their duties, as were a number of journeys between Waterloo and Salisbury, and between 1973 and 1987 they worked boat trains along the Weymouth Harbour Tramway. They also proved useful on railtours, in particular on branch lines where a '33/1' and a 'TC' set resolved any difficulties that would have occurred running-around conventional stock.

The class in general were to be seen on every conceivable type of passenger and freight working on both the Southern and other Regions, often far in excess of their original expectations, and were to be found working cross-country services from the Wessex area; they also found employment on selected Royal Trains, boat trains and other specials.

In 1973 the entire class had been renumbered into the '33/0' series, with sub-classes: '33/1' for those converted to push-pull operation and '33/2' for the Hastings line group. The 31st October, 1987 saw the first '33/1' member of the class named when at a ceremony at the reopened Templecombe station No. 33112 was named *Templecombe*. Between April and December 1988 No. 33114 received the name *Sultan*, and during its short period of glory propelled class '442' Wessex Electric No. 2413 from Southampton to Fareham on 28th July conveying the Minster of Transport and other guests to inaugurate the commencement of the Solent electrification scheme. Later the name was returned to the original holder, No. 33025.

A decline in services requiring the class '33s' had slowly taken place; with classified overhauls ceasing in May 1986 the run-down of the class was to follow. The electrification to Weymouth again reduced their workload, although they made appearances on summer Saturdays during 1988/9 with a working from Bournemouth to Weymouth then a round trip to Bristol before returning to Bournemouth. During the same period they also made a reappearance on short workings from Waterloo to both Salisbury and Yeovil Junction, and following problems with Sprinter diesel units the class returned in push-pull mode on Portsmouth-Bristol-Cardiff services in December 1988. Again the class came to the rescue between the 11th and 15th December, 1988

An unidentified push-pull fitted Crompton type '3' heads round the curve from Dorchester South past Dorchester Junction signal box to join the former GWR line for the remaining journey to Weymouth. The junction with the Western Region line in the foreground had been simplified to a simple ladder junction when this photograph was taken during in early 1986.

J.E.R. Jackson

During the final weeks of push-pull operation between Bournemouth and Weymouth a number of Crompton type '3' locomotives appeared with headboards '1967 Push Pull 1988'. No. 33113 pulls out of Bournemouth depot onto the down line at Branksome station to commence duties on 26th March, 1988. *D.M. Habgood*

Crompton class '33' No. 33119 propels a '4TC' unit forming the Weymouth section of a Weymouth-Bournemouth-Waterloo service on 14th May, 1988 between Spa Road bridge and Skew bridge at Radipole. *D.M. Habgood*

Crompton class '33' No. 33109 runs into Upwey with a down train on 22nd August, 1988. *D.M. Habgood*

A trio of push-pull fitted Crompton type '3s' wait in the up west siding at Southampton Central during engineering works in December 1980. The usefulness of the class in hauling electric units over non-electrified lines during engineering diversions cannot be over-emphasised, a facility sadly lacking on today's modern railway. *Author*

Class '442' 'Wessex Electric' No. 2409 approaches Parkstone station up the 1 in 60 incline from Poole on 31st March, 1997. The factory buildings shown to the right in earlier photographs have been replaced by apartment blocks. *J.D. Ward*

following a derailment at Parkstone when a push-pull service was operated over the up line.

A number were transferred outside the old Southern Region; by 1990 of the original 98 locomotives only 56 remained active. Further withdrawals and transfer to the Private sector took place, where their versatility kept them active.

A popular candidate for preservation, by late 2007 twenty-four had achieved such status. The Swanage Railway had two, Nos. 33034 and 33012, the latter hauled the last wagons off the Old Road on 3rd May, 1977. Now restored in green livery with her original number, D6515, she carries the name *Stan Symes* after the former Bournemouth driver. A number of the others have changed ownership several times and all are not in running condition. At the time of writing a small number of the class remain in the private sector certified to work on the rail network. One of the most successful smaller diesel-electric locomotives they have given over 40 years' service and will always be associated with the part they played in the Bournemouth electrification scheme.

The 1973 renumbering of the '33/1' sub-class fitted for push-pull working was:

33101	6511	33106	6519	33111	6528	33116	6535
33102	6513	33107	6520	33112	6529	33117	6536
33103	6514	33108	6521	33113	6531	33118	6538
33104	6516	33109	6525	33114	6532	33119	6580
33105	6517	33110	6527	33115	6533		

The stock provided to replace the 'REP'/push-pull arrangement with the electrification through to Weymouth was in itself unique. The 24 five-car units of the '442' class were a mixture of traditional traction equipment and the latest in coach design, and they were compatible for operation with both class '33/1' and class '73' locomotives. However, within 19 years they had become incompatible with any other stock in use on the Southern Region (and later South West Trains).

The Waterloo-Bournemouth-Weymouth line is not an InterCity route but owing to its length it required stock of that calibre as it carried a regular number of commuters together with a substantial amount of business travel between Waterloo and Southampton and beyond, also seasonal leisure traffic to the New Forest, the Bournemouth area and through to Weymouth. Therefore the quality of the stock had to be capable of retaining and enhancing this mix of traffic.

With electrification through to Weymouth it also allowed the provision of one class of stock for the entire route, a choice of which was to prove successful. Based around the BR Mk III bodyshell developed to its ultimate potential as an electric-multiple-unit, with its well formed rounded ends it was a stylish design that cut a dash as it effortlessly sped through the Wessex countryside. Although between April 1992 and December 2004 some units were employed on Waterloo-Portsmouth services, they were essentially designed for the Bournemouth line and warrant a detailed description.

Compared with previous Southern Region emu stock which had all been based around the Mk I carriage design, the '442' units were state of the art, adapting the basic 63 ft Mk III design recently employed for locomotive-hauled and HST stock. The most notable improvement, the first on British Rail, was the provision of electrically-operated plug type doors with individual press button operation, an over-ride operated from the guard's compartment allowing selective opening as a safeguard for any coaches not alongside a platform. A further safety device prevented the driver starting the train should any doors not be closed. Further refinements included electrically-operated vestibule doors at the gangway ends, full air-conditioning, and air bag suspension, whilst the braking was undertaken by electro-pneumatic disc brakes. Other innovations included a public address system operated from the guard's compartment, and a card-operated public telephone for passenger use.

Modifications had to be made to the existing body shell for the motor brake luggage vans, as there had to be sufficient strength to support the additional 15 tons of electrical equipment. This was obtained by using a design BREL had used when building generator vans for Iarnród Éireann (Irish Railways). The idea of placing all the power motors and associated equipment under one coach in an emu appeared unorthodox at the time, but it had been the system adopted by the former London Brighton & South Coast Railway for its overhead DC electric stock. Only the technology had improved, although one might be forgiven for thinking this was not completely the case: in a traditional British compromise to cut costs, traction motors and other control equipment were removed from the class '432' ('4REP') units and installed in the new power cars. Whereas the '4REPs' had eight English Electric type '456' 400 hp traction motors, only four were fitted to each of the new units giving a power output of 1,600 hp. Although this cascading of old equipment denied the new units the benefits of chopper control and other refinements, the used equipment was well proven, in good condition and estimated suitable for a further 20 years' service. No collector shoes were mounted under the motor coach, these were carried on the 1st, 4th, 7th and 10th bogies giving each trailer one shoe set each, power being fed to the motor coach via jumper cables. To provide power for auxiliary equipment including doors, lighting, air conditioning and buffet equipment, static converters to convert the 750 volt dc line current to 415 volt ac were mounted under the trailer seconds.

The formation of the units from the Waterloo end was driving trailer first class, trailer second class, motor buffet second class, trailer second class, and driving trailer second class, producing a combined weight of 199 tonnes with seating for 50 first class and 248 second class passengers.

The driving trailer first contained 7 x 2 sets of seats in open plan next to the driving cab and entrance doors, followed by six compartments of six seats, then a toilet and entrance doors, giving a total seating capacity for 50 first class passengers. The introduction of compartment seating was a breakaway from the standard Mk III layout but assisted the movement of passengers through the train during busy periods. Originally the 14 open plan seats were to be second-class accommodation, but during the building stage it was decided that this area would also be first class thus making the entire coach one class.

This was followed by a trailer second containing a mixture of seating for 80 passengers: on one side of the centre corridor 10 sets of 2 x 2 seats with facing tables, the other side having two blocks of 8 uni-directional seats facing the centre of the coach with two blocks of 2 x 2 seats with tables in the centre. Also on that side of the coach a toilet is situated at each end before the entrance vestibules.

The centre coach being the motor brake luggage second was originally designed with two compartments for luggage and parcels, one either side of the central guard's compartment. A 14-seat second class open compartment was situated at one end next to the entrance vestibule. Shortly after a number of units had been delivered it was decided that was required less space for parcels, resulting in a change of plan allowing the luggage compartment next to the buffet to be converted into a lounge with seats and tables, the two sets of luggage doors being replaced by windows. Sets that had been delivered earlier were modified between August 1988 and April the following year. Further seating was added between April 1997 and January 1999 when the remaining luggage space was reduced further allowing another 12 seats to be installed. Then between July 1999 and March 2001 an additional five seats were fitted into the buffet area.

Next came a further trailer coach except that two sets of unidirectional seats have been removed to provide space for a wheelchair, thus reducing the seating capacity to 76, although two tip-up seats are provided within the wheelchair space. The toilet at that end was suitably equipped for the disabled and fitted with a power-operated door.

Finally there was the driver trailer second, again with access doors behind the driving cab, with face to face 2 x 2 seating at the cab end followed by 2 x 2 uni-directional seating, a toilet and vestibule and entrance doors forming the inner end. Both driving trailers had styled driving cab ends fitted with corridor connections allowing access to an adjoining unit.

Following initial teething problems and subsequent minor improvements the class settled down and performed well. By the very nature of its third rail electric system and its massive commitments in the London area the Southern has always been able to adapt to its unique situation, the class '442' units being no exception to the rule. During their life they have undergone various modifications: in 1989 retention toilets replaced the conventional toilets; there were also four increases in seating capacity from their original design specification of 300 to 333 passengers per unit. They were also the last main line carriages in the country to retain compartments for first class passengers, and they served the Waterloo-Weymouth line well.

In January 2006 unit No. 442402 was the first to enter the Bombardier depot at Ilford to receive refurbishment, and by October 10 units had been dealt with. However, in the everchanging world of the franchised railway system the situation can change very quickly, it then being announced that the class would not form part of the new South West Trains franchise due to commence on 4th February, 2007. The '442' units would be withdrawn after 3rd February and be handed back to the leasing company Angel Trains, whose property they had been since 1st April, 1994.

The influx of Desiro '444' and '450' units had made the '442s' non-standard, as they were the last units (heritage stock excepted) with traditional buffers and buckeye couplings plus non-standard electrics and control equipment which prevented their use with other stock - although they had never had the universal choice of multiple-unit operation as did their predecessors.

As the new '444' class entered service the '442s' were withdrawn, the first '442' workings being taken over by class '444' units on 16th October, 2006. By Saturday 13th January, 2007, which was expected to be their final day, there were only 16 units remaining in service. However, owing to delays in the new stock entering service between four and six units continued in use.

During their final week units Nos. 2405/10/12/13/19 were noted mainly working Waterloo-Poole services, the 7.25 am Weymouth-Brockenhurst was also worked by members of the class on both 22nd and 24th January. The final day of operation, 3rd February, saw units Nos. 2405, 2410, and 2412 in service. The latter worked the South West Trains staff farewell tour from Waterloo to Windsor, Twickenham, and Shepperton before returning to Waterloo for the final working, the 9.05 pm Waterloo-Poole, thus bringing down the curtain on 19 years of Wessex Electric operation. Then with their future undecided a number went into storage at the former Eastleigh works.

The privatisation of the railways in 1996 had seen the units acquired by the train leasing company Angel Trains from whom South West Trains had leased them. Returned to the leasing company their future appeared in doubt owing to their incompatibility with anything else. In March 2007 announcements appeared in the railway press that a unit was to be leased to Hull Trains to be hauled by a EWS class '67' with a driving van trailer in the formation, to cover rolling stock shortages.

However, this scheme fell by the wayside, but interest was taken up (by train operating company Southern) for use on services on the Brighton line. At the time of writing 17 units are undergoing upgrading and driver training commenced on 9th June, 2008. At an auction on 14th June, 17 of the nameplates formerly carried by the class were sold raising £5,970, the proceeds going to the Naomi House Children's Hospice near Winchester.

Names of class '442' units

2401	Beaulieu	2413	(un-named)
2402	County of Hampshire	2414	(un-named)
2403	The New Forest	2415	Mary Rose
2404	Borough of Woking	2416	Mum in a Million 1997 - Doreen Scanlon
2405	City of Portsmouth	2417	Woking Homes
2406	Victory	2418	Wessex Cancer Trust
2407	Thomas Hardy	2419	BBC South Today
2408	County of Dorset	2420	City of Southampton
2409	Bournemouth Orchestras	2421	(un-named)
2410	Meridian Tonight	2422	Operation Overlord
2411	The Railway Children	2423	County of Surrey
2412	Special Olympics	2424	Gerry Newson

Chapter Eleven

The Evolution of Signalling along the Line

To describe fully the signalling and its history in the area covered by this work would require a volume in itself, therefore many details of alterations and additions to both signal boxes and associated equipment along the line have been described in the general text. However, a number of general points and other items of interest are covered in this chapter, in particular a description of early signalling, a subject much neglected in many books covering signalling history.

When the line to Dorchester first opened there had been few developments in signalling, there were few trains and speeds were slow, thus operating practices were extremely hazardous compared with modern railways. Yet there were few serious accidents and the railway was considerably safer than other forms of transport of the period.

The rules of signalling in 1845 were very basic, virtually involving the use of a revolving disc signal as shown below.

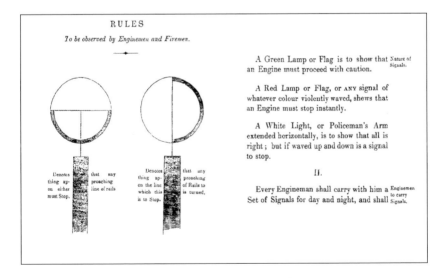

However, in 1848 it was found necessary to introduce auxiliary signals, the forerunner of distant signals at places where the approach view of the station signal was difficult. The rule book of the period gave simple clear instructions on the working of these signals:

> DISTANT AUXILIARY SIGNALS. Must be worked strictly in conjunction with the station and junction signals; that is to say whenever a DANGER SIGNAL is shown at a station or junction, its auxiliary Distant Signal must show DANGER likewise.

SECTION I.

INSTRUCTIONS AS TO DISC SIGNALS.

STATIONARY AND DAY SIGNALS.

BRANCH LINE DISC SIGNALS AT JUNCTIONS, &c.

DIAGRAMS. DISC SIGNALS.

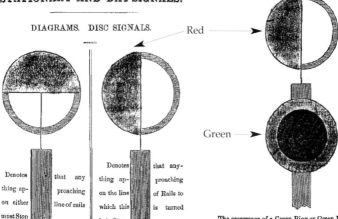

Red

Green

Denotes that any thing approaching on either line of rails must Stop.	Denotes that anything approaching on the line which this is to Stop.	that anything approaching of Rails to is turned

The occurrence of a Green Ring or Green Light under another Signal denotes that it relates to a Branch Line, and must be attended to thereon, but may be disregarded by persons upon the Main Line.

DISTANCE OR AUXILIARY SIGNALS.

8. At the Stations, at Junctions, and at other places on the Line, Distance or Auxiliary Signals are placed in advance of such Stations, Junctions or places; these, when they show a *Stop* Signal, are intended to warn the Enginemen and Guards that similar Signals are exhibited at such Stations, Junctions, &c.

These Auxiliary Distant Signals must be worked strictly in conjunction with the Station and Junction Signals; that is to say, whenever, and so long as, a *Danger* Signal is shown at a Station or Junction its Auxiliary Distant Signal must show *Danger* likewise.

The Distance Stop Signal must always be turned on immediately a Train passes it, and also at the same instant or before the stationary Signal is turned on. In the case of Junctions great care must be taken not to turn off the Stop Signals for the Branch till a sufficient time has elapsed after putting on the Signals for Main Line to prove *that no Main Line Train is approaching.*

9. Enginemen are required to stop their Engines and Trains in obedience to a Distance Signal. Having done so, they must, without a moment's delay, move gently forward as far as the line may be clear from obstruction, *at a speed not exceeding five miles per hour, until the whole Train is well within the Signal,* so that their Train may be protected by the Distant Signal from any Train or Engine following, and then await a Signal from the Station or Junction to proceed. Should it not be practicable to draw the Train far enough forward for the Signal to afford sufficient protection, the Guard or Breaksman must at once hasten back with the necessary Signals to protect the Train. When this occurs to an Engine without a Train, this duty will rest with the Fireman, the Engineman being responsible for the duty being properly performed.

SEMAPHORE SIGNALS.

25. These Signals are fixed on posts, and are constructed with one or two arms for day, and lamps for night, worked by hand-levers. The Signal is invariably made on the *left-hand* side of the post, as seen from an approaching Train. The position of the right-hand arm has reference to the right-hand Line, and is consequently a Signal for Trains running in a contrary direction.

26. The Stop Signal is, in the day, shown by the arm on the left-hand side being raised to the horizontal position, thus:—
And at night by a Red Light.

27. The Caution Signal—to Slacken Speed and Proceed Slowly— is, in the day, shown by the arm on the left-hand side being raised half way, thus:—
And at night by a Green Light.

28. The All Right Signal is shown, in the day, by the left-hand side of the post being clear, the arm being within the post, thus:—
And at night by a White Light.

29. When both arms are raised horizontally, both Lines are stopped.

GENERAL RULE.

30. An unlighted Signal after dark, or a signal blown down, or evidently not in proper working order, must be considered a Stop Signal, and the same precaution used, except it is a Siding Signal habitually not lighted, or not used at night.

Drivers and guards are required to STOP their trains at the distant signals when at danger. HAVING DONE SO, they must without a moments delay, move gently forward, AS FAR AS THE ROAD MAY BE CLEAR, to await a signal from the station or junction to proceed; and to be within the Distant Signal as far as possible, for protection against following trains.

With the sparse service of the day this system was deemed adequate, although strict adherence to the written timetable had to be followed, as there was no form of communication with other stations along the line. The Worgret accident described on page 71 of Volume One clearly illustrates the folly of breaking away from those basic principles.

The 1864 rule book as illustrated *opposite* and *below* clearly demonstrates that signalling had advanced, although still leaving much to be desired.

GENERAL SIGNALS.

1. A *White Light* by night, or an arm extended horizontally by day, shows ALL RIGHT.

2. A *Green Light* by night, or a *Green Flag* by day, is to show that an Engine must proceed with CAUTION.

3. A *Red Light* by night, or a *Red Flag* by day, or *any Signal, of whatever colour, violently waved*, shows that an Engine *must* STOP *instantly*.

4. Detonating Signals are to be *carefully* attached (label upwards) to the Rail upon which a Train is coming, by bending the lead clip round the upper flange of the *outside* Rail, and are exploded by the Train passing over them; *Red Signal Lights* have directions for use printed upon them; both these Signals indicate STOP. These Signals are to be used in addition to those formerly mentioned, and not in substitution for those Signals. During Fogs, all the Signal Lamps must be kept lighted, *as if it were night*, and Detonating Signals used to ensure the stoppage of Trains when necessary.

JUNCTION AND BRANCH LINE SIGNALS.

5. At all the Junctions the Branch Line Signals must always show the *Stop* Signal towards the Branch Line, and no Engine can pass from the Branch Line on to the Main Line until the *Stop* Signal for the Branch be taken off.

6. The Pointsmen must not take off the stop signal, or show the *All Right* Signal to a Train proceeding either to or from a Branch Line, unless they be certain that the Main Line is clear, and no Train approaching, and also that the *Stop Signals* are shown to any Train approaching on the Main Line; and in like manner they must not show the *All Right* Signal to a Train approaching from a Branch Line, unless they be certain that the *Stop* Signals are shown, so as to stop any Train approaching from or to the Branch Line. Pointsmen must never, under any circumstances, turn off the *Stop* or *Danger* Signal upon the Branch Line until after they have turned on the *Stop* Signals upon the Main Line. *The Danger Signals should invariably be turned on so as to stop Trains on the Main Line, previous to the Stop or Danger Signal on the Branch Line being turned off.*

7. Enginemen, on approaching Junctions, must shut off their steam at a sufficient distance (not less than 800 yards), and have their Trains under such control as will enable them to stop before reaching the Junction, whatever Signal may be shown.

The single line was operated in the fashion of the period by strict adherence to the working timetable assisted when required by written train orders. Policemen worked the signals and points at the various loops and controlled movements, it being recorded in December 1847 that clothing for 86 pointsmen and gatemen on the line cost £3 11s. 9d. per person. The few signals that existed were of the revolving disc type designed by Albinus Martin, one signal usually sufficed to indicate both directions. When the station signal was in the all-clear position it gave the driver clearance to run into the crossing loop. No starting signals were provided, the policeman giving authority for the train to proceed, either verbally or in written form.

Even the introduction of the electric telegraph could lead to incidents unless clear concise messages were sent. The telegraph was usually housed in the booking office, the policeman and pointsmen having to walk to the various points and signals to work the levers, none of which had any form of locking.

With the doubling of the line the 'Time Interval' system was adopted and with the electric telegraph an early form of Block working was instituted. However, this was not entirely satisfactory: a clerk would wire forward the departure of a train to the next station, but that station would not telegraph its arrival to state 'Train Out Of Section', so that the late or non-arrival of a train at the next station was not immediately reported back. Thus in the event of the train coming to a halt in the section it could well be struck in the rear by a following train!

In the booking office the clerk was often busy resulting in the telegraph instrument being operated by whoever happened to be about at the time, the policeman could be anywhere about on the track as were the pointsmen. This state of affairs gave rise for misunderstandings and confused messages. In short, although the electric telegraph provided a chain of communication along the line, it was not wholly dependable as a signalling system and the signals were still free to conflict with the points, there being no form of interlocking.

At greatest risk were the numerous level crossings along the route, although after the introduction of the electric telegraph relay bells were sometimes provided and later telephones. However, as late as 1935 crossings Nos. 11 and 12, just west of Holmsley, were without any form of communication. Some crossings were provided with auxiliary signals by 1857. In 1859 the Traffic Committee were asked 'for ladders to the high signals on the Dorchester line'. It was recommended that these be 'placed where required owing to gatekeepers being lame or old men', it is on record that one such keeper on the Wimborne-Ringwood section was a Crimean War veteran with a wooden leg.

Unfortunately, few details remain of the early signalling along the line. A few references from surviving records reported that in June 1857 the company accounts showed that the carriage department was credited for one auxiliary signal installed at Moreton, crossing lodge No. 3, and crossing lodge No.10 with two auxiliary signals at both lodge No. 9 and Beaulieu Road, and three auxiliary signals at Eling. Whilst Lyndhurst was credited with two auxiliary signals and one safety signal in June 1859, an auxiliary signal was also provided at lodge No. 26 and one 'high' signal at Totton. A second auxiliary signal was credited to lodge No. 3 in June 1860 at a cost of £22. In December 1865 it was recommended that semaphore signals be erected at Wimborne Junction, and in April 1866 that a ground signal be placed in Southampton tunnel.

The Signals

The disc signals were soon replaced by early forms of semaphore, some of which were 'slotted post signals' which had three positions, horizontal for 'stop' lowered 45 degrees for 'caution' and lowered vertically into the slot in the post for 'all clear'. Needless to say a signal arm that disappeared to give a 'clear' indication was unsatisfactory if it jammed in the slot or became broken, and was soon replaced by the well-known two-position lower quadrant arm with its 'fail safe' counter-weight system.

However, a few disc signals remained for a considerable time. It was not until 11th January, 1892 that the up and down distant disc signals were replaced at Avon Lodge crossing between Ringwood and Hurn.

Even the use of semaphore signals was of little help at night with the poor standard of signal illumination. Until the early 1890s the lamp indication at night for clear was a white light (green usually being used as a caution signal), but with the more widespread use of lighting in towns near railway lines the white signal light became very difficult to identify. This resulted in green being adopted as the 'clear signal'.

One of the great difficulties for engine drivers until the 1920s was the fact that distant signal arms were painted red and at night a red light was exhibited when the arm was in the 'on' position, just the same as stop signals. This situation tested a driver's route knowledge to the extreme and in the case of a driver becoming disorientated could lead to disaster.

This situation was overcome after 1903 with the introduction of the 'Coligny-Welch Distinguishing Distant Signal Lamp', an idea imported from the United States, although only the three companies that later formed the Southern Railway and the Great Eastern Railway took up the device in the UK. This lamp as well as allowing light to pass through a bulls-eye lens and then through the signal arm spectacle as normal also created a 'chevron' illumination next to the spectacle plate which mimicked the 'V' shape cut into the end of the signal arm. The chevron was displayed in both the 'on' and 'off' positions.

Provision of the new lamps was slow; it was not until 1908-9 that great progress was made and not until the early part of 1910 that signals between Redbridge and Lymington Junction were equipped, although Millbrook had received them in the August of the previous year. By the end of 1910 the line to Bournemouth and beyond and the Old Road had been equipped

No further developments in distinguishing distant signals took place until 1925 when the Ministry of Transport adopted the principle of yellow arms and lights for distant signals. Again the change over was slow and haphazard, only Christchurch on the lines covered in this work having received yellow arms and lamps by July 1927. In September it was decided that 'fishtail' lights would be removed from all distant signals fitted with yellow arms and spectacles, resulting in Christchurch having the Coligny-Welch equipment removed on 25th October.

During April 1928 a concerted effort was made to modify all distant signals west of Southampton, a majority of locations in the Bournemouth area being changed during the first week of May. Crow crossing and Ringwood survived until 8th May, with Avon Lodge and Hurn going the following day. The honour of being the last outpost on the Old Road with the old distant signals fell to Ashley Heath, which was changed on 10th May, leaving only Bournemouth Goods Junction and Bournemouth Central where they remained until the new Bournemouth Central box was brought into use on 8th July, 1928.

The majority of signals were illuminated by oil lamps requiring frequent filling and trimming, which involved staff climbing signals in all winds and

Above: The up starting signals at Hamworthy Junction were a fine example of LSWR lattice post junction signals with co-acting arms, the higher signals being visible to the driver of an approaching train above the station buildings and the lower signals easily visible when starting from the platform. The left side signals controlled the Old Road to Broadstone, the right side signals the route to Poole across the Holes Bay curve

G.A. Pryer Collection

Right: Broadstone had two sets of LSWR lattice-post 'gallows' type signals which survived until the closure of the Old Road. Illustrated here is the up main (from Hamworthy Junction) starting signal routeing trains to Wimborne, the left-hand arm directing trains onto the Somerset & Dorset line.

G.A. Pryer Collection

weather, which was also costly in labour and the amount of oil consumed. During 1909 the long burning signal lamp was evaluated and, proving satisfactory, resulted in a decision in the December to equip Dorchester and five stations in the London area likewise. Following several other satisfactory reports, in May 1914 it was decided that the remaining 4,300 signal lamps illuminated by ordinary paraffin oil and 500 with coal gas be converted into long burning oil lamps at a cost of £7,500, the expenditure to be spread over five years.

In style the signals west of Southampton covered the entire gambit of both LSWR and Southern railway designs. However, a few deserve special mention. At sites where a bridge, building or curve in the track could affect the sighting of a signal a very tall signal with a lower co-acting arm would be provided. One such example was the up starting signal at Totton, which as well as having a co-acting lower arm suspended from a bracket also carried on the upper part the up distant signal for Redbridge. Ranking amongst the tallest signals on the Southern, it was also a landmark above surrounding buildings for a considerable distance when approaching Totton by road from the west!

Other interesting signals were lattice post 'gallows' type junction signals which once graced the up ends of Broadstone station.

The reversing of up trains into the platform at Dorchester South required the services of a 'wrong road' signal, often referred to as a 'bow tie' signal as the arm was in the shape of an elongated cross; when in the 'off' position it displayed a purple light. This interesting signal was replaced by an elevated disc in February 1952.

The early wooden signal posts were superseded by the distinctive lattice steel posts of the LSWR, which in turn were replaced in Southern Railway days by rail-built posts constructed from second-hand bullhead rail. During the 1930s lower quadrant arms on signals started to be replaced by upper quadrant arms: the first upper quadrant signal between Southampton and Dorchester was brought into use during early 1930 with the replacement of the up home at Dorchester South followed by the up starting signal at Millbrook.

All signals at Southampton Central and Millbrook were of the upper quadrant type following the remodeling of both stations during 1935. Although in general replacement was a slow process, with new arms only being fitted when necessary, at Tunnel Junction, Southampton the up line signals were still equipped with lower quadrant arms in May 1963 although the down line signal arms were upper quadrant mounted on their original posts. Both Broadstone and Ringwood retaining a number of lower quadrant signals until closure.

Between Dorchester Junction and Weymouth the signalling was of Great Western origin until the section was transferred to the Southern Region, although a number of GWR signals remained for many years. At Weymouth major alterations to the station and its layout and the construction of a new signal box in 1957 saw the introduction of Southern Region signalling, including rail-built upper quadrant signals, although two wooden post GWR signals remained as a reminder of the former owners!

Ground signals, often referred to as ground discs or in railway parlance as 'dummies', fulfilled two purposes, some indicated the position of a set of points, others authorized a move as far as the line was clear towards the next signal

Southampton Tunnel Junction signal box was the oldest to survive on the line sitting in the cutting where the Southampton & Dorchester line was joined from Northam Junction by a direct chord in 1858. The box dated from the 1860s and survived until October 1966, originally it had a 13-lever frame (later increased to 14). It was unusually placed at right-angles to the track, the signalman looking through the frame towards Southampton tunnel. Photographed in November 1968 the disused structure is overshadowed by the adjoining houses in Northam Road.   *R.K. Blencowe Collection*

Somerset & Dorset Railway small 4-4-0 No. 45 passes Parkstone box with a down train for Bournemouth West. Parkstone was a typical small LSWR type '1' box having been modified with the cross-bracing timbers covered by lapped horizontal boards in later years. Although the lantern type ventilator remained on the roof, the original valences had also been removed except for a small section to the rear of the door. Note the gradient post signifying where the gradient changed from 1 in 50 to 1 in 300 through the station.   *Dr J. Boudreau Collection*

only. Ground signals had also originally exhibited a red danger light; in 1905 trials were carried out using firstly a white light and later a purple light as the danger light. In March 1907 it was decided that the use of the white light and the abolition of the back light had proved satisfactory, and it was decided that the white light would by adopted as the danger light for ground signals. (In later years it became red, as with running signals.)

At that time a common sight on the LSWR was the Stevens 'pillar' or 'flap' shunting signal. The flap was painted red and when it dropped down to the horizontal position a green light was exposed; sadly by the early 1950s these unique signals had been replaced by standard disc (dummy) signals.

Today the flickering flame of an oil lamp on a semaphore signal is almost extinct on the line west of Southampton. At the time of writing the sole survivor is the down branch starter at Hamworthy Junction. Elsewhere even where the mechanical signalling frame still exists, the superior piercing glow of colour-light signals with the additional in-cab protection of the Automatic Warning System (AWS) is a far cry from the disc signals of 150 years ago.

Signal Boxes and their Equipment

The first signal boxes were few and far between and only erected where absolutely necessary. One such situation is highlighted by the Board of Trade report of August 1866 for the new junction at West Moors which, although brief in its description of the signalling, states, 'the siding chock block should be connected and worked from the junction stage'. This statement implies that just a raised platform was provided for the levers and not a signal box.

The LSWR account journal for December 1869 shows that G. Witt was authorized to build a 'signalman's hut' costing £45, and that Messrs Stevens & Sons were to supply and fit locking apparatus at Wimborne station in December 1870 at a cost of £154 1s. 6d. The accounts in May 1872 show payment of £37 0s. 9d. for the construction of a new signal box at No. 10 gatehouse, the first crossing on the Old Road beyond Lymington Junction. There was also a payment to Messrs Bull & Sons for repairs to the signal box at Lymington Junction in April 1867. One early box was situated at Tunnel Junction, Southampton located in the 'V' of the junction it was equipped with a lever frame at right angles to the track. Closed on 2nd October, 1966 it had served for over a century.

It was not until after the introduction of the Regulation of Railways Act of 1871, which extended the Board of Trade's powers to the inspection of new lines and alterations of existing works, that the signal box developed. The LSWR from that moment fitted all new lines, junctions, and siding connections with locking frames. This included the new line between Broadstone and Poole, with boxes constructed at Broadstone and Poole in 1872. In 1874 with the line extended boxes were provided at Parkstone and Bournemouth West, which according to the Board of Trade report were equipped with Saxby & Farmer frames; Broadstone box had a lever frame with both numbered and lettered levers.

From that time the provision of boxes was quickly undertaken. In March 1884 the Traffic Committee recommended additional signal boxes as block sections

Ringwood East signal box, an LSWR type '1' box dating back to the 1870s. Following alterations to the signalling layout in January 1929 the box was reduced to a ground frame. This photograph was taken in later years when alterations had included the loss of the original box type roof vent, and the addition of a porch at the top of the stairs entering the box.

South Western Circle/Eyers Collection

All the signal boxes on the Bournemouth Direct Line of 1888 were of the LSWR type '3A' of which Sway was a classic example; although the lantern type roof vent had been removed it still retained all the features of its original design. Equipped with a Stevens 17-lever frame with 4¼ inch centres, the box was taken out of use on 26th February, 1967. *Author's Collection*

should be erected at 'No. 6 Woodfidley Crossing, No. 16 Crossing [sic], No.18 Woolsbridge Crossing, and No. 21 Uddens Crossing'. In the event No. 16 was replaced by No. 15 Crow Crossing, each location being equipped with a ground level variation of a type '3' box, fitted with a Stevens 'knee' frame (Uddens in latter days was equipped with an Evans O'Donnell frame). In order to reduce the long section between Wareham and Hamworthy Junction an additional block section was approved for Keysworth Crossing in 1898 at a cost of £380.

At a number of locations the adjacent crossing gates were not interlocked with the signals and were hand-operated independently of the signal box thus being devoid of any interlocking. In April 1885 the thrifty management agreed to the £70 cost to work the gates at Moreton from the signal box, by fitting some old gates and machinery from Christchurch. By 1889 the cost of controlling Wool gates from the signal box was estimated as £170.

A further Act in 1889 with a deadline for compliance of interlocking added urgency to the matter. The whole undertaking was completed using three successive basic designs, which the Signalling Record Society have classed into groups: type '1', 1873-1877; type '2' 1877-1884; type '3' 1884-1897; needless to say there were variations to suit circumstances. Thus during the period from the mid-1870s the trusted Absolute Block system with mechanically operated and locked points and signals, later assisted by track circuiting, became standard. The LSWR employed block instruments of the Preece one- or three-wire patterns, a majority of the lever frames, signals and other equipment being supplied by Messrs Stevens & Son, the principal signalling contractors to the LSWR. The quality of the workmanship was demonstrated by the fact that at several locations the equipment lasted until the 1960s, indeed it was not until circa 1970 that the last Preece's one-wire instruments were taken out of use.

Although as previously stated Stevens had quickly become established as the principal signalling contractor to the LSWR, a number of early frames were of different origin; unfortunately much of the detail has been lost in the passing of time. However, it is recorded that a Dutton 27-lever frame existed in Ringwood West box until 1929 when replaced by a frame to the Stevens' pattern at the time Ringwood East was reduced to a ground frame. Ringwood East had also been one of the last places to have signal wires running from overhead posts.

Reverting to signal box design, a majority of the boxes of the 1873-1897 period either were constructed on a brick or stone base with timber upper works and a hipped slate roof as standard. With the early boxes the timber framework was outside the weather boarding thus creating traps for rain water and causing decay, a matter resolved by placing the weather boarding on the outside which became standard on later boxes.

In 1894 a further design of signal box was produced, the type '4', usually of brick construction up to the eaves with a slate hip roof. It was realised that windows in the front of the box were obstructed by both the lever frame and block shelf, so the designer grouped the windows where they were of greatest value, at the front corners. Again there were variations to suit certain situations, this most successful design remained in use during the Southern Railway period, a late example being Wareham in 1928. Although the type '4' had been introduced for a number of years, a new 19-lever box constructed at the level

Increased traffic required additional block sections be established, one such was Woodfidley Crossing signal box situated in the New Forest east of Beaulieu Road. It was a typical ground level signal box of the period to be found throughout the LSWR. Opened on 8th August, 1884 it was equipped with a nine-lever Stevens knee frame extended to 11 levers in November 1916 with the opening of a War Department siding. This box altered very little over the years but closed on 23rd October, 1966.

C. Chivers Collection

Holton Heath signal box, opened in May 1915 as 'Holton' and renamed Holton Heath the following year, was constructed to control the sidings serving the Admiralty cordite factory. A standard type '4' structure it remained in use until 3rd November, 1968 when it closed and the equipment was removed. However, owing to the fact the Admiralty had paid for its construction it remained derelict for a number of years whilst the legal situation was resolved before its demolition.

Author

Increased traffic during World War I required the signals at Holme crossing between Wareham and Wool be interlocked with the gates resulting in a new six-lever ground frame and building being opened on 9th April, 1917 replacing the previous crossing arrangements. The new structure was a ground frame version of the LSWR type '4' signal box. Closed on 21st April, 1965 the crossing was the first in Dorset to be equipped with automatic half-barriers. *R.K. Blencowe Collection*

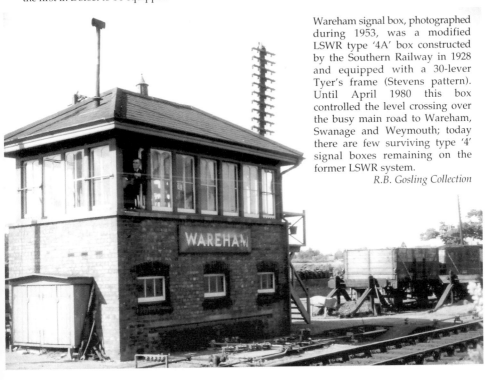

Wareham signal box, photographed during 1953, was a modified LSWR type '4A' box constructed by the Southern Railway in 1928 and equipped with a 30-lever Tyer's frame (Stevens pattern). Until April 1980 this box controlled the level crossing over the busy main road to Wareham, Swanage and Weymouth; today there are few surviving type '4' signal boxes remaining on the former LSWR system. *R.B. Gosling Collection*

Right: The cramped interior of West Moors signal box photographed in May 1959, with the rim of the gate wheel in the right corner, and the instrument shelf above the levers. The Preece's one-wire block instrument for the section to Ringwood is on the extreme left.

G.A. Pryer Collection

Below: Lymington Junction signal box was a case of using a previous design, this type '3' box was opened in July 1915 many years after the introduction of the type '4'. When opened Preece's one-wire block instruments controlled both the main line and the Old Road with Tyer's No. 6 tablet on the single line to Lymington Town. Standard SR three-position block was provided on the main line from 1961. The original small panes of glass in the windows had been replaced by the time this photograph was taken in April 1967. *C.L. Caddy*

crossing end of West Moors station in 1904 to replace the previous type '2' box situated at the junction with the Salisbury & Dorset line had many similarities to the previous type '3' boxes.

During the early 1930s the Southern Railway introduced a box, of brick construction but with a flat concrete roof. With this model the lever frame was usually placed along the back wall of the box (back to traffic) leaving the front and side windows unobstructed. Boxes of this design were erected at both Southampton West and Millbrook, opening in June 1935, equipped with Westinghouse 'A2' frames.

Thus it was with this selection of boxes that the lines west of Southampton were controlled until boxes of British Railways design were erected at Weymouth in 1957, Dorchester South in 1959 and Brockenhurst A in 1965.

Although with earlier boxes the chosen building material was wood or a combination including brick or stone, the original Poole (1872-1880), Broadstone, Parkstone and Wimborne boxes were of superior brick construction. Wimborne was exceptionally tall to allow the signalman a view over the station, which was situated on a curve.

A most unusual box was Totton, originally named Eling Crossing, then Eling Junction 1925-1950. Thrifty as ever the LSWR had constructed it from a former crossing keeper's cottage (No. 2), as block working and interlocking started to spread. The roof was removed and an upper storey constructed to take the locking frame and it became a signal box. The ground floor (the original cottage) then contained the interlocking and lead-off connections. As the signal box occupied the same area as the cottage had done it was a roomy structure by LSWR signal box standards - and must have seemed spacious indeed when it contained the original 17-lever Stevens' frame. However, this spaciousness was to prove very useful: when sidings were added on the down side (west of the level crossing) in 1895 six more levers were added and the advent of the Fawley branch caused an extension to 35 levers - achieved without any enlargement of the building itself!

Before 1878 a signal box had existed at Dorchester situated on the up side on the site of the later goods shed extension, with a further box along the line opposite Mansfield's private siding, named Chalk Sidings signal box, the sidings being to the east of the Wareham Road overbridge. However, the construction of the new down platform and revised signalling arrangements at Dorchester in 1878 required a new station box. Owing to the curve of the new platform and the engine shed lying alongside the down main line, the new box had to be built to a 'crows nest design' with the end of the operating floor overhanging the down main line to afford the signalman a view past the engine shed and over the canopy of the curved down platform. As with Tunnel Junction the lever frame was at right angles to the running lines. Owing to the box being the last before reaching the GWR line the signalman had to use two sets of bell codes: LSWR codes to boxes to the east and GWR codes to Dorchester Junction. Also the block instruments used to the latter box were of GWR pattern, and despite the need for close co-operation between the two signalmen a telephone was not provided until 1900!

Another box of exceptional height was erected at Christchurch with the construction of the Direct Line, situated near the junction of the branch from

Totton signal box is unusual in the fact that it is a conversion from the Southampton & Dorchester Railway crossing keeper's cottage, note the original windows, doorway and scullery still in position, the operating floor being just simply built on top of the original bungalow. Originally named Eling Crossing and containing a 17-lever frame increased to 22 in 1895 and to 35 with the opening of the Fawley branch, its ample size allowed for the additions. The original slate roof was replaced by an asbestos structure in later years, the box being taken out of use on 28th February, 1982 and demolished when the area came under the control of Eastleigh panel box. *Author*

Brockenhurst West, opened in April 1936 and renamed Brockenhurst B in April 1939, was a non-standard Southern Railway design containing a Westinghouse 'A2' frame. Closed on 19th October, 1978 and demolished, the Westinghouse frame was saved and today is in use on the Swanage Railway in the replacement box constructed at Swanage. *Author*

Dorchester signal box was a modified type '1' with standard windows and hipped roof. It was unusual in that it was at right-angles to the running line. as was the 31-lever frame, it was also high and overhung the down line, this gave the signalman a view past the engine shed, seen in the background, and over the roof of the curved down platform behind the camera. It is seen here during 1959 after being replaced by a BR standard type box further up the line. To the left is the original 1847 goods shed with its later extension, alongside which is the backing signal to admit trains into the up platform.   *Author*

Christchurch signal box required to be elevated to enable the signalman to clearly see over the Fairmile Road bridge. The box, an LSWR type '3A' equipped with a 39-lever Stevens 4⅛ inch lever frame, opened in 1888. This February 1963 photograph shows the removal of the down dock siding. Passing on a down train is British Railways Standard class '4' 4-6-0 No. 75079 constructed in January 1956 and withdrawn after only 10 years' service in November 1966; today she is preserved on the Mid-Hants Railway.   *J. Read*

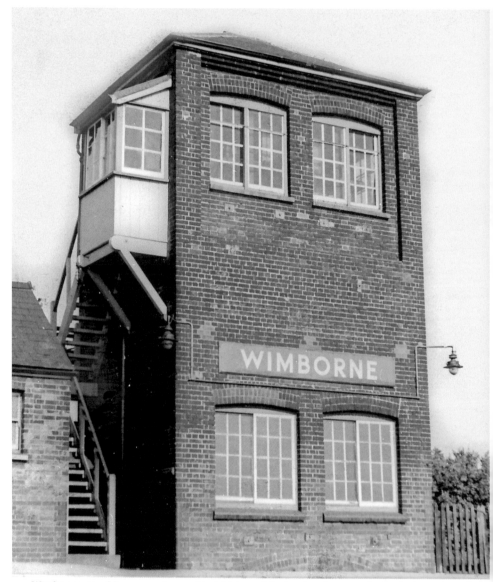

Wimborne signal box was of a great height to enable the signalman to obtain the best view of the curved layout, part of which would otherwise be obstructed by the platform canopies. Of all-brick construction, there is very little documentary evidence of either its date of construction or original equipment. In later years it contained a 23-lever Stevens 4¼ inch frame extended to 29 levers in 1929. Reduced to what must have been the tallest ground frame on record in July 1966, it was abolished on 8th January the following year.   *C.L. Caddy*

Ringwood; the height was required for the signalman to see the approach of the new line over the top of Fairmile Road bridge.

A further box in an elevated position was the new box at Bournemouth Central opened in July 1928. Constructed above the roof of the down platform canopy, it gave a clear view of the engine shed and the line towards and over Beechy Road bridge in the down direction, although the signalman's vision in the up direction was obstructed by the overall roof of the station. However, track circuiting was in use by that time so vision was not quite so important; in fact the reason the box was in that lofty position was probably because there was very little other space to put it! Equipped with a 60-lever Westinghouse 'A2' type frame, this was retained to work all the points and signals following their conversion to electric operation in December 1966 with the remodelling of the layout.

When Pokesdown station was rebuilt in 1930 the new signal box fitted with a Westinghouse 'A2' frame, but for reasons never fully discovered it was a completely non-standard structure 16 ft 2 in. by 12 ft 2 in., elevated 10 ft and was of unusual construction being clad in steel sheeting which was a cross between the traditional corrugated iron and the modern material in use today, described at the time as 'Patent Protected Metal Sheeting'.

At other locations the alteration of layouts at times involved the installation of a longer lever frame, but instead of constructing a new box an extension of the existing building was undertaken. The opening of the Corfe Mullen cut-off in 1885 involved the replacement of the original 17-lever frame in Broadstone box with a Stevens 33-lever frame. To accommodate this the box was extended to twice its previous length in matching style, and apart from a slight difference in the shade of the brickwork there is nothing to suggest the entire structure was not original. In 1950 when Broadstone required a new frame, a second-hand 32-lever Westinghouse 'A2' frame from Lockerley was installed against the back wall.

Ringwood West box had also been extended, with its wooden top section and brick base the extension is detectable by the fact the locking room windows are off-centre. This followed a recommendation in February 1904 that Christchurch Road crossing be interlocked and worked from the signal box at an estimated cost of £326, which would allow the removal of some unnecessary signals and effect a saving of about £22 a year in maintenance charges.

In an effort to avoid extending boxes Stevens frames were often fitted with push and pull levers; when normal the lever stood half-way in the frame, being pushed to clear one signal and pulled to clear the other, this method of operation usually being restricted to shunting signals.

Economy was also the watchword, and the removal of a signal box to a second site was not unknown. In September 1889 it was recommended that a disused signal box at Nursling be placed at Totton station level crossing to work the gates which were then interlocked with the signals at a cost estimated to be £170.

In January 1891 closing out switches were installed in the following boxes: New Milton, Hinton Admiral, Bournemouth Goods Junction, Ringwood East, West Moors, Wimborne Junction and Poole East. This allowed the boxes to close on Sundays, the LSWR looking towards saving wages during quiet periods.

Above: The interior of Bournemouth Central box photographed during 1988 showing the 60-lever 4 inch centre Westinghouse 'A2' frame. From 11th December, 1966 the mechanical frame controlled a layout with all points motor controlled and all signalling colour lights with magazine train describers between Bournemouth and Brockenhurst and bell block to Branksome. Bournemouth Central box closed on 15th December, 2003 along with Branksome when they were replaced by a panel housed in the former parcel office. *Author*

Right: The interior of Broadstone box photographed in May 1959. The 32-lever Westinghouse 'A2' frame with 4 inch centres was second-hand retrieved from Lockerley and installed during 1950 in SR fashion along the back wall, giving the signalman a clear view out of the front windows. On the block shelf to the right is the Preece's single wire block instrument to Wimborne, at the left-hand end is the Preece's 3-wire block instrument to Poole B box.

G.A. Pryer Collection

Pokesdown signal box opened on 27th April, 1930 replacing the original structure with the reconstruction of the station. Equipped with a Westinghouse 22-lever type 'A2' frame with four inch centres, like many boxes it retained its Preece's one-wire block instruments until 1961 when replaced by the standard SR three-position block. The box was of unusual construction being clad in steel sheeting which was a cross between the traditional corrugated iron and the modern material in use today, described at the time as 'Patent Protected Metal Sheeting'. The box closed on 3rd December, 1972, photographed here on 5th June, 1961 with 'Merchant Navy' class 4-6-2 No. 35019 *French Line CGT* passing on an up train. *C.L. Caddy*

Ringwood West signal box was a typical LSWR type '1' opened during the 1870s, a close look at the base of the structure shows that the locking room windows are off-centre and reveals an extension to the right side of the box. There had been two extensions to the lever frame, the first in September 1904 when the level crossing was put under control of the box with additional levers and gate wheel and further alterations carried out in January 1919 when a new 32-lever Stevens pattern frame was installed and renamed Ringwood with the reduction of Ringwood East to a ground frame. *South Western Circle/Eyers Collection*

It is also interesting to note that train describers replaced block instruments in Tunnel Junction and Northam Junction boxes also other boxes to Eastleigh East on 15th May, 1899. The Tunnel Junction describer only displayed limited indications: Fast Special Excursion or Fruit, Dorset Line Slow Passenger, Dorset Line Goods, Bournemouth and Weymouth Fast, Royal Train. By April 1910 both Poole boxes had been equipped with platform-operated 'detached vehicle' indicators, also to be used if a train was allowed to remain at the platforms for an unusual period.

The Working of Single Lines

The safe working of single lines required equipment that made it impossible for a second train to be admitted onto the single line section from either end until the previous train had cleared the section. Originally this was accomplished as described earlier by strict observance of the timetable, to be later replaced by a simple Train Staff or on busier routes the Train Staff & Ticket. However, the introduction of electric locking allowed the Train Staff system to be superseded on busier lines making for more flexible working. The new system usually employed the 'Electric Train Staff', the 'Electric Tablet' and later the 'Electric Key Token'.

The LSWR used the tablet system, and the first line to employ the system was West Moors-Alderbury Junction. This followed recommendations in August 1884 that the Tyer's tablet train signalling apparatus should be tried on the Salisbury & Dorset single line, 'with such modification if any as the experience of the Caledonian Railway who are working the system may suggest'.

Using Tyer's No. 1 instruments the experiment was successful. No doubt it was the involvement of the LSWR in the Somerset & Dorset affairs which led to a further trial on the new Broadstone-Corfe Mullen cut-off the following year, resulting in Tyer's No. 1 being installed over the Somerset & Dorset Joint main line between Wimborne and Bath in 1886.

From about 1889 the LSWR used the Tyer's No. 3 instruments for new work. With both the No. 1 and No. 3 instruments, once a tablet was withdrawn it could only be placed in the machine at the other end of the section. Greater flexibility was allowed with the subsequent No. 6 instrument, introduced in 1892, where a tablet could be replaced in the machine from which it was withdrawn, i.e. if a train enters a section and needed to return to its starting point, for example if the locomotive failed or the line was obstructed. A further advance in signalling technology with the No. 7 instrument (1898) allowed for provision of an intermediate tablet instrument at an intermediate siding, allowing a train to be 'shut in' at the siding so that a further train could enter the (now clear) section. However, the LSWR used very few No. 7 instruments in places where it specifically wanted to take advantage of this facility.

The Ringwood-Christchurch-Bournemouth East line was controlled by Tyer's No. 6 electric tablet, as was the Lymington branch, although the latter was replaced by a simple wooden train staff for 'One Train Working' operation in April 1967, the branch again reverting to the most basic form of single line control.

The Swanage branch was also equipped with Tyer's No. 6, but the section from Worgret Junction to Corfe Castle was changed to Tyer's No. 7 in 1914 (to provide 'shut in facilities' at Furzebrook Siding) and then to Tyer's key token in 1961. The section from Corfe Castle to Swanage remained Tyer's No. 6 until downgraded to 'One Train Working' in 1967 with a wooden train staff.

The Fawley branch was operated originally by Tyer's No. 7 electric tablet, but later by Tyer's electric key token, as was the section of line between Broadstone and Hamworthy Junction following its singling in December 1932. Broadstone box also contained a Tyer's electric tablet machine (originally No. 1, replaced about 1948/1950 by No. 6) for the single line section over the Somerset & Dorset to Corfe Mullen Junction. Broadstone was also equipped with Whittaker tablet exchange apparatus, a common feature on the Somerset & Dorset.

West Moors signal box housed a Tyer's No. 6 electric tablet instrument for the single line section over the Salisbury & Dorset line to Verwood. However, with the economies of the pre-war years, from August 1931 a miniature electric train staff machine was also installed to work the long section to Fordingbridge allowing Verwood to switch out at quiet times.

Following the singling of the Hamworthy branch in November 1905 a diamond-shaped staff sufficed to cover the branch goods working until July 1938 when the Air Ministry sidings were opened, at which point the 'No Signalman Key Token' was introduced. It is an economic system of working a single line branch, which dispenses with the need for a signalman at the terminus end but offers a greater degree of freedom in operating the traffic where a second train can be allowed on the branch after the first has cleared the single line and its token replaced in the instrument.

On withdrawing a token from the instrument (which is painted blue as opposed to the normal red) the Hamworthy Jn signalman had to insert the key into a lock on No. 37 lever, 'loop to down branch points'. He could then unlock the lever, reverse the points and let the train onto the branch, then reset the points and lock the lever 'Normal' again before withdrawing the key token from the lock and handing it to the driver By this means, the signalman was prevented from setting the points to let another train onto the branch until either the token had been inserted in the instrument at Hamworthy Goods (located in the goods office), which then allowed the Hamworthy Jn signalman to withdraw a second token, or the train had returned with the same token. No bell signals were used with this mode of working, but a tablet showing 'Locked' or 'Free' is fitted to the instrument. When a token is withdrawn from either end, the tablet shows 'Locked' and the word 'Free' only appears when no keys are out. Whilst the tablet shows 'Free', the person at either end may withdraw a token, which action electrically locks the opposing moves.

Single line operation had also been applied on two occasions over the Direct Line. Firstly, at Hordle between Sway and New Milton during 1948 and 1949, when Hordle Intermediate and Hordle Cutting signal boxes together with facing crossovers were installed as a temporary measure during civil engineering work. The second occasion was during the Bournemouth electrification work in 1966, when at various periods single line working was introduced between Christchurch-Hinton Admiral, Hinton Admiral-New

Photographed in 1977, the interior of Hamworthy Junction signal box showing the Stevens 59-lever 4⅛ inch centre frame. On the block shelf are the two Preece's 3-wire block instruments controlling the sections to both Holton Heath and Poole B. Over the years the simplification of the layout and signalling had resulted in 39 of the levers becoming spare by 1990. *Author*

The 'No Signalman' token instrument at Hamworthy Junction used for working the branch to Hamworthy Goods. On withdrawing a token from the instrument the signalman must insert it in the lock on lever No. 37 to lock the lever 'Normal' before handing it to the driver. *Author*

Lever No. 37 with the token in the lock. Once locked the signalman is prevented from setting the points to allow another train onto the branch until the token has been inserted into the machine at Hamworthy Goods which allows the Junction signalman to withdraw a second token, or the train has returned with the same token to Hamworthy Junction. *Author*

Right: Woolsbridge signal box was a typical ground level signal box of the period to be found throughout the LSWR. Opened on 8th August, 1884 it was equipped with a nine-lever Stevens' knee frame. Renamed Ashley Heath and reduced to a ground frame with the opening of Ashley Heath Halt on 1st April, 1927, it also doubled as a booking office, the window of which can be clearly seen in the photograph. Final closure came on 8th January, 1967 when opening of the gates by hand became the option for the remaining months of operation.   *S. Drew*

Milton, and New Milton-Sway. As with the previous work temporary facing crossovers were laid and token instruments used to control the working.

The signal box at Dorchester South was reduced to a ground frame in June 1970 when the new up platform was built and the area came under the control of Dorchester Junction. In September 1984 it was closed altogether and replaced by a new ground frame outside, the lever frame being removed in due course and the box converted to staff use. However, in June 1985 when the line to Moreton was reduced to single track, it was reopened as a signal box and equipped with a new panel to control the single line and the points at Moreton, with Absolute Block on the up line and Track Circuit Block on the down line. In July 1986 the panel took over the control of Dorchester Junction and Dorchester West station on the line to Castle Cary, and in 1987 it gained control of Weymouth.

An item of interest that came under the control of the signalling system was the luggage platform (also referred to as a portable footbridge) at Brockenhurst. Owing to both the booking and parcel offices being away from the two island platforms, the luggage bridge could be swung across the up loop line to allow luggage and parcels to be wheeled across. A ground frame, which was released by levers in both A and B signal boxes, controlled its operation which today is supervised by Brockenhurst panel.   *Author*

Crossing No. 32 at Stoke, between Wareham and Wool, is the only crossing on the line remaining under control of a crossing keeper. Owing to the configuration of the road layout to date it has been impossible to replace the hand-operated gates by automatic barriers. Although the original crossing keeper's cottage has been demolished the crossing hut remains and a portakabin has been added for the crossing keeper's use. *Author*

Conclusion

On Monday 15th December, 2003 the two conventional signal boxes at Bournemouth and Branksome were replaced by a panel housed in the former parcels office at Bournemouth station. With Brockenhurst box to the east and Poole box to the west as fringe boxes, the new panel covers the same 16 route miles as the previous installations. It is questionable as to why it had not at least taken in both Poole and Hamworthy boxes. Indeed, when the scheme was first considered the then Railtrack was looking to replacing all signalling between Totton and Weymouth!

However, it is interesting as the new system is the first to use the Siemens SIMIS-W computer-based interlocking employing axle counters rather than track circuits for the detection of trains. The entire control area was monitored by 98 axle counters, the control centre at Bournemouth having visual display unit-based controls using a Windows NT operating system. The only alterations to the previous layout are that the down platform at Bournemouth has became bi-directional over its entire length using a new crossover at the west end and is signalled as two separate platforms. Whilst at Branksome the down platform became available for up departures with the introduction of a new signal.

Thus the latest signalling technology had arrived. At the time of writing, panels at Eastleigh, Brockenhurst, Bournemouth and Dorchester South control almost the entire line with only a small enclave of mechanical signalling remaining between Poole and Wool, the operational signal boxes at Poole, Hamworthy Junction, and Wool all dating back to the 19th century. In Bournemouth carriage sidings, overlooking the latest rolling stock, stands Bournemouth Carriage Sidings ground frame, which until 1st November, 1965 was Bournemouth West Junction signal box, an LSWR type '3A' structure dating back to 1888, a monument to a glorious past.

Chapter Twelve

Architecture and Infrastructure

A General Overview

Any work covering the history of the Southampton & Dorchester and associated lines would not be complete without a brief examination of the architecture along the route, remembering that stations are not the only buildings; goods sheds, engine sheds, staff accommodation and many other structures including bridges and viaducts make up the infrastructure.

Just as plagiarism was rife amongst the literary world in Victorian times, there is little doubt the same applied in the world of architecture, it being a well-known fact that Victorian architects were great copyists of earlier designs despite the widely used term 'Victorian Architecture'. In truth much early railway architecture was a selection of various ideas and styles. It also has to be realised with the earlier railways in particular that there was little previous experience to draw upon. This resulted in a variety of styles, some followed existing designs, such as warehouses, market halls, waterworks, gasworks and other industrial buildings of the period, whilst others were simply at the whim of the railway engineer.

It also has to be remembered that in the 1840s the three basic building materials were stone, brick and timber. It was not until the mid-19th century that iron and steel were added to the combination, demonstrated by the success of the Crystal Palace in 1851, after which a structural revolution began. In the late 1850s 'company styles' began to develop, as each railway company grew larger and reflected a degree of uniformity, there being many examples on both the LSWR and GWR to name but two.

The responsibility for the design of buildings along the railway was that of the appointed Engineer, in the case of the Southampton & Dorchester William Scarth Moorsom. Moorsom had previously been Engineer of the Birmingham & Gloucester Railway, which opened in 1841, and much of the architecture produced for that line with a little modification was reproduced on the Southampton & Dorchester. There were two reasons for this, firstly why waste a perfectly good set of drawings, and secondly the financial circumstances of the Southampton & Dorchester would not have allowed for designs of a new or more flamboyant style. Again with economy in mind, and perhaps wishing to see continuity, the same designs were later used at Hurn and Christchurch on the Ringwood, Christchurch & Bournemouth Railway of which Moorsom was also Engineer.

At the time of their construction there was a general consensus of opinion amongst a majority of railways that in order not to offend tradition or the landed gentry through whose land railways often passed, country stations should be of a style that suited the surroundings. Thus the 'Mock Tudor-Gothic Rectory' style developed, and this was followed on the Southampton & Dorchester. Unfortunately, whereas most companies endeavoured to build

The original station building at Wareham, replaced by the new station in 1886, it survived until the early 1970s as the station master's house. Although several extensions have been unsympathetically added, the building still retained its original character. Beyond stands the original goods shed with the 1928 signal box to the left; in the foreground is the roof of one of the original crossing cottages. Photographed on 25th March, 1967 as British Railways Standard class '4' 2-6-0 No. 76064 arrives with a down Weymouth train.   *C.L. Caddy*

A pre-1911 view of Wool looking west; the similarities with Eckington station on the Birmingham & Gloucester Railway confirm the theory of the same basic set of architect's drawings being employed. To the left is the small goods shed and to the right the up side waiting shelter added at a later date.   *Author's Collection*

Wool Railway Station.

superior stations at principal towns as a symbol of their status the Southampton & Dorchester failed miserably on this count at both Southampton and Dorchester! The other stations between Southampton and Dorchester appear to have been divided into two groups: Lyndhurst Road, Holmsley, Ringwood, Wimborne, Poole (Hamworthy) and Wareham were classed as a higher grade than Redbridge, Beaulieu Road, Wool and Moreton which were graded as second class, no doubt owing to their lower traffic potential. However, in the case of Redbridge within 25 years a substantial addition had been made to the main building, and later a single-storey office extension was added to the west end with the unusual feature of a central passageway providing access to the platform.

Indeed, improvements were continually carried out to improve the accommodation of waiting passengers, usually following complaints of the lack of facilities. An example was reported in the *Western Gazette* during October 1876:

> The South Western Railway Company have now completed some alterations to the station at Lyndhurst Road, which give additional accommodation to the public. As on each side of the line waiting places of shelter have been provided, the want of which has been felt for a long time past.

Allowing for slight variation and subsequent alterations and extensions the connection between the Birmingham & Gloucester and Southampton & Dorchester becomes clear. Both consist of 'Tudor-Gothic' style buildings constructed as two rectangular units set at right angles to each other with separate pitched roofs, blind openings in the gables and one gable wall containing an oriel window. The second class buildings were of similar style although less elaborate, the oriel window being replaced by a single sash window with the upper rooms partly in the roof space. An extensive article on the subject cites Droitwich Road on the Birmingham & Gloucester and Lyndhurst Road on the Southampton & Dorchester as compatible buildings, whilst Eckington compares with the Southampton & Dorchester second class buildings.

A further degree of similarity existed between the up platform canopy (Birmingham bound) at Bromsgrove station on the Birmingham & Gloucester Railway and those at both Ringwood and Wimborne on the Southampton & Dorchester, all three stations having canopies of hipped slate roof construction without any glazing. The Ringwood canopy situated on the up platform was sited beyond the station building. Theories that these canopies were later additions could be dismissed by their rather crude design, which would not have been acceptable to either the Midland or LSWR companies, added to which the chances of both companies arriving at the same design are extremely remote.

The original station at Brockenhurst was of a different design, the details of which are difficult to determine. At a Traffic Committee meeting in June 1848 the want of accommodation at this station was raised. The Directors,

> ... regretted the inconvenience but as there was a possibility of the Lymington branch being built they did not consider it warranted in making any outlay at Brockenhurst, as the station would have to be moved a mile further west.

The exterior of Lyndhurst Road station; both the brick extension under the oriel window in the end gable and the wooden structure were later additions to this original station building. The Tudor-Gothic style complete with stonework around the windows is clearly shown and compares with the later additions.   *South Western Circle/Eyers Collection*

Wimborne looking east with the main station buildings behind on a lower level. Both the up and down side shelters are of a design employed at Bromsgrove on the Birmingham & Gloucester Railway. Note the high signal box allowing the signalman a good view in either direction.
                                                                                    Author's Collection

In the event the station was not moved, however, it is certain the original building was extended to form a two-storey structure in line with the platform, flanked at each end by a two-storey building of two end gables. A flat-roofed canopy supported by timber uprights covered the platform area along the entire length of the station building, whilst on the down platform a simple shelter with a steeply-sloped roof was supported by a number of brick columns. However, there is a strong suspicion that this configuration is not original and certainly at the west end a bay platform covered by a small train shed was added for the Lymington branch train.

The original Hamworthy Junction station was of similar design to Brockenhurst except that the centre section was shorter, the down side timber waiting shelter having curved arches along its front as did Wareham, Wool and Moreton.

Further evidence of comparable ideas exist in the tunnel mouths at Moseley on the Birmingham & Gloucester and the west end of Southampton tunnel, where the portals, instead of having straight wing walls, sweep round in a curve to meet in the centre at an angle, these in both tunnels have distinctive pillar-like key stones.

Stations and associated buildings of the 19th century

Dorchester, the largest and most important station on the original line could never be described as inspiring. The large train shed was neither elegant nor well proportioned, and completely overshadowed the single-storey station building on its north side. Unfortunately few photographs exist of earlier days showing the exterior of the station, which featured a selection of Roman-Doric pilasters, a parapet and a cornice of no obvious significance. Over the years improvements had been carried out in an attempt to update the facilities available. In 1866 an additional waiting room was provided for gentlemen allowing separate accommodation for ladies, and further improvements were carried out during the 1880s. More light was shed on the station following the removal of the train shed during 1938, after which a standard Southern Railway steel canopy was erected.

The undistinguished station building at least saved the station master from living over the business. At Dorchester the station master was originally classed as the superintendent of the line, this being reflected in his residence; this was constructed in 1858 at a cost of £250 and situated at the end of the station approach overlooking Weymouth Avenue. Featuring a 'double hipped' roof this building was large compared with many officials' houses, and certainly made the terrace of six early railway cottages in the station approach look humble.

The original goods shed was constructed of brick with a low-pitched hip roof on wooden trusses. The sidewalls were constructed of a series of semi-circular blind arches, a number containing round-headed windows with iron radial glazing bars for the small-paned windows. In August 1884 it was proposed to enlarge the goods shed and carry out other alterations at Dorchester station at an

The exterior of Dorchester station photographed during 1969 showing the Roman Doric-style pilasters and parapet finish to an otherwise uninspiring building. However, it was functional and served well remaining in use for 139 years. *Author*

The up platform of Dorchester photographed in April 1967. The Southern Railway style canopy added after the removal of the overall roof was, apart from the subway, the only major improvements ever made to the station. *G.A. Pryer Collection*

Dorchester goods shed: the original building of 1847 extended on the left end in the same style in 1884 and with the later 1897 extension to the right. The round-headed iron-framed windows with radial glazing bars, sometimes referred to as 'Ironbridge Windows', were once a common feature of railway and other industrial buildings. The disc signal mounted on the post to the right was the backing signal to allow trains to reverse into the up platform.   *South Western Circle/Eyers Collection*

estimated cost of £854. However, it was recommended that only one half of the proposed extension to the goods shed should be carried out, the addition being added to the west end of the original structure in the same style including the round-headed iron windows. A later addition approved in 1897 was built onto the east end of the original, although in the style by then adopted by the LSWR.

Round-headed iron-framed windows were also used in the construction of the engine shed which stood opposite across the main line. The shed building was of brick construction having a slated roof with louvres, the entrance to the two-road shed being via two brick arches of limited clearance. A two-road wooden extension constructed during the 1880s was built onto the south side of the original building. In a cost saving exercise some of the south side iron windows were removed from the original leaving open arches, the windows then being inserted in the south wall of the new building.

A considerable amount of building work was carried out over the years at Dorchester. In November 1856 G.J.G. Gregory was paid £53 16s. 11d. for building work at the station, followed by repairs the following year, whilst in 1858 Messrs Bull & Sons were paid £525 for building cottages at Dorchester.

The original Southampton & Dorchester station at Blechynden was only of a temporary nature of which no details appear to exist. Its replacement was constructed after the line had been taken over by the LSWR and was an ill-equipped affair which came in for a great deal of criticism. A single-storey building of understated style stood on the up side, whilst a small shelter sufficed on the down side.

In general the goods sheds and associated facilities along the line at its opening reflected the mainly rural nature of the route, and apart from Dorchester only Brockenhurst, Ringwood, Wimborne, Poole (Hamworthy) and Wareham could boast a reasonable size goods shed. A small building without direct rail access sufficed at Wool, whilst other stations appear to have had no covered goods accommodation provided.

Ringwood goods shed followed the same design as Wareham, likewise alterations took place over the years. The original end entrance can be seen boarded over whilst sliding doors have been built into the original side wall, and the original slated hip roof replaced by a simple asbestos version. To the right is the corrugated-iron animal feed store standing on piers to reduce the chances of vermin infestation. *South Western Circle/Eyers Collection*

Wareham goods shed photographed on 26th March, 1983. Only two of the original windows survived on the side; originally the track entered the building through the first arch on the side via a wagon turntable. Severely damaged by fire in April 2003 this Grade II listed building is at the time of writing being restored and converted into office accommodation retaining the iron-framed windows. *Author*

The sheds at Ringwood, Poole (Hamworthy) and Wareham were served by sidings that originally entered the sheds via wagon turntables with movements either being handled by a horse, or the wagons manhandled into position. These three buildings were of brick construction, Ringwood and Wareham with slated hip roofs and, as at Dorchester, the walls were of brick constructed in the form of semi-circular brick arches, a number having doors for access whilst others again had iron-framed round-headed windows. Today, albeit in a distressed condition, Wareham is the sole survivor of this style of goods shed and is a listed Grade II building.

Poole (Hamworthy) differed in that the roof was not of hipped but of pitched construction with a skylight along the ridge extending almost its entire length, although this may have been a later addition. The building, a two-road shed, was also long and narrow with the rail entrances through the south end wall, again accessed via a wagon turntable. The original goods shed at Brockenhurst was of the same style as Dorchester but shorter, with semi-circular brick arches, iron-framed rounded-top windows and a hipped roof.

Unfortunately, at Wimborne there is a certain amount of conjecture as to the exact construction of the goods shed. No photographs of the structure appear to have survived, and indeed it is not shown on several plans. It is inconceivable that Wimborne was without a facility; the point being proved by both newspaper reports and Board minutes following the goods shed fire of 1879. A clue to the type of building is shown to the left of the station in the drawing of Wimborne in Volume One (*p.64*) which depicts it looking not dissimilar to other early goods sheds on the line. As with several other buildings in the drawing the proportions may be a little overstated but there is no reason to suggest any of the buildings were simply added by the artist for effect. Nor has any photographic evidence survived of Christchurch goods shed in its original form prior to its enlargement in 1894.

As big an enigma as Wimborne goods shed are the engine sheds at Ringwood and the original at Poole Junction (Hamworthy Junction). The latter, constructed at the opening of the line, was situated at the west end of the station on the north side and was served by a siding off the up line and consisted of a single road structure. Surviving general station plans suggest it was a narrow brick building of which little is known apart from the fitting of skylights in June 1859. The shed was replaced during 1864 by a new building situated in the 'V' between the Hamworthy branch and the main line. Although of a superior architectural style to earlier buildings it was still adorned by round-headed iron-framed windows!

Several other small engine sheds of a temporary nature also existed along the line. A timber shed was erected at Totton in conjunction with the doubling of the line to Brockenhurst, the shed being used to house the engineer's ballast engine. A further timber shed of this nature was also erected at Wareham to the west of the level crossing, again used by the engineer's ballast engine.

The new station at Totton opened in 1859 and differed from the original small stations along the line in that it was a single-storey building affording no residential accommodation for the station master - indeed, in later years, his office consisted of a wooden hut situated further down the platform. The main

Poole station photographed on 24th August, 1963 with passengers waiting for a down train, whilst a Hampshire diesel-electric unit stands in the up platform. To the extreme right, fenced off, is the point where the former Poole Quay tramway entered the public road.   *C.L. Caddy*

Parkstone station, photographed in 1977, was constructed by the Poole & Bournemouth company and to fit in with in with the aspiring new suburb was constructed of the local brick in various shades to highlight the structure. With the living accommodation within the building it was superior to the earlier stations between Southampton and Dorchester.   *M.J. Tattershall*

building, constructed of brick with stone surrounds to both the windows and doors and stone capping to the gables of the main block, has stood the test of time and today is still pleasing to the eye. However, the down platform shelter of timber construction was undoubtedly either reconstructed or added in later years and was typical of the functional structures required to serve the purpose.

Likewise the station at Millbrook added in 1861 was a utilitarian structure of timber constructed in great haste and added to as the occasion arose. Pokesdown's original station could also be best described as an 'economy job', situated in a cutting and reached by a flight of steps from an overbridge, the wooden buildings standing on the island platform. Again, like many stations, the platform soon proved too short for the longer trains and was lengthened in 1906.

A further example of how vulgarity could arise amongst otherwise pleasing station design occurred with the construction of West Moors (1867), a station that arrived as an afterthought with the opening of the Salisbury & Dorset line. It was once described as 'like a row of terraced houses taken out of an industrial street and deposited on the edge of Dorset'. The station never had a canopy; if the platform and other railway related fittings were removed the description summed it up perfectly.

Moving forward to the 1870s we find the station buildings on the section between Broadstone and Bournemouth West are of yet a different design, mainly by reason of their construction by a separate concern. All four stations, Broadstone, Poole, Parkstone and Bournemouth West were constructed of local brick, which gave a distinctive mellow appearance. Broadstone developed over a period of time. A covered footbridge was authorized in 1887. Originally the booking office was situated on the island platform, but in 1901 a plan was submitted showing how a new booking office and parcel office could be provided on the down side platform with the original booking office being added to the waiting room. Poole station had many alterations and additions over the years, mostly unsympathetic to each other. Unfortunately, these, together with its situation, never gave Poole the station it deserved!

Parkstone set in the leafy suburbs of Poole, was a distinctive gabled building with living accommodation above. The design was pleasing with the use of lighter coloured bricks to highlight the window and door lintels and laid in several layers around the building at different levels. In 1888 a footbridge was added at the west end of the station, the plate girder sides resting on brick supports and staircases. The covering consisted of glazed side panels, with a corrugated-iron roof being added eight years later. Further improvements were carried out in 1896 when a rear extension was added to the station house, to be followed by the replacement of the original basic down platform shelter by a standard LSWR structure of the period and a new extended canopy erected on the up platform during 1897.

Bournemouth West was of the same style as Parkstone although slightly larger, consisting of gable sections at the ends, and again the use of decorative brickwork was evident. With the enlargement of the station during the 1880s, the south end of the building was extended to include a new booking hall and additional canopies added to the exterior of the station including an imposing glass-roofed porte-cochère.

The down side of Bournemouth Central viewed before World War I with not a motor vehicle in sight. The massive columns of the side wall that support the roof girders are imposing as is the end screen to the roof. To the left the covered porte cochère to shield passengers arriving and departing by carriage was a facility in keeping with Bournemouth's high standards.

South Western Circle

The interior of Bournemouth Central looking westwards taken shortly before World War I, clearly shown is the 95 ft-wide roof which stands 43 ft above the platforms. It has been remarked that Bournemouth Central was only second to Waterloo for its grandeur and design. However, some of the elegance appears to have been lost behind the mass of advertising material that covers all available space.

South Western Circle

Other piecemeal developments took place with the extension of existing and additional platforms including canopies of LSWR design. The original small goods shed of brick construction to match the station survived until the end. However, the single-road engine shed situated on the south side of the original station approach was swept away with the 1880s improvements, and no evidence has survived to determine its design.

Bournemouth Central can quite rightly be classed as 'The Jewel in the Crown' of stations on the LSWR, and at its opening the *Christchurch Times* stated it was 'second to none of the provincial stations throughout the company's system'. There is no doubt that the LSWR wished to please both the authorities and the inhabitants of Bournemouth and with the new station they certainly succeeded, as it lay discreetly in a cutting thus attempting to save the inhabitants the sight of an actual railway station!

The massive roof, 350 ft long, 95 ft wide and 43 ft high spanned four tracks and the two platforms and the majority of the station's accommodation was housed under this great roof, supported on 12 massive deep-latticed girders each weighing 17½ tons on supporting piers built into the high screen walls. Nine longitudinal glazed ridge-and-furrow bays provided the roof glazing with deep glazed end screens on curved transoms to cover each end of the roof structure. Additional light was provided at the higher level of the sidewalls by three lancet windows in the 22 bays between the supporting pillars.

The south (down) side had 22 bays, the brickwork of the massive sidewalls being adorned with cornice work at first-storey level. On the north (up) side a second-storey flat was provided above the refreshment room for the manager. The up bay platform at the east end was accessed from the main platform by a series of 13 arches, eight of which were under the main wall of the building, a further 13 blind arches on the outer wall supporting the separate arcaded roof.

A view of the west end of Bournemouth Central showing the large glazed end screen, the down bay platform to the right added in 1900, and the short canopy five years later.

South Western Circle

Bournemouth Central viewed from the east end during 2006 showing the restored roof and end screen.   *Author*

Bournemouth Central from a view under the roof during 2006 clearly showing the restored roof, girder work and brickwork which has, as far as practicable, restored the station to its Victorian glory.   *Author*

From its opening accommodation had been provided on a grand scale for all classes with three classes of ladies waiting rooms, and the entrances on both the north and south sides were protected by a good porte-cochère. However, the station very quickly proved to be a 'wind tunnel' and as early as December 1885 the company's Engineer referred plans to the Traffic Committee for erecting screens on the platforms as additional protection from the wind.

By the turn of the century improvements were required to the station. In December 1899 plans for a bay platform at the west end of the down platform, a new parcels office and cloakroom, and alterations to the existing offices on the down side were approved. Again with the extra platform accommodation the denizens of Bournemouth had to be protected from the weather, and in November 1905 additional roofing for the down platform was authorized at an estimated cost of £780.

With the removal of the down bay in 1928, the canopy was replaced with a steel structure of Southern Railway design, the new signal box being placed above. The 1928 improvements also saw the carriage dock and siding at the east end on the down side removed and the platform extended eastwards with a large parcels office added to the end of the main building.

In general the LSWR had provided the best at Bournemouth, but unfortunately the ambience of the station was devalued by the erection of an inferior engine shed in the yard adjacent to the west end of the station. Although the later structure further west was an improvement, its nearness to the station always cast a shadow over the scene.

Although Bournemouth symbolized the status of the company, other stations were not without style. By the 1880s a set of standard designs had been evolved to give what in today's language would be a corporate image. However, whereas today this would be slavishly followed in each building to the last detail, the designs of the LSWR had variation to suit both location and local requirements.

For the new stations on the Bournemouth Direct Line and other reconstructions of the period the 'Flemish-Queen Anne' style was adopted, which had already been put to use further up the line where Worplesdon (1883) was identical to New Milton, the latter also having the adornment of Dutch gables. Both Sway and Hinton Admiral were of the same design, although without the Dutch gables as if to demonstrate they were in a lower order than the fast developing township of New Milton. All three stations had standard LSWR canopies to provide shelter on the down platforms.

Whereas the previous three stations had living accommodation provided, Christchurch, which was built on a gentle curve although in the same style, was a single-storey building. This had good quality accommodation for passengers who were also provided with a covered footbridge to reach the up platform, to the north of which land was available for additional platforms. This provision was never required, although the existing platforms were lengthened in 1897.

Brockenhurst, although rebuilt in the Queen Anne style, differed in the unusual fact that the main station buildings were isolated from the platforms, which were only accessible via a footbridge. Also provided was a new goods shed. The up platform was provided with a standard canopy of the period, whilst the down platform canopy of older design had a curved corrugated-iron roof.

The exterior of Wareham station constructed in 1886 in the Flemish-Queen Anne style popular with the LSWR at that period. The gables complete with ball finials are of particular interest, one having a decorative stone panel containing the LSWR crest. Today the up platform shelter, which is of standard LSWR design of the period is Grade II listed. *Author*

Hamworthy Junction was a station that for a number of years escaped the attention of the painters, the faded old Southern Railway livery still visible when visited by the photographer in March 1963. In the foreground are examples of an SR rail-built signal to the left and a traditional LSWR lattice post signal to the right, both having been equipped with upper quadrant arms. BR Standard class '4' 2-6-0 No. 76012 stands in the down bay platform. *C.L. Caddy*

Further west the new station at Wareham (1887) is regarded as the most elaborate example of the company's Queen Anne style, with two gables, one displaying the LSWR coat of arms the other in the Dutch-Flemish style complete with ball finials, with the steeply-angled red tile roof supporting a cupola complete with weathervane. The platform canopies were of standard LSWR design of the period and a footbridge mounted on brick staircases linked the platforms. Today, the station (including the shelter and lamp standards) is Grade II listed. In stark architectural contrast just off the ends of the platforms the two crossing keeper's cottages (Nos. 28 & 29) of 1847 remained, as did the original station building which was retained as the station master's residence until its demolition.

Two further stations opened during 1893 as part of the final direct route to Dorchester and Weymouth. First Branksome which was situated awkwardly in a cutting at the top of the 1 in 60 Parkstone Bank, which necessitated the booking office and main station buildings being situated at road level with the platforms reached via flights of stairs. Mathew Shaw of the London Constructive Iron & Bridge Works of Millwall supplied a covered lattice footbridge supported from the upper level, whilst two standard LSWR canopies covered the platforms below.

Whilst Branksome, then a rapidly developing suburban area, required a station of reasonable proportions, it is difficult to understand why the reconstructed station at Hamworthy Junction needed to be so lavish in view of the reduced and rapidly failing passenger service on the Hamworthy branch. Furthermore there was very little development in the area surrounding the station at that period. The new structure retained part of the original up main building with an extension added to the west end; the two platforms were reconstructed, the down side being an island with a loop to serve the Hamworthy branch. A subway connected the two platforms, which were covered by large canopies of standard LSWR design.

The final important station to be constructed between Southampton and Dorchester in the 19th century was Southampton West which opened in November 1895. Again the Flemish-Queen Anne style was adopted with subtle differences from other stations of the period.

It was a single-storey structure of brick under a steeply-angled red tile roof, with stone used for window dressings and other decorative work. The down side buildings were surmounted with a cupola and weathervane, whilst on the up side there was an 82 ft-high clock tower, its cupola top the principal distinguishing feature of the station. A covered footbridge in iron on brick supports connected the platforms at the London end of the station.

The Crossing Cottages

The crossing keeper's cottages of the Southampton & Dorchester, of which at one time there were 46 spread along 60 miles of railway, are worth a study in themselves. However, there are several points of interest that deserve mention. What could be described as the standard design of a single-storey building was placed at many minor crossings and at stations such as Brockenhurst and Wool.

Uddens crossing gatehouse No. 21 was of unusual design, no doubt to please the owner of Uddens estate who was a Director of the Southampton & Dorchester company. The lodge had pedimented gables with a little Dutch-Flemish influence. The adjacent signal box/ground frame was typical of LSWR design of the period. Today both the lodge and all other remains of the railway at this point have been demolished. *South Western Circle/Eyers Collection*

Crossing cottage No. 30 at Wareham, with No. 29, situated on the opposite side of the line, were provided at the opening of the line, and resembled a number of toll houses of the period. Containing three main rooms and a scullery they were the answer to a working man's prayer in 1847, but by the time this photograph was taken in August 1966 they uninhabitable and were demolished the following March. *Lens of Sutton Association*

There were also a few two-storey cottages: West Moors (19) and Dolmans Lane (20) of original design, whereas Woodsford (38) is thought to have been a standard cottage with an additional storey added.

Four further cottages were added later by the LSWR. One such was at Rushton level crossing between Wareham and Wool where in July 1900 it was decided to provide a gatekeeper and erect a cottage at an estimated cost of £275, for which about 20 perches of land would have to be purchased.

In addition there were gate lodges of non-standard design in locations where the gentry and other matters had to be considered. For example Lord De Mauley, a Southampton & Dorchester Director, and later Sir John Josiah Guest had interests in the vicinity of Oakley crossing (No. 26) near Canford Manor so it had Tudor-style windows as did Syward (41) with slight variations; both were minor copies of Moorsom's smaller stations. Another Director Edward Greathed owned Uddens estate, hence Uddens crossing (21) had the most ostentatious lodge along the line, a two-storey building with two sections at right angles to each other, two end walls with Dutch gables, and a tile hung wall on the gable end housed the front door which had a miniature Dutch gable over the porch.

The four lodges at Christchurch Street, Ringwood, (17), Wareham (29 & 30) and the gate lodge at Dorchester (43) were representative of certain toll houses and the gate lodges of large estates of the period, and were obviously placed where it was wished to give a good impression of the company. Of superior design to the other single-storey lodges, they consisted of three main rooms, the end two being formed of octagonal-shaped sections with bay windows in the front elevation, although there were minor variations within the four buildings. Later the bay windows were removed from the Ringwood lodge (17), it has to be assumed at the time of laying the third line for the Christchurch branch in 1862. Again these lodges were clearly of a design employed on the Birmingham & Gloucester Railway, and an example of almost identical proportions existed for many years at Alstone crossing, Cheltenham.

In general the lodges could only be described as small houses even by the standards of the mid-19th century, and as early as 1852 there were reports of building work being carried out at various gate lodges. This process was reported in the accounts for many years as alterations and extensions were carried out to make life a little more comfortable for the occupants, who no doubt like the majority of occupants of tied cottages in the 'good old, bad old days' were reluctant to complain of their conditions! Added to the various alterations carried out, gate lodge No. 1, situated at the east end of the 1859 Totton station, was dismantled and following the cleaning of the bricks etc. was rebuilt at Lymington Junction for an unspecified purpose!

Today a few lodges survive, often extensively rebuilt in private ownership. At the time of writing No. 8 lodge with its patterned brickwork stands alongside the crossing at Brockenhurst station. It is the best surviving example, albeit substantially modified in the past with a large lean-to at the rear and extensions to the main building at the east end, clearly shown by the off-centre crossing number plate, the plainer brickwork of the extension and the additional chimneystack.

Crossing cottage No. 8 at Brockenhurst; the two windows to the left mark the extent of the original building it being extended twice at the right-hand end and had the original small windows replaced. The original patterned brickwork highlights this as one of the original standard crossing cottages, albeit much modified; still occupied when photographed in September 2007. *Author*

Pure pre-war suburbia, with a terrace of shops as a background. Bournemouth Corporation trolleybus No. 283 turns off Christchurch Road into Seaborne Road in the mid-1960s. To the right of the trolleybus stands Pokesdown station with its attendant lock-up shops. Pokesdown station was a modern Southern Railway design of the 1930s familiar in the London suburbs, indeed if the trolleybus was red, one could be forgiven for thinking one was in the metropolis. *C.L. Caddy*

Staff Cottages

By the very nature of railway work a certain amount of staff accommodation had always been provided, thus over the years a considerable number of houses were constructed, the details of which are far too complex to describe fully in this work. Their construction was, however, an ongoing programme for a number of years.

In 1885 a pair of cottages was erected at Hurn with two additional cottages added at Moreton the following year and a single cottage provided at Woodfidley in 1893. A dormitory for enginemen was built on land adjoining the engine shed at Dorchester in 1894, whilst further cottages were constructed in 1897, bringing the total to 23 plus a dormitory at Dorchester alone. Further cottages were erected at Moreton during 1897 and in the same year the cost of six cottages built at Wool was estimated at £1,672 including the purchase of land, and although the work was approved it was noted the cost appeared high! Staff cottages were also provided at Bournemouth West in 1896, and the same year there was also an upgrading of existing property when earth closets were replaced by flush toilets at the five cottages outside Poole station at a cost of £114 3s. 3d.

The difficulties of providing accommodation for staff in country districts was further demonstrated in January 1906 when it was recommended that a cottage be rented by the company at £2 12s. per quarter and sublet to the signalman at Woodsford Crossing at a rent of 4s. per week, the landlord keeping the house in repair and paying the rates and taxes. There were few houses in the neighbourhood and the owner would not let direct to the signalman.

Stations and associated buildings of the 20th century

The reconstruction of Pokesdown station in 1931 (with the exception of the World War I station at Holton Heath) was the first new station on the line since the end of the 19th century; it also demonstrated the new architectural styles the Southern Railway frequently used to promote its electrification programme. A single-storey building in brick with stone dressings, modern windows and doors complete with adjoining lock-up shops produced a very contemporary looking station.

Indeed, after the introduction of Bournemouth's trolleybuses that passed the door, had they been red, one could be forgiven for thinking that a little piece of suburban London had reached Bournemouth! A covered concrete footbridge gave access to the two low level platforms, which were covered with standard Southern Railway steel canopies.

Apart from modifications at Brockenhurst, the only major rebuilding works carried out between the wars was complete reconstruction of Millbrook and the partial rebuilding and extensions at Southampton Central, as fully described in the main text. Thereafter, other than repairs to war damage, no further major construction took place until August 1966 when the up side buildings of Southampton Central were demolished, their replacement of concrete construction consisting of a four-storey structure with station facilities on the ground floor and office accommodation above. However, the station facilities provided only limited accommodation for both passengers and staff resulting in renovation work in 1988 when an improved booking hall/ticket office, enquiry office and a new buffet and bookstall were brought into use. At the same time minor alterations were made to the down side facilities including the surviving parts of the 1935 buildings, the destroyed centre section having been replaced by a new glass-fronted structure during 1980.

The year 1969 saw the rebuilding of Wool station using the 'CLASP' system, which had been developed for industrial buildings and the post-war school building programme. The up side shelter, also of CLASP construction, could be described as a high-class bus shelter. The following year Poole was reconstructed using the same method, the modular design of the system allowing for a larger building, and in both cases their lack of architectural interest leaves little to remark on.

The life of the rebuilt Poole station was short. By 1991 further reconstruction had taken place, again with new buildings on the up side, described as a 'Grand Marquee' building of wood and glass, four steel masts with cables supporting the barrel-vaulted roof constructed from coated plywood. However, the new buildings were not without problems when defects were discovered upon their completion. Again further improvements were carried out at Wool during 2005 when a new shelter was provided on the up platform and the station forecourt was rearranged to assist with the arrival and departure of connecting bus services.

Finally one must not forget the restoration of Bournemouth Central as described earlier, which has given the station back much of its former glory and a place in the annals of railway architecture.

Poole station looking west during July 2008, the station building with its curved roof on the right-hand platform is the third building on the site, the platforms with their sharp curve being a throw-back to the original station.   *Author*

Bridges, viaducts and other structures

Bridges and viaducts have by their nature seen more change than the majority of buildings along the line, generally their replacement being hastened by fatigue, the increased weight of locomotives and stock, and the advantages of superior materials. A number of the timber structures, built as an expedient to facilitate the opening of the line, were soon replaced. By 1858 the wooden bridges at Millbrook, Redbridge, a bridge east of Brockenhurst, and Rockley viaduct were all subject to a 20 mph speed restriction for all traffic, athough a number of timber structures survived a considerable time; in September 1892 the *Southern Times* reported that the replacement of three wooden bridges between Wareham and Wool was taking place.

In May 1885 the Engineer recommended that certain cast-iron bridges on the line between Ringwood and Dorchester be reconstructed in wrought iron. The company records of the same period also make reference to the strengthening of the Avon viaduct at Ringwood and the reconstruction of overbridge No. 120 (Culliford Road bridge) near Dorchester station. Also in connection with the new direct line, several cast-iron bridges on the original line between Christchurch and Bournemouth East were replaced by wrought-iron structures.

Even their iron and steel replacements did not always have a long life, the use of even heavier locomotives requiring their replacement. Rockley was an example: the seven-span wrought-iron viaduct was only 38 years old when replaced in 1923 by a single-span bowstring girder structure. On the other hand, a similar viaduct between Redbridge and Totton survived until 1964, whilst one of two viaducts on the Old Road at Ringwood had pre-cast concrete decks fitted to the original piers in 1961.

A number of the original and replacement brick bridges survived, albeit many strengthened and altered, including the bridge that carried the line over the entrance to Canford House, situated just south of the viaduct over the River Stour at Wimborne. Often referred to as the 'Lady Wimborne Carriage Road Bridge' it is one of the most ornately carved railway bridges in the country. There is a distinct possibility that the ornate hamstone facings were added at a later date to at least part of the original bridge structure, as the Canford Estate was not sold by Lord De Mauley to Sir John Guest until 1846 by which time the railway was in an advanced stage of construction. The later improvements are substantiated by the fact the new owners engaged architects to improve the buildings on the estate, and the surviving drawings of the bridge by the architect Sir Charles Barry are dated 1853. Also the Guests were lavish entertainers of the great and good of the time including Royalty, thus the entrance to their estate had to reflect their position in society.

Other bridges of particular interest included the now-demolished bridge over the River Stour at Wimborne which consisted of three plate girder spans supported on brick and stone piers with a brick archway on the river bank each side. The bridge over the River Piddle west of Wareham is now Grade II listed, although the steel span over the river is a replacement; the brick arch each side built on the skew and the brick quadrant retaining walls at either end, although much renewed, are today considered one of the chief original civil engineering features of the line. Likewise the iron bridge carrying the Wareham Road over the line east of Dorchester is also Grade II listed. Viewed from the adjacent footbridge, the railings, a feature of the older bridges, are visible.

Bridge No. 14 carrying a footpath across the line near Deer Leap crossing, south of Lyndhurst Road. The cast side girders bear the inscription 'W. & J. Lankester 1848 Southampton' and it was still in use during the summer of 2007 when this photograph was taken. *Author*

Bridge No. 68 that originally carried the A31 across the line at Ashley, west of Ringwood, replaced a level crossing and is slightly newer than bridge No. 14 near Lyndhurst although of the same general construction. A bridge of the same style, No. 74, still survives in Leigh Lane east of Wimborne although much surrounded by trees and vegetation. *L. Tavender*

One of the earlier bridges No. 14 still survives to this day carrying a pathway over the line near Deer Leap crossing, south of Lyndhurst Road. The cast side girders carry the inscription 'W. & J. Lankester 1848 Southampton'. West of Ringwood Ashley bridge, now demolished, was of similar construction. Still standing is bridge No. 74 over the disused earthworks at Northleigh Lane, Colehill near Wimborne. It has a span of 28 feet; four wrought-iron girders with brick jack arches between support the road surface above. The side balustrades 3 ft 10 in. high are formed of cast-iron railings with pattern work long the upper section, indeed, the design has similarities to bridges on the Birmingham & Gloucester Railway, although in this case there is certainly a time gap. In fact bridge No. 74 was not built until the mid-1850s replacing a crossing and lodge No. 25.

The later construction of the Bournemouth Direct Line saw a different style of construction. The viaduct crossing the River Avon at Christchurch consists of three 60 ft bow lattice girders spans across the river with a 40 ft bow plate girder span each side spanning the riverbank. Likewise, the overbridges on the line are not without interest, the majority being of a standard design executed in brick and distinctive in that they consisted of twin arches, resulting in the up and down lines being slewed out to pass through. However, the jewel in the crown of the Direct Line and the Bournemouth extensions are the two magnificent brick viaducts that span the head of the Bourne Valley at Branksome. The nine-arch viaduct carries the new line from Branksome towards Bournemouth and the 10-arch curved viaduct formed the connecting spur between Gas Works Junction and Bournemouth West. Built high above the valley floor, the former still carries the main line to Weymouth, whilst the latter remains disused since the closure of Bournemouth West, now a reminder of Bournemouth's railway history.

Owing to the nature of the countryside construction of the original line required few tunnels, the infamous 528 yard Southampton tunnel has already been well documented, whilst the only other tunnel was under the A349 Wimborne-Poole road near Merley and is a mere 37 yds long and of cut-and-cover construction. The vaulted roof was supported by eight arches, the ones at the tunnel ends being 9 ft

Bridge No. 75, a later replacement across Leigh Road, Wimborne, was of conventional plate and girder construction. However, with only 14 ft headroom the Hants & Dorset bus company had to ensure none of its Poole-based Bristol KSW6B highbridge double-deckers ever strayed onto that route.   *Author's Collection*

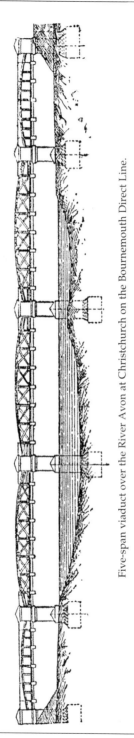

Five-span viaduct over the River Avon at Christchurch on the Bournemouth Direct Line.

One of the two pile-supported bridges that carried the Old Road across the River Avon and its flood plain west of Ringwood still survive as part of the Castleman Trailway.

Author

In this pre-1914 view looking along the line from Bournemouth West Junction towards Branksome, the nine-arch brick viaduct carrying the direct line between Gas Works Junction and Branksome station across the Bourne Valley can be seen to the right. *South Western Circle*

wide, whilst the intermediate six are 3 ft wide, and set into the brickwork of each arch are cast-iron inserts to give extra clearance to allow a carriage door to be opened in the tunnel without the top of it striking the brickwork. It is understood these were fitted during the 1880s at the request of the Board of Trade.

On the Bournemouth extension line the tunnel under Holdenhurst Road on the approach to Bournemouth Central station is only 48 yds long, and the one under the crossroads at Cemetery Junction 69 yds, both these being twin bore tunnels. Whilst the 822 yd Bincombe tunnel and the 41 yds-long Bincombe South tunnel are on the former GWR section forming the summit of the line out of Weymouth, and are still in use.

The footbridge adjacent to the level crossing in Poole High Street has served since 1872 when the railway first arrived in Poole. On the girder work can be read the inscription 'Ransome & Rapier London 1872'. A photograph of the bridge under construction is shown on page 115 of Volume One. *Author*

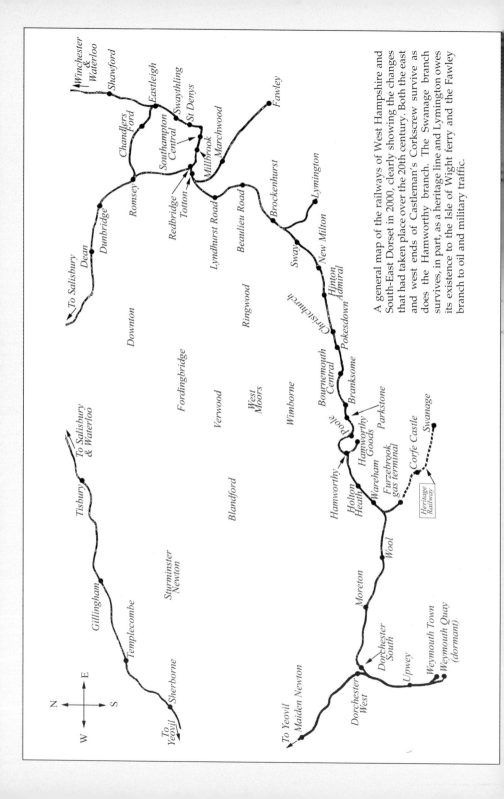

A general map of the railways of West Hampshire and South-East Dorset in 2000, clearly showing the changes that had taken place over the 20th century. Both the east and west ends of Castleman's Corkscrew survive as does the Hamworthy branch. The Swanage branch survives, in part, as a heritage line and Lymington owes its existence to the Isle of Wight ferry and the Fawley branch to oil and military traffic.

Chapter Thirteen

Into the 21st Century

Thus the Southampton & Dorchester Railway entered the 21st century much reduced, with the early demise of the Ringwood-Christchurch branch and the loss of the Old Road to Beeching. The scale of the other and the Beeching cuts was relatively light, only the stations at Boscombe and Bournemouth West being closed, although many have been reduced in status, in an entirely different world. Gone were the monopolies they had previously enjoyed over a majority of goods and passenger traffic, now their future trade ruled by costs, convenience, contracts and politics.

By the end of the 20th century the area west of Southampton had developed beyond all expectations. The New Forest had become a popular residential and holiday area, housing had covered large areas of land in the Ringwood and Wimborne area with ribbon development stretching westwards from Ringwood through Wimborne to Poole. The 2001 census showed Wimborne having a population of 6,500 with a further 7,030 in adjoining Colehill. Ringwood housed 14,400 against the 6,220 a century before. The combined population of Bournemouth and Poole had reached 301,732, Dorchester 16,160 and Weymouth and Portland 63,648. So it is against these statistics that we move forward into the future.

Industry has always been light in the area with many disappearing over the years, but fortunately others are reborn or arrive. The introduction of sand trains between Wool and Neasden brought much needed freight traffic to the line, the first departing on 2nd June, 2000 hauled by EWS class '66' No. 66124, although from April 2005 the contract was transferred to Freightliner which early in 2007 introduced a new rake of wagons for the working.

To accommodate the wagons in the up siding at Wool station, the empty stock works through to Dorchester South where part of the train is shunted into the down siding before the engine runs round via Dorchester Junction and takes the first part to Wool before returning to Dorchester to repeat the process. The sand is brought to Wool by road from a pit at Woodsford, west of Moreton. There had been proposals to install a siding at milepost 132 just west of No. 38 crossing. Unfortunately the capital outlay required caused the scheme to founder; had it been proceeded with it would have been within a very short distance of the old LSWR ballast pit at Woodsford.

The £7 million restoration and refurbishment of Bournemouth station was completed during 2000 and a commemorative plaque was unveiled by the Mayor of Bournemouth, Councillor Ben Gower FCA, on 4th August to mark the occasion.

Improvements were also taking place with passenger services. The first Virgin Voyager train reached Bournemouth on 16th September, 2001, when unit No. 220006 arrived with the 1.11 pm from Manchester. It was a sign of future travel on cross-country services. On 29th September the final locomotive-hauled Virgin service ran from Weymouth with class '47' No. 47810 hauling the 9.20 am Weymouth-Liverpool, and No. 47805 arriving with the 9.13 am from Liverpool.

A new traffic to the Dorset area is the transportation of sand from Wool to Neasden. During August 2006 a Freightliner-liveried General Motors class '66' prepares to shunt sand wagons at Wool. *Author*

The 1930s architecture of Pokesdown station forms a backdrop when history was made on 9th July, 2003 as British Railways Standard class '5' 4-6-0 No. 73096 steams through the station hauling the return working of the first passenger-carrying steam train between Poole and Waterloo for 36 years. Owing to signalling problems which caused delays, the special worked as a normal stopping train calling at New Milton, Christchurch, Bournemouth and Poole, it being estimated around 100 passengers took advantage of this unique event. *A. Wild*

The 15th October, 2002 saw the official launch of the fleet of class '450' Desiro trains, a fleet of 155 units to replace slam door stock, which was due to, be phased out by 2005. The new fleet consisted of 110 four-car class '450' units running on mainly suburban services and 45 five-car class '440' units for main line services.

The new units were gradually introduced into the Network as they arrived from their German builders and underwent their acceptance trials. The first two units Nos. 450007 and 450008 arrived at Bournemouth depot on the 18th and 31st December respectively. Weymouth received its first visit on 23rd January, 2003 with the arrival of unit No. 450007 on trial, topped and tailed by class '33s' Nos. 33103 and 33202.

To maintain the new Desiro fleet a £30m depot had been constructed at Northam, east of Southampton on the site that had originally been Northam engine shed. Construction commenced in February 2001 with the officially opening on 2nd July, 2003, the first new 750V DC third-rail depot to be constructed for over 30 years.

The Desiro units had undergone extensive testing between Bournemouth, Dorchester South and Weymouth before the first unit entered revenue earning service on 5th October, 2003 when units Nos. 450015 and 450026 worked the 10.30 am and 1.30 pm Bournemouth-Weymouth services and the 12.23 pm and 3.23 pm return services. On 7th December unit No. 44401 of the '444' sub-class worked a test train between Weymouth and Wool.

Whilst the new units were making their debut on the line, other historic events were taking place. The 17th May, 2003 saw the final working of HSTs on cross-country services to and from Bournemouth. On 9th July to celebrate the 35th anniversary of the end of Southern Region steam, BR Standard class '5' No. 73096 worked a special from Poole to Waterloo. History was made on the return journey when owing to long delays arising from signalling problems at Wimbledon No. 73096 worked as a normal stopping train calling at New Milton, Christchurch, Bournemouth and Poole. It was estimated that around 100 passengers took advantage of this unique event when for the first time since 1967 ordinary fare-paying passengers travelled on the Southampton-Bournemouth line hauled by a steam locomotive.

During the early hours of 7th April, 2003 the Grade II listed goods shed at Wareham, the only survivor of the original goods sheds constructed on the Southampton & Dorchester, was severely damaged by fire, the roof being almost totally destroyed and the wooden doors charred. The previous day the local authority had turned down an application to convert the premises into residential accommodation!

Chandlers Ford station, on the Romsey-Eastleigh line, closed in May 1959 and was reopened on 18th May, 2003 when a new service operated by diesel units commenced between Romsey and Totton via Eastleigh and Southampton Central.

Following the introduction of many of the new units, South West Trains introduced a new timetable from 12th December, 2004. Based on the well-tried former Southern Railway regular interval service principle, it was the first major attempt to amend the timetable introduced with the 1967 Bournemouth electrification. The Waterloo-Weymouth service now departed at 35 minutes past the hour and on the hour from Weymouth, but retimed to provide a larger gap from Virgin trains between Basingstoke and Bournemouth. The five minutes past the hour Waterloo-Poole service and the 39 minutes past the hour Waterloo-Southampton service were also retimed to avoid delays.

When the railway first arrived at Southampton nobody could have foreseen the growth that was to take place. It became the principal ocean liner port in the British Isles served by the leading shipping companies of the day. This traffic with its attendant boat trains has gone, superseded by long haul airliners, so have conventional cargo vessels and the labour intensive business of loading and unloading cargo from assorted ships into railway wagons. Nowadays massive ships stacked sky high with containers are swiftly unloaded by giant cranes and the containers dispatched by trains from the Freightliner depots at the Maritime Terminal and Millbrook. Today there are two terminals handling the transport of new motor vehicles, and a stone terminal. On the passenger front, although a leading port for cruise liners, they are only served by the occasional boat train, whilst the Royal Pier area and parts of the old docks have been redeveloped for non commercial purposes.

Gone is the civil engineering depot at Redbridge and the Eling Tramway along with many private sidings in the Southampton area, whilst on the plus side Freightliner has a locomotive maintenance and wagon repair depot at Millbrook and South West Trains the Desiro maintenance depot at Northam.

Down Southampton Water at Fawley the products of the refinery once moved by numerous tank trains are now sent through pipelines to major distribution centres, leaving only a limited amount of rail traffic. However, a substantial traffic to and from Marchwood military port travels over the Fawley branch. During recent years there have been plans to construct further container terminals on the west side of Southampton Water which would be accessed from the Fawley branch; to date this development has been forestalled by opposition.

A general view looking west of the Freightliner locomotive maintenance facility at Millbrook during September 2005.   *Author*

To the older generation Southampton will always be synonymous with the great liners of the past. The ill-fated *Titanic* sailed from Southampton in 1912 and many Southampton men in her crew were lost. More fortunate were the *Mauretania*, *Aquitania*, and the pride of the British Merchant Navy the *Queen Mary* and *Queen Elizabeth*; they all appeared to have a living spirit, and were admired by thousands. However, times change and as we move into the 21st century the scene at Southampton has changed. With a population in 2001 of 217,445 it is still an important passenger centre. South West Trains operate the main line service between Waterloo and Weymouth, there are various long distance cross-country services (now run by Arriva Cross-Country), and services between South Wales and Bristol to Portsmouth and the South Coast passing through the station. During 2004 Southampton Central handled 300 passenger trains for South West Trains, Virgin, Wessex Trains and Southern, also approximately 58 freight trains for EWS and Freightliner each day.

The demise of slam-door stock had slowly taken place since the introduction of the Desiro units, the new units being used from 4th April, 2005 to operate the stopping service between Brockenhurst and Wareham. The last official slam-door train ran on South West Trains on Thursday 26th June: the 11.35 am Waterloo-Weymouth service consisting of '4CIG' units Nos. 1396 and 1398 and '4CEP' unit No. 3536. Each of the 'CIG' units contained a coach formerly in '4CEP' units, coaches Nos. 10202 and 510242, thus making them the last two Eastleigh-built coaches in main line revenue-earning service. Following arrival at Bournemouth at 1.20 pm the stock proceeded to Branksome carriage sidings, whilst passengers for Weymouth continued aboard a class '442' unit.

However, there is an exception to the rule. As the Lymington branch is worked as a separate line from Brockenhurst, the Railway Inspectorate have given a dispensation for the use of slam-door stock on this branch with a speed restriction of 45 mph. Classed as a heritage line, two refurbished '4CIG' units, No. 1497 (originally No. 1883) now named *Freshwater* and painted in BR blue and grey and unit No. 1498 (originally No. 1888) now named *Farringford* and painted in Southern Region green, were named at Brockenhurst on 12th May, 2005 and run as three-car sets. To add to the effect, at Brockenhurst, Lymington Town and Lymington Pier stations BR-style totem nameboards were fixed to station lampposts.

Although several steam excursions had run to Waterloo commencing at both Wareham and Poole, history was again made on Saturday 18th June, 2005 when unrebuilt light pacific No. 34067 *Tangmere* worked an excursion throughout from Weymouth and return.

The following month saw the final liquid petroleum gas tank train depart from Furzebrook on 15th July, the remaining small flow being transported by road, thus concluding freight operation on the remaining section of the former Swanage branch. Although physically connected to the Swanage Heritage Railway, it awaits signalling alterations to enable through running on and off the national rail network.

Withdrawal of the class '442' units introduced in 1988 took place as the new Desiro units entered service, the first regular Desiro workings commencing on 16th October, 2006, with Saturday 13th January, 2007 expected to be the final day for the '442' class. Unfortunately delays in new stock delivery resulted in four and six units remained in service the following week.

'Battle of Britain' class 4-6-2 No. 34067 *Tangmere* has just arrived at Weymouth on Saturday 18th June, 2005 following the first return working to Waterloo of a steam train since the end of steam in July 1967. *Author*

Class '442' 'Wessex Electric' No. 2421 stands under the roof of Bournemouth Central station in October 2005. Whilst the great Victorian structure has endured the passage of time, the '442' units incorporated a little from the past in their traction motors and associated equipment being recovered from the '4REP' units. *Author*

During their final week class '442' units Nos. 2405/10/12/13/19 were noted mainly working Waterloo-Poole services, the 7.25 am Weymouth-Brockenhurst was also worked by members of the class on both 22nd and 24th January. The final two workings from Weymouth took place on Friday 2nd February with unit 2410 departing at 4.00 pm and unit No. 2412 departing at 11.11 pm. The last day of operation, 3rd February, saw units Nos. 2405, 2410, and 2412 in service, the final working being the 9.05 pm Waterloo-Poole, thus bringing down the curtain on 19 years of Wessex Electric operation.

The Desiro unit, No. 450127, was delivered early in January 2007, and with the classes firmly established, and the '444' class working the majority of the Weymouth trains, unit No. 44012 was named *Destination Weymouth* at Weymouth station on Friday 6th July, 2007. The nameplate was unveiled by World Champion Gold Medal sailor Richard Glover assisted by Jacob Bowyer, a pupil of St John's School, Weymouth who had won a competition for drawing a modern train. The ceremony, attended by the Mayor of Weymouth and Portland Councillor David Harris, pupils from St John's School, Railway and Council officials. Albeit only an electric-multiple-unit, *Destination Weymouth* is the third locomotive to carry the Weymouth name.

From 9th December, 2007 the previous hourly service to Weymouth was doubled to two trains an hour until the late evening, the Brockenhurst-Wareham stopping service being withdrawn with the introduction of the new timetable. In the summer of 2008 Weymouth enjoyed 28 trains between Waterloo and Weymouth and 30 return workings. Today Southampton can be reached from Waterloo in 1 hour 13 minutes, Bournemouth in 1 hour 45 minutes and Weymouth in 2 hours 48 minutes. Never before has the line west of Poole been so well served by through trains from the capital. At Wareham a 30 minute rail service in conjunction with an hourly bus service to and from Swanage gave rail-bus transport superior to anything provided before.

To the east at Lymington the first branch to be opened after the completion of the original Southampton & Dorchester Railway is still operating from Brockenhurst, where there is a real junction with passengers changing into a branch train. It serves a growing area of residential development and the Isle of Wight ferry to Yarmouth. It celebrated its 150th anniversary on 12th July, 2008.

Following the withdrawal of the '442' units the future of South West Trains Bournemouth depot looked insecure. Fortunately, during early 2008 the depot became a mini-refurbishment centre with various classes of electric stock undergoing upgrading.

During recent years the operational side of the railway has constantly changed to suit the commercial situation, likewise the infrastructure and associated buildings are changing as town and country evolve in the 21st century. The uncontrolled growth of lineside vegetation has reduced the view to be seen from the passing train and likewise the view of the railway from the countryside.

Much disused land has been redeveloped, the infilling of the upper reaches of Poole Harbour has moved the site of Holes Bay Junction away from the water's edge and changed the surrounding landscape; apart from the main line the area is now occupied by industrial premises. To the east side of Poole the embankment dividing Poole harbour from Poole Park has been reclaimed on the harbour side and now forms Baiter Harbourside Park.

The class '442' 'Wessex Electrics' only had days left in service on the Weymouth-Waterloo line as unit No. 2405 waits to depart with the 7.00 am Weymouth-Waterloo service on 20th January, 2007, the first Southern departure that day which was the 150th anniversary of the railway opening between Dorchester and Weymouth. *J.D. Ward*

The modern scene at Brockenhurst on 1st September, 2007. On the left in the Lymington bay is one of the class '421' emu heritage units used exclusively on the Lymington branch. In the down platform is a Virgin Voyager, and a class '450' emu stands in the up loop. *Author*

At Bournemouth the magnificent 10-arch curved viaduct between the former Gas Works Junction and Bournemouth West Junction, although disused, still stands. A short distance away the approaches to the former terminus at Bournemouth West and part of the station site is now part of Wessex Way and other road improvements. The Midland Hotel still stands, once situated opposite the station entrance, it now houses a sports bar - 'Champions'. The goods yard at Bournemouth Central has become a retail park, and the up side of Boscombe station had been occupied by industrial units.

The former engine shed site at Dorchester is now a small housing estate, so is the goods yard and surrounding land at Moreton. At Hamworthy Junction the railway cottages have been demolished and the site incorporated in a housing development. Recently the railway cottages at Ashurst (Lyndhurst Road) have been renovated. At the time of writing the fire-damaged 1847 goods shed at Wareham is being refurbished as modern office accommodation providing a ground floor of 1,570 sq. ft, and a mezzanine first floor of 1,260 sq. ft, all set within the listed building in which the round top iron-framed windows have been replaced.

At Poole Network Rail has obtained planning permission to remove the remaining three goods yard sidings and replace them by two electrified sidings, which can be used for emergency train maintenance in the event of restricted access to Branksome. A scheme is also being discussed to reconstruct the station for the third time in 35 years. The existing station building is to be replaced by

The modern face of freight traffic is shown as Freightliner-liveried General Motors class '66' No. 66540 *Ruby* passes Millbrook station on 1st September, 2007 taking the line into Southampton Western Docks with a train of containers. Across at the quayside a cruise liner waits to sail, all the land between the station and the ship having been reclaimed for the pre-war Western Docks scheme.   *Author*

a new structure largely constructed of glass, closer to Towngate bridge although without any significant changes to the platforms. The work will form part of a £50 million plus Poole Gateway development to include a transport interchange, an 11-storey hotel, six blocks containing 265 flats, office space, cafes and a multi-storey car park.

The changing fortunes of industry were clearly demonstrated when the old-established brewery of Messrs Eldridge Pope at Dorchester ceased brewing. Only 17 years previously the brewery had expanded its property taking in the old station and goods yard. The entire site was sold for redevelopment during 2005, and at the time of writing housing and retail outlets are being constructed, with plans for another new station, which it is hoped will be Britain's first solar-powered railway station in the country.

In this ever-changing world it is difficult to foresee the future. As these words are being written in June 2008, we can be certain that more than 160 years ago, in 1847, when the first train steamed into Dorchester station, neither Charles Castleman, nor his associates could have imagined such vast changes.

The modern electric railway in 2008 is illustrated by class '444' Desiro unit No. 444020 approaching Wool with the 2.07 pm Weymouth-Waterloo service on 21st July.   *Author*

Chapter Fourteen

Epilogue to the Old Road

Once a railway closes and the track is lifted both nature and redevelopment can quickly change the scene. In some places parts of the line remain as a permanent memorial of past glories such as the original brick bridge of the Broadstone-Hamworthy Junction line crossing the Upton Cross-Hamworthy Road a few feet from the later structure carrying the Holes Bay cut-off. Unused but not a traffic hazard, on such a busy road with adjacent property its removal would be a major operation.

Within a short time of the Old Road's closure parts of the trackbed were used for road improvements. The first major work, begun in April 1967, was the Wilverley Post improvement scheme, at the time estimated to have cost £74,985. Part of the trackbed in the vicinity of Holmsley station was converted into a road to eliminate the crossroads on the A35 Bournemouth-Lyndhurst Road and carry the C10 Burley-Lymington Road under the A35 Bournemouth-Lyndhurst Road making 1¼ miles of 20 ft wide road through the former railway cutting to Hag Hill from Holmsley station. At the time plans were discussed to extend the road westwards along the trackbed to Ringwood providing a bypass for Burley, to date no further progress has been made in that direction.

The trackbed of the former Poole & Bournemouth Railway between Broadstone and Holes Bay Junction has been incorporated into the Broadstone bypass. Known as Broadstone Way, it commences on the Poole side of the bridge that carries the A35 Upton Road over the former line at Fleetsbridge. After passing under the bridge the road follows the old trackbed and passes the site of Creekmoor Halt, at which point a pelican crossing and a set of bus-activated traffic signals allows buses to cross the bypass between Creekmoor Lane and York Road.

Further along, the road runs parallel to the embankment of the original Broadstone-Hamworthy Junction section of Castleman's Corkscrew. One of the original brick arches is still in position as this is part of the Castleman Trailway, a 16 mile footpath and cycleway that runs along the former trackbed for most of the way from Ringwood to Upton. The bypass terminates on a roundabout just short of the original Broadstone station, today Broadstone Leisure Centre, and housing covers the site. Only the station master's house and railway cottages remain, the former Station Hotel has now been renamed the 'Goods Yard'. Fortunately parts of the station building were recovered and have been re-erected at Medstead & Four Marks on the Mid-Hants Railway.

At Ringwood the station has disappeared under a new road aptly named Castleman Way and industrial premises occupy much of the site, only the former seed warehouse and the Station Hotel are reminders of past glories. At the east end of the site only Crow Arch bridge remains to signify that a railway passed that way, to the west of the town the two viaducts survive and are now incorporated into the Castleman Trailway.

Surprisingly, Holmsley station survived the transformation at Wilverley Post. Unoccupied until 1969, it was sold and work commenced on restoration, then in December 1972 it was purchased by the Arnold family who, by the summer of 1973, had converted it into tearooms. In recent years a change of owners has brought many improvements, resulting in a restaurant and tearooms displaying photographs of the station and other railway memorabilia. Additionally there is a snack bar and tea garden outside, all retaining the atmosphere of the old station.

Apart from Holmsley no other station buildings remain standing along the Old Road. The site of Wimborne station is now absorbed into the nearby market and industrial estate. At West Moors the site of the station is now occupied by sheltered housing, whilst at Ashley Heath Halt a section of the up platform was restored by local residents during 1994, which complete with name board, stands as a memorial to the line.

Only 10 of the 46 crossing cottages along the entire original route survive, those demolished include the unique and flamboyant two-storey building at Uddens, and Oakley with its Tudor-style windows. Of those remaining No. 8 at Brockenhurst station still has the look of a crossing cottage, as does No. 15 Crow crossing, and the two-storey cottage No. 19 at West Moors. Many of the others have been upgraded and had additions to bring them up to modern standards.

Apart from railway buildings, those associated with Castleman and his family still survive. Allendale House in Wimborne is now an adult education centre, St Ives House near Ringwood a residential home and Glasshayes at Lyndhurst now the very comfortable Lyndhurst Park Hotel. The building originally used by Castleman as a solicitor's office, now Nos. 6 and 8 Christchurch Street, Ringwood, is still standing albeit now with a shop front added. The Bible used by E. & C. Castleman when administering oaths for clients remains in use with their successors 'Meesons' in their office at Market Place at Ringwood.

Little remains of the branch from Ringwood to Christchurch: 60 years of nature had taken control of the trackbed, the supports of one of the viaducts on the outskirts of Ringwood, later rebuilt for double track, still show where they were constructed for three tracks. The building at Avon Lodge still survives, now set in a very select estate. The station at Hurn was reopened as the Avon Causeway public house in 1972. At first it was laid out internally to represent a railway to the point of having several railway carriage compartments in the bar and numerous items of railway memorabilia. Outside a modern Metro-Cammell Pullman coach No. 340 and a small Fowler industrial shunter placed on a length of track alongside the platform are an extra attraction used for a number of functions. At Christchurch the original station building has gone, although the tank traps from World War II are now listed as a National Monument.

In recent years conservation has become popular resulting in sections of the trackbed along the Old Road being developed as the 'Castleman Trailway' between Upton and Ringwood, and in places where the old railway is either inaccessible or been redeveloped alternative routes are signposted to lead back to the trackbed. Commencing north of Upton Country Park one can proceed along a good section of embankment south of Broadstone, after which one can rejoin the former line. Along this section the cut and cover tunnel of vaulted construction is passed through where it passes under the A349 near Merley. Shortly after this the trailway leaves the former trackbed as it descends Oakley Hill (B3073) before turning east and passing beneath the ornate hamstone bridge, known as the Lady Wimborne Carriage Road bridge, that carried the line over an entrance to the Canford Estate.

The trackbed is rejoined at Stapehill as the trailway continues to Dormans Crossing, where a further section leads towards West Moors. From West Moors the route continued to the outskirts of Ringwood, passing the site of Ashley Heath Halt, before crossing the two railway viaducts over the River Avon and entering the west side of Ringwood.

Many great writers have over the years drawn heavily on railways including Castleman's Corkscrew in their work. Thomas Hardy the celebrated Dorset novelist worked on his first novel *Desperate Remedies* and other works whilst living at Weymouth between 1869 and 1871; he acquired a house in Wimborne during 1881 and spent his later years at Dorchester. In his novels, Hardy used pseudonyms to name many places which were based on Dorset towns and villages (i.e. Casterbridge for Dorchester and Warborne for Wimborne), there being several references to the railways of the period, and in *Desperate Remedies* the mention of a gate lodge.

Holmsley station features in *The Wrong Box* written in 1889 by Robert Louis Stevenson who once resided at Bournemouth. In the novel the station, under the name of Browndean, is the scene of a train crash.

The Lady Wimborne Carriage Road bridge, photographed from the east side, formed one of the most ornately carved small railway bridges in the country. Restored in recent years, it now spans the Castleman Trailway.   *Author*

Bibliography

Books

Atthill, Robin, *The Somerset and Dorset Railway*, David & Charles, 1985.
Biddle, Gordon, & Nock, O.S., *The Railway Heritage of Britain*, Michael Joseph, 1983.
Bird, John H., *Southern Steam Sunset*, Runpast Publishing, 1997.
Brown, P.A., *Many and Great Inconveniences*, South Western Circle, 2003.
Bradley, D.L., *Locomotives of the London & South Western Railway*, 2 vols., RCTS, 1967.
Bradley, D.L., *Locomotives of the Southern Railway*, 2 vols, RCTS, 1976.
Clark, R.H., *Southern Region Chronology and Record*, Oakwood Press, 1964.
Fairman J.R., *The Fawley Branch*, Oakwood Press, 2002.
Faulkner, J.N., & Williams, R.A., *The LSWR in the Twentieth Century*, David & Charles, 1988.
Henshaw, David, *The Great Railway Conspiracy*, Leading Edge, 1994.
Lucking, J.H., *Railways of Dorset*, RCTS, 1968.
King, Mike, *Illustrated History of Southern Pull-Push Stock*, OPC, 2006.
Mitchell, B.R., *British Historical Statistics*, Cambridge University Press, 1988
Moody, Bert, *Southampton Railways*, Waterfront Publications, 1992.
Pattenden, N.H., *Special Traffic Arrangements*, South Western Circle, 2008.
Popplewell, Lawrence, *Bournemouth Railway History*, Dorset Publishing Company, 1974.
Pryer, G.A., *A Pictorial Record of Southern Signals*, OPC, 1977.
Pryer, G.A., *Signal Boxes of the London & South Western Railway*, Oakwood Press, 2000.
Pryer, G.A., *Signal Box Diagrams of the Southern Railway*, (various).
Stone, Colin, *Rails to Poole Harbour*, Oakwood Press, 2007.
Tavender, Len, *Ringwood Papers No. 3: Southampton, Ringwood & Dorchester Railway*, 1995.
Vaughan, Adrian, *Railwaymen, Politics and Money*, John Murray, 1997.
Webb, Michael, *Steam Days in Dorset*, Waterfront Publications, 2002.
Winkworth, D.W., *Southern Titled Trains*, David & Charles, 1988.
Wolmar, Christian, *On the Wrong Line*, Aurum Press, 2005.

Magazines & Periodicals
Back Track
British Railways Staff Magazine
Rail
Railway Magazine.
Railway Observer
Railway & Travel Monthly
Railway World
RC&HS Journal
South Western Circular
South Western Gazette
Southern Railway Magazine
Southern Way
Steam Days
Trains Illustrated

Index